WHITE ON GREEN

Also by Peter Oborne:

Wounded Tiger: A History of Cricket in Pakistan

Basil D'Oliveira: Cricket and Conspiracy The Untold Story

(with David Morrison) *A Dangerous Delusion: Why the West is Wrong about Nuclear Iran*

The Rise of Political Lying

The Triumph of the Political Class

Not the Chilcot Report

Also by Richard Heller:

A Tale of Ten Wickets

The Network

WHITE ON GREEN

Celebrating the Drama of Pakistan Cricket

RICHARD HELLER AND PETER OBORNE

**SIMON &
SCHUSTER**

London · New York · Sydney · Toronto · New Delhi

A CBS COMPANY

First published in Great Britain by Simon & Schuster UK Ltd, 2016
A CBS COMPANY

Copyright © 2016 by Richard Heller and Peter Oborne

1 3 5 7 9 10 8 6 4 2

Simon & Schuster UK Ltd
1st Floor
222 Gray's Inn Road
London WC1X 8HB

www.simonandschuster.co.uk

Simon & Schuster Australia, Sydney
Simon & Schuster India, New Delhi

The author and publishers have made all reasonable efforts
to contact copyright-holders for permission, and apologise for
any omissions or errors in the form of credits given.
Corrections may be made to future printings.

A CIP catalogue record for this book
is available from the British Library.

ISBN: 978-1-4711-5641-0
Ebook ISBN: 978-1-4711-5643-4

Typeset in Garamond by M Rules
Printed and bound by CPI Group (UK) Ltd, Croydon, CR0 4YY

MIX
Paper from
responsible sources
FSC® C020471

Simon & Schuster UK Ltd are committed to sourcing
paper that is made from wood grown in sustainable forests and support the Forest
Stewardship Council, the leading international forest certification organisation.
Our books displaying the FSC logo are printed on FSC certified paper.

To the memory of Liz and Lindsay
and to both Felixes, Giles, Tom and Rupert,
and to all the amazing cricket players
and cricket lovers in Pakistan

Contents

Acknowledgements

This book would have been impossible without the unstinting help of many others, especially in Pakistan. However, we are especially indebted to two people.

Qamar Ahmed is based in Karachi when not pursuing his trade as doyen of the world's cricket reporters. In 2014, he followed Richie Benaud and John Woodcock (of *The Times* of London) into the highly select club of people who have reported 400 Test matches. His reporting career began at Lord's in 1974 (a controversial rain-hit Test between England and Pakistan). At the time of writing, he had covered 418, in both print and broadcast media, including the BBC. To put this figure in perspective, this is more Test matches than Pakistan have ever played, and constitutes nearly 20 per cent of all the Test matches in cricket history. To this total can be added 732 one-day internationals. It is hard to imagine that anyone else could have seen, let alone recorded, such a high proportion of the history of any sport.

In a country whose media are often partisan, Qamar has stood out as a journalist of integrity. A graduate in English literature from Sindh University in Hyderabad, he can express himself equally forcefully in English as in Urdu, but he has never allowed any personal or factional agenda to influence his output. He has earned the trust of generations of Pakistan cricketers and for that reason was instrumental in securing many of the interviews in this book: we are especially indebted to him for those of Misbah-ul-Haq and Younus Khan.

Qamar's cricket memories reach back into the 1950s, when he had a successful career in Pakistan's domestic cricket as a slow left-arm bowler. He was the only bowler to dismiss each of the five Mohammad brothers in first-class cricket: Wazir, Raees, Hanif, Mushtaq and Sadiq. He was close to Test selection, but as with so many other Pakistan players he was a victim of caprice. For many years after, he produced match-winning performances for club and media teams. One cricket skill is still with him, in his 79th year. He is an excellent judge of a sharp single, invariably giving a decisive call to his partner at the right moment to cross a busy street in Karachi. Outside of cricket, Qamar appreciates literature and bon mots. He is as generous to other people's as to his own. When he has the time he is a brilliant cook, and he is a generous supplier of wondrous mangoes from his family's farm.

In Lahore, Najum Latif made a similar contribution to this book. On his own initiative he secured a groundbreaking interview with Dr AQ Khan, and we are grateful to him for the opportunity to publish the greater part of this. Najum also secured many interviews for us from his own long list of contacts within Pakistan cricket where he has earned their respect, trust and friendship. We were especially pleased that these included Israr Ali, Pakistan's oldest surviving Test cricketer – a quest which lasted over two years. Sadly, Israr Ali died as this book was being prepared: our interview was the last he ever gave.

Although a back injury ended his promising career as a seam bowler, Najum made lasting friendships at school and college with many eminent cricketers, particularly Saeed Ahmed and the late MK Mantri of India. He has become not only a distinguished historian of Pakistan cricket but, even more importantly, one of its conservators. He founded and still curates Pakistan's first (and still only) cricket museum at the Lahore Gymkhana club and has set down the oral memories of many great Pakistan cricketers, being especially close to Fazal Mahmood in his final years. Apart from cricket, he has been a conservator of wildlife. He raised wolves with his daughter at Sahiwal and adopted lions and tigers at Lahore Zoo, one of many organisations for whom he puts in countless unpaid hours as a writer and administrator. He is equally at home with films and books as with cricket.

Mueen Afzal was a wonderful host in Lahore and Sharjah. After a distinguished career in public service, academia and private business he is an especially informed devotee of Pakistan cricket and observer of its administration under different governments. He was a rich source of memory and analysis, and we thank him particularly for his profile of his long-time friend Shaharyar Khan.

Arif Abbasi supplied us with a wealth of detail on Pakistan cricket, and often pungent analysis of its problems, past and present. In three separate spells of high office in its administration, he was instrumental in modernising its finances, improving and extending its infrastructure and raising its international profile, particularly in the organisation of two World Cups. We look forward to the imminent publication of his own memoirs, entitled *Inside Outside*, in Pakistan. Arif was a rare supporter of women's cricket in a difficult era, and we are especially grateful to him for introducing us to the amazing Khan sisters.

Afzal Ahmed in Karachi was indispensable to us, with his extraordinary eye for detail. He not only weeded out many errors in the manuscript but also supplied many positive suggestions of his own, together with rare archive material from his personal collection.

Many others were also remarkably generous with their time and energy, whether in interviews or in other essential contributions to this book. With one exception (a former player who sought $1,000 for a half-hour interview) no one ever refused a request for information or a meeting. We thank:

The late Abdul Rahman Chughtai, Abdul Qadir, Aftab Baloch, Aftab Gul, the late Agha Saadat Ali, Aleem Dar, Valoise Armstrong, Asad Azeem Shan, Fakir Syed Aizazuddin, Arif Chugtai, Arish Butt, Ashiq Qureshi, Athar Viqar Azeem, Mrs Azmat Humayun, Basalat Mirza, Bina Muneer, Michael Blumberg, Syed Iftikhar Ali Bokhari, Syed Zulfiqar Ali Bukhari, Kamal Chinoy, Pia Chinoy, Faisal Choudry, Alain de Botton, Faizan Siddique, Farasat Bokhari, Feryal Ali Gauhar, Ghulam Yaseen, Farrukh S Goindi, Hameed Masih Meetha, Hanif Mohammad, Hussain Malik, Nawabzada Mohammad Idrees Khan, Nawabzada Dr Mohammad Fateh ud-Din Khan, Ijaz Chaudhry, Ilyas Khan, Imran Ayub, Imran Bucha, Imtiaz Ahmed, Intikhab Alam, the late Israr Ali, Jabbar Mirza,

Jamil Rana, Javed Jabbar, Javed Ashraf, Javed Zaman Khan, Jawed Iqbal, Jugnu Mohsin, Kamal Azfar, Hamza Kardar, Shahid Hafiz Kardar, the late Khalid Aziz, Khalid Butt, Khalid 'Billy' Ibadulla, Dr Abdul Qadeer Khan, Mrs Henny Khan, Justice Abdul Sami Khan, Shaharyar M Khan, Khan Shehram Eusufzye, Marianna Karim, Maqsood Ahmad Khan, Shaiza Khan, Sharmeen Khan, Kiran Baloch, Dr Ambereen Latif September, Majid Khan, Dr Mansoor Ahmed (Director-General Health and Radiation Protection, Khan Research Laboratories), Alex Massie, Mehmud-ul-Hasan, Mehr Mohammad Khalil, the late Mian Mumtaz Ahmed, Misbah-ul-Haq, the late Chacha Mohammad Sharif, Mr & Mrs Syed Mohsin Ali (Mitchell's Fruit Farms Renala Khurd), Mohsin Hasan Khan, Moin Khan, Munawar Hussain, Mohammad Farooq of Okara, Mohammad Zafar, the late Mukhtar Bhatti, former president Pervez Musharraf, Mushtaq Mohammad, Nadeem Omar, Nasreen Ilahi, the late Naqi Shamsi, Raama S Cheema, Raees Mohammad, Naghma Raheela, Rashid Latif, Saeed Bakhsh, Najam Sethi, Nawabzada Abdul Khalik Nasiruddin, Pervez Sajjad, the late Khalid Qureshi, Maulana Shaikh Fazal-ur-Rahman Bin Mohammad Al-Azhari (SF Rahman), Rana Muhammed Arshad (secretary, Mohammadi Mosque), Saad Bari Cheema, Sabin Agha, Saeed Ahmed, Salim Altaf, Samina Abbas, Sadiq Mohammad, Savail Meekal Hussain, Shafqat Rana, Mrs Asma Shah, Dr Imran Ali Shah, Dr Junaid Ali Shah, Shahbaz Kalia, Shahid Javaid Khan, Babra Sharif, Angela Simone Sharpe, Duncan Sharpe, Shaukat Virk (executive director Dr AQ Khan Trust Hospital), Shujaat Ullah Khan, Professor Shaista Sirajuddin, Sultan Mahmud, Brigadier Taimur Dotani, Tanveer Hanif, Tariq Javed, Tariq Haroon, Tauseef Ahmed, Lt-Gen (retired) Tauqir Zia, John Taylor, Dr Pippa Virdee, the late Waqar Ahmed, Wasim Bari, Wasi ud-Din, Wazir Mohammad, Yahya Ghaznavi, Younus Khan, the late Dr Zafar Altaf, Zaheer Abbas, Dr Zaituna Shah, Zia Burney, Zia ul-Hassan Mian. Sadly, Waqar Ahmed and Dr Zafar Altaf passed away as this book was being completed.

In Lahore, we thank all the courteous and efficient staff of the Lahore Gymkhana Club, particularly the librarian Fauzia Shafique, and all the other library staff.

In Karachi, the wondrous Sind club was again a perfect base: our special thanks go to its affable secretary, Shuja Baig, the librarian Aisha Begum, and to Umar, the squash professional, whose leg-breaks remain as unfathomable on the new surface of the nets as on the old.

At the Pakistan High Commission, we acknowledge the support and hospitality of the high commissioner, HE Syed Ibne Abbas; the press attaché, Muneer Ahmad, was unfailingly courteous and helpful.

At Lord's, we were always able to count on the expert assistance of Neil Robinson, the librarian, and Adam Chadwick, the curator and of all the staff working in the library or the archives.

We thank Ian Marshall at Simon & Schuster for his faith in this book, especially when it grew much longer than expected. As in *Wounded Tiger*, Tom Whiting was a sympathetic and sensitive editor and we thank Marie Lorimer for managing the demands of the index. We are grateful to our agent, Andrew Gordon.

The generous help we received in Pakistan gave us far more material than we could use in this book. We take full responsibility for our final choices, and for any lingering errors which escaped our scrutineers.

Note on sources

Unless otherwise stated, all direct quotations are from personal interviews with the people concerned, and all cricket statistics and analysis derived from them are from the online *CricketArchive* database. Some interviews were by Richard Heller alone, as indicated. He is the 'I' in their text.

Introduction

THE DRAMA OF PAKISTAN CRICKET

The story of Pakistan cricket is intensely and uninterruptedly dramatic. The basic narrative lurches constantly from triumph to disaster and back again. The main characters touch dazzling heights of heroism or astonishing depths of villainy, and the same character can shift between hero and villain at dizzying speed. There are regular comic, even absurd, performers but they too can change into figures of grandeur or infamy. And the extras in the chorus line – like Ruby Keeler in *42nd Street* – can wake up as stars.

Even the dullest stories in Pakistan cricket – for instance, one of those domestic matches in the early 1960s where two sides bat forever to secure a first-innings lead on a sedated pitch – acquire an epic quality. One starts to empathise with the journeyman bowler on each side, usually a slow left-arm finger-spinner, a Sisyphus who wheels away for 70 or 80 uphill overs and yields around two runs off each one.

Outside of statistical sources, historians rarely encounter an objective, factual narrative of any episode in Pakistan cricket, except, curiously, in the autobiographies of early Pakistan cricketers which are often reticent. Whenever we spoke directly to former players or officials or even onlookers, they nearly always gave us a vivid narrative with sharp characters, crisp dialogue and a clear point of view. Richard, who has written fiction and screenplays, announced during his first visit to Pakistan that its cricketing history had the contents of fifty novels.

However, we could not find any to cite when we researched this book. Perhaps Pakistani novelists thought themselves unable to match the real characters and real events in their country's cricket.

As is frequently observed, cricket has become a shared experience for Pakistan, instilling a sense of identity in a sprawling nation of many cultures, languages, ethnicities, communities, clans and other networks, value-systems and strands of faith. We discovered this especially in Chitral, a remote and beautiful district in the Hindu Kush mountains which until recently was an independent kingdom, and have included Alex Massie's fine description of the experience of playing cricket there. As with all of Pakistan, Chitral's relationship with cricket has been shaped strongly by television coverage, which is why we talked to two distinguished directors.

We are amazed that so many worthy analyses of Pakistan have been published with no mention of cricket. It would be wrong to say that it unites the country: in fact, few topics are more likely to divide Pakistanis than the performance of their cricket team. As bemused neutrals, we have sat through countless passionate arguments about team selection, captaincy, choice of bowlers and field settings and about wider issues of management and administration. Pakistan cricket supporters, we believe, are more likely than those of any other country to assume the worst motives behind any failure in performance or any decision they disagree with. No, cricket does not unite Pakistan but it gives millions of Pakistanis something which they all care about and, so it follows, a common repository for their emotions.

For that reason, we came to see cricket as a bridge to understanding the collective subconscious of Pakistan. The drama and turbulence of Pakistan cricket are echoes of the drama and turbulence of the nation's history. This was a theme of *Wounded Tiger*, Peter's history of Pakistan cricket, but this was inevitably restrained by the demands of narrative and balance.

In this book, we have chosen to ignore those demands, although for the convenience of readers we have put the contents more or less into narrative order. This book is *not* a history, and it does not offer any kind of structured analysis. Instead, we have presented a series of characters or episodes that seemed to us to provide some kind of dramatic connexion to Pakistan cricket. We have used our freedom to describe some of these in depth – and to allow all of our chosen characters as much as possible to speak in their own words. We hope that they will thereby bring readers emotionally closer to Pakistan cricket and to the country itself.

We made all our selections because we thought them interesting and entertaining, but they are not completely random. We believed that their stories illustrated certain recurring themes in Pakistan cricket.

However, at a very late stage, one name virtually imposed itself upon us. Our friend and collaborator Najum Latif secured an interview with **Dr AQ Khan**, 'the father of Pakistan's nuclear bomb'. This was a remarkable achievement, the first of its kind for a decade. Dr Khan is of course a deeply contentious figure in Western eyes and the subject of enduring controversy. But for the great majority of Pakistanis he is a national icon, so that his relationship with cricket is immensely illuminating. We therefore cited large tracts of this interview, verbatim, without judgement or commentary of our own, as they relate to cricket. We especially enjoyed his account of his early experience, shared by so many other Pakistanis of his age, of following Pakistan cricket through a shared radio in a public place. Dr Khan also had much to say about his role as a patron of Pakistan cricket. His Khan Research Laboratory team has employed some of Pakistan's greatest players, notably Misbah-ul-Haq, who scored more runs for them than for any other team in Pakistan's domestic cricket.

There are some heroes in our other selections, but most of our names have faded. Behind their unremarkable, sometimes pitiful, statistics were some amazing back-stories.

We had the good fortune to meet **Zaheer Abbas** on the very day he became president of the International Cricket Conference, and to share his thoughts on how to use his new status and his moral authority as a cricket icon. Zaheer scored more first-class runs than any other Asian batsman. He is very likely to keep that distinction forever. Zaheer is generally remembered as a supreme artist, sometimes endearingly fallible, but his memories at our meeting showed an intriguingly different, almost artisan, self-image.

Zaheer's great contemporary **Majid Khan** had already made a huge contribution to *Wounded Tiger*. He is a grandee of Pakistan cricket, a guardian of standards from another era. For this book, he gave us not only a penetrating analysis of the historic problems that have damaged Pakistan's domestic cricket, but also a cogent plan to overcome them, worked up with his son Bazid, also a Test cricketer. The reception of this plan offered a wry commentary on the fate of reformers in Pakistan cricket.

We met two current heroes, **Younus Khan** and **Misbah-ul-Haq**, one voluble and extrovert, the other more measured and reserved, but both imbued with a sense of responsibility to their team and their country. We learnt how they had set themselves to create a moral partnership as well as a cricketing one and had led other players to pull Pakistan cricket out of a dark pit of failure and corruption.

We met four other heroes, less well known to the public, who also served Pakistan cricket nobly at a terrible time. **Mehr Mohammad Khalil** and **Judge Abdul Sami Khan** shared their memories of the terrorist attack on the Sri Lankan cricketers in Lahore in 2009. Both kept their heads and did better for Pakistan on that day than many more senior people: Judge Abdul Sami Khan as liaison officer in the minivan carrying the match officials, Mehr Mohammad Khalil as the driver of the stricken team coach who managed to drive the Sri Lankans to safety as the bullets were flying.

Against a background of extreme state-organised repression of women, and in the face of official indifference or hostility, the remarkable **Khan sisters** returned from England to their native Karachi to create Pakistan's first international women's cricket team. With the support of their father they faced down ridicule, feuding, legal battles and death threats. They had to smuggle their new Pakistan kit onto their aircraft and hide in the toilets to change into it. After calamitous initial results, their team set new international records – but they were then supplanted by their rivals, who in a kinder environment took Pakistan women's cricket to a higher level.

From **Wasim Bari**, Pakistan's great wicketkeeper, and **Abdul Qadir**, the leg-spinning genius who revived a dying art, we heard of the power of childhood dreams and the prodigious work needed to make them come true. All over Pakistan, children and young people are dreaming the same kind of dreams and working as hard to fulfil them – but sadly, as we discovered from the **young people in a sandstorm in Lahore,** they have less confidence than before that their work will be recognised and rewarded.

Intikhab Alam became a hero with the very first ball he delivered for Pakistan. He still enjoys showing how it took a wicket and put him into the history books. Since then he has served Pakistan almost continuously for over 55 years as player, captain, coach, manager and administrator. He has survived many crises, but none more important than the horrors of Partition, which affected so many early Pakistan cricketers. Intikhab's account has the pathos of being told through the eyes of a terrified five-year-old child.

Another great survivor was **Israr Ali,** the oldest living Pakistan Test cricketer at the time of our meeting. Sadly, he died only weeks later. Immensely dignified, with the aura of history, he was still endearingly vain about his appearance as he received us at the farm he established a few hours' drive from Lahore. Israr endured some cruel treatment as a cricketer, and then a much more cruel blow from life itself.

Four others also illustrated the power of bad luck. **Raees Mohammad** was the only one of the five famous brothers not to play Test cricket. In one match, he was certain of winning his first cap on the evening before, only to have it snatched away from him the next morning. His legacy was delivered through his three younger brothers, for whom he was a coach and a mentor.

Khalid 'Billy' Ibadulla was so disappointed by the selectors that he made history by leaving his country and becoming the first Pakistani to qualify for an English county. When finally given a Test cap, he made a statement as the first Pakistani to score a century on debut. Finally he made another life in a third country, as a coach and a fly-fisherman.

Duncan Sharpe inherited much of the story-telling gift of his ancestor, WM Thackeray. He told us how he became the first Anglo-Indian to play Test cricket for Pakistan; he will almost certainly be the last. But he too had his heart broken by the selectors, and made a second life in a faraway country.

Aftab Baloch joined the very select club of batsmen who scored a first-class 400. But his was one of the least watched and least rewarded. In making it, he set a record which is so obscure that he did not even know that he owned it when we told him.

Two of our characters were in different ways non-conformists and paid a penalty for it. We could not resist opening this book with **Prince Aslam**, heir to a princely state of pre-Partition India. He was a prodigious cricketing talent and an outsize personality who scattered bright memories like sequins to his contemporaries. Fatally, he refused to adapt his princely lifestyle in a Pakistan where it had become both censured and unaffordable. He died sad and alone, two years after his last first-class cricket match. By contrast, **Shaharyar Khan** was also born a prince of a pre-Partition state but made a much more successful transition to modern Pakistan. He served with distinction as a diplomat and, twice, as chairman of the Pakistan Cricket Board. His longtime friend Mueen Afzal has provided unique insight into his character and achievements.

Aftab Gul was a more serious (and far more intelligent) non-conformist than Prince Aslam. He was a radical student leader and lieutenant of ZA Bhutto, and became the only Test cricketer to make his debut when out on bail for criminal charges. He endured a period of exile in England but returned to become a radical lawyer. As cultured as he is irreverent towards all authority, Aftab Gul keeps alive all the causes he believed in, especially the Bhutto who offered Pakistan the promise of transformation in the late 1960s.

Many Pakistan cricketers have been deeply devout men, and almost the whole team became visibly religious during the past decade. But none made such a deep journey into faith as **SF Rahman**. A leg-spinner and a one-cap Test player in the 1950s (yet another member of the 'unlucky club') he was also a dapper dresser, accomplished ballroom dancer and a popular clubman. He made a second life as a renowned and prolific Islamic scholar, and an emotive preacher who won a national following without the help of broadcast media. His views were austere, at times unpalatable to Western ears, but his personality was warm and generous.

SF Rahman joined Pakistan's only official visit to the United States, which was part of **AH Kardar**'s early mission to make the world aware of Pakistan as a nation. To this end, Kardar became the only Pakistan captain to become a contestant on an American prime-time television quiz show. A few years earlier, with the same flag-showing mission, Pakistan stopped to play a match in Egypt: it finished early to allow for sightseeing.

Although Pakistan's army has had a decisive impact on the country's history, it never much approved of cricket and certainly did not encourage its officers to play it. However, for about three years Pakistan cricket came under the influence of two strong-minded soldiers, General **Pervez Musharraf**, the country's military ruler, and his personal nominee as head of the **PCB** (Pakistan Cricket Board), General **Tauqir Zia**. Both men talked to us candidly about their agenda for Pakistan cricket – which ranged from major new infrastructure to the size of players' beards. General Tauqir Zia has the unusual distinction of being praised by **Shoaib Akhtar** in his memoirs. For convenience, we have provided a short summary of all the people injured or insulted by the fastest man who ever bowled for Pakistan.

At the time of writing, Shoaib was planning a movie career. He would find it hard to match **Mohsin Khan**, one of Pakistan's batting stars of the 1980s. He is the only successful cricketer to win more movie roles than Test caps. Recalling much of his original dialogue, he told us the story of his journey from cricket to Bollywood and back.

Pakistan staged the greatest mismatch in cricket history: victory by an innings and 851 runs. We wanted to find out what really happened. We asked an enterprising journalist, Khan Shehram Eusufzye, to trace surviving participants. This became almost another 'Quest for Corvo'. He sent us back regular gnomic emails announcing, 'Research going well' but the quarry was always elusive. Finally, he traced two members of the losing Dera Ismail Khan team of 1964 and they told us the touching story of the youngsters playing pick-up games on the parade ground who found themselves pitted against the mighty Railways team. One of them narrowly missed a second chance of a cricket career – instead he became President Zia-ul-Haq's personal pilot.

Like Blanche DuBois in Tennessee Williams' *A Streetcar Named Desire*, Pakistan cricket has always depended on the kindness of strangers. We profile two modern benefactors. One is the late **Dr Mohammad Ali Shah**, subject of a delightfully comprehensive biography called *The Legend Unfolds*, whose work is carried on by his family. Another is **Nadeem Omar**, an industrialist with an unusual 'hinterland' of other interests, including singing. His corporate team is helping to rehabilitate Mohammad Amir, the brilliant young fast bowler jailed over match-fixing. Another benefactor is **Aleem Dar**, who also gave us the personal story of his beginnings as an umpire in Pakistan.

There is a strong sense of stewardship in Pakistan cricket, as ex-players take on a special responsibility for preparing the next generation. From a past age, we have told the story of **Master Aziz**, with particular help from his greatest pupil, Hanif Mohammad. Master Aziz was separated at Partition from his adored 12-year-old son. For reasons we cannot explain, the separation was almost permanent, although the boy became one of India's most popular Test cricketers, the all-rounder Salim Durani. In place of his own son, Master Aziz mentored dozens of young Pakistanis and helped some to greatness.

In the current era, two former wicketkeepers, **Moin Khan** and **Rashid Latif** have set up celebrated cricket academies in Karachi. Their personal styles are contrasting, but their objective is the same – producing young players with the character to match their talent.

Pakistanis have been unmatched as cricket innovators. They gave the world reverse swing and the doosra. But their most important invention is **tapeball**, an electrifying street version of the game which has the potential to develop as a sport in its own right. We discovered its appeal in an exciting match in Karachi and talked to two players who have managed to become tapeball professionals.

One of the recurring legends in Pakistan cricket is the sudden discovery of a genius who gatecrashes his way into the Test team. The best-known representatives are the teenaged fast bowlers, Wasim Akram and Waqar Younis. At the other end of the scale is the remarkable **Miran Bux**, propelled into the Test team at the age of 47 – the second oldest debutant for any country. **Tauseef Ahmed's** story was the most dramatic of all. He was a net bowler, asked to give practice to Pakistan's powerful batting line-up in 1980 before the Karachi Test against Australia. He did so well that the selectors put him in the team. We talked to Tauseef – and to the still-disappointed bowler he supplanted, **Ilyas Khan**, whose Test career was over before it began.

This legend still has the power to make young people dream. That is why we conclude with the story of **Arish**, a club cricketer who abandoned his life in England to come back to Pakistan and ask for a trial with the Test team. As he said himself, only in Pakistan could such a request be made, and only in Pakistan would it be granted.

We hope that this cast of characters might bring readers closer to Pakistan – and that readers will enjoy meeting them.

Richard Heller
Peter Oborne
December 2015

I

THE LOST PRINCE OF PAKISTAN CRICKET

Early Pakistan cricket is dominated by three figures: AH Kardar, Fazal Mahmood and Hanif Mohammad. All three were dedicated, even heroic characters, but each rather solemn. As in all drama, Pakistan cricket needs its jesters as well as its kings – and in its first phase we kept discovering one name which seemed to fill that role.

Prince Mohammad Aslam Khan was a left-arm spin bowler whose first-class career spanned from 1955 to 1978. His figures are respectable but not compelling: 84 wickets from 28 matches (all in Pakistan) which cost him 22.63 apiece, from 861 overs at the economical rate of 2.20. Like many bowlers of his type at that time, he had to bowl many long end-holding spells on dead pitches. He had two successful overseas tours, one with the Pakistan Eaglets, which groomed many of Pakistan's early stars, but never broke into the Test side.

However, behind these figures was a magician, who could bowl any kind of left-arm spin at will, orthodox and unorthodox, and bamboozle the greatest batsmen of his time. Several of his contemporaries told us independently that he (not Saqlain Mushtaq) was the true inventor of the doosra, although he gave it no name. His left-arm version would have turned sharply from off to leg. As with later practitioners, there were doubts over its legality, but umpires then were more relaxed than today.

Bill O'Reilly once wrote: 'You can never become a good attacking bowler if you do not develop a bowling "temperament". A happy-go-lucky, good-natured and carefree outlook is of no use whatever to an ambitious and competent bowler. He must be prepared to boil up inwardly on the slightest provocation, and opportunities are so common that there is no need even to cite one.'[1]

This advice was wasted on Prince Aslam. His life was a long party, in which cricket was included. His disposition was sunny not sullen, and except on one memorable occasion, he never boiled up on or off the field. He loved company, and didn't care for rank or status. He was a talented musician and singer, who jammed with hundreds of pick-up bands. He loved practical jokes – all harmless, except for one pompous victim who had it coming to him. He spent money lavishly on friends and hangers-on and even total strangers in need, and was always ready to share his bottle of Johnnie Walker Black Label whisky.

He was equally generous as a cricketer, regularly sharing his secrets with other players, even rival left-arm spinners. He was an exhilarating coach, who loved to gather children, rich and poor, to pass on his tricks.

Our files grew thick with anecdotes. Many were hard to believe, but they revealed how legends collected around him. One adjective came up repeatedly: non-conformist. Here was a man who never compromised in his chosen lifestyle and never allowed the Establishment to dictate his behaviour.

As a cricketer, he demanded the right to play in his own way – so long as he took wickets. Bowling was his passion. All other aspects of the game were secondary, although he was a fine fielder anywhere in the inner circle, who could throw with either hand. He was also a talented batsman but preferred to lurk at number 9, smash some crowd-pleasing sixes and then get out, in order to rejoin his current girlfriend or his current party. His time-keeping was fitful: when team-mates struggled to matches on time on foot, or by bicycle, or jammed into buses and carts, Prince Aslam often drove up late in his convertible. He sometimes left unimportant games early if he felt he had taken enough wickets.

1 Cited in A Rajan, *The Twirlymen* (Yellow Jersey, 2011), p.189.

But this fun-loving genius had a full share of secret sorrows. His cricket career ended with a fine flourish, but there was no afterlife. He died suddenly, young and alone.

Prince Mohammad Aslam Khan was born on the Ides of March in 1935, first child of the Nawab of Manavadar, and heir to an independent princely state in Gujarat, in pre-Partition India, with a population of around 26,000. He had two full brothers and three full sisters. When Prince Aslam was ten his father took a second wife, by whom he had another five children, the last born in 1963. Through his mother, aunt and grandmother, Prince Aslam was also a scion of the princely house of Mangrol, in Gujarat.

It was a magnificent inheritance, but perhaps also a fatal one. He played cricket like a prince when Pakistan wanted toilers and strivers, and in life he could not break free of the habits and expectations of a prince when these were no longer realistic or sustainable.

Manavadar was a prosperous state, a centre of the cotton industry and famous for a local sweet known as kuvar-pak, made from aloe vera. His father had succeeded in 1918 at the age of seven and his grandmother became Regent. She was a remarkably good ruler, promoting free education and pioneering a free health service over 20 years ahead of Britain's. The British gave her a high decoration, the gold medal of the order of Kaiser-i-Hind, and elevated Manavadar to the status of a second-class state. They asked her to continue her regency, but she stepped aside in 1931 for her 20-year-old son to rule in his own right. The Nawab, Prince Aslam's father, was a brilliant sportsman who played several first-class cricket matches for Western India, but was even more famous as a patron and player of hockey. He was founder and captain of the world-famous Manavadar hockey team, which toured New Zealand and won every match, and he also played for All-India in the Western Asiatic Games in 1934.

Prince Aslam spent his first twelve years in Manavadar, living at the Zorawar Bagh Palace. This period seems to have been idyllic. As heir to the throne, he was indulged by his family, especially his grandmother, and by his father's retainers. In the poetic words of his younger brother,

Prince Idrees Khan, he grew up 'with all the bloom of the kingdom'. Private lessons were undemanding and he had full scope to develop his love of sport. He enjoyed hockey, wrestling and squash (the palace had the first squash court in India), and became an excellent horseman and a crack shot with a variety of guns. He also learnt to perform well on the mouth organ, and on Pakistan's version of the harmonium, in which one hand works the bellows and the other plays a scaled-down piano keyboard. In later life, if there were no pick-up musicians available, he often performed as a one-man band, supplying his own percussion as well.

But cricket was his first love. He had no formal coaching, and like so many talented slow bowlers he taught himself by spinning balls or fruit or other suitable objects from hand to hand. As with other sons of famous sportsmen, he may have wanted to try a different sport from his father's. Perhaps he also sensed that spin bowling would be a better outlet for him as a solo artist than being part of a hockey team.

The one blight on his childhood was asthma, a family malady, and he took anti-asthma remedies all his life. Unfortunately, one of these was hot tea and brandy at night – a routine preventive measure at the time but dangerous for a child's development, both physically and psychologically.

When Prince Aslam was 12, he left his promised kingdom forever. At the Partition of India, in 1947, his father, along with his cousin and overlord, the Nawab of Junagadh, tried to accede to Pakistan. India refused to accept their declaration, claiming that it was unlawful and ignored the wishes of the Hindu majority. (At the same time, India accepted the accession of Kashmir from its Hindu ruler despite its substantial Muslim majority.)

Prince Aslam was sent with his mother and family, including his new-born brother, Prince Idrees Khan, to Karachi, while his father remained in Manavadar to confront an Indian invasion. A member of the Nawab's Arabian palace guard was killed and he ordered the end of all resistance. He became a prisoner, spending some time in jail, sleeping on straw, before being removed from his state and confined in the town of Songadh. Nehru's powerful deputy, Sardar Patel, tried to induce him to cede Manavadar to India, even offering him full princely privileges and the chance to write his own treaty with the Indian government. He refused and remained a prisoner until 1951, when he was released as part of the exchanges under the Liaquat Ali-Nehru Pact.

The Nawab had lost most of his property and had been unable to transfer all his money to Pakistan. His wife and family lived in much reduced circumstances in Karachi, although they occupied a large property, known as Manavadar House, in an elegant neighbourhood close to the former Hindu temple of Guru Mandir. Things improved when the Nawab joined them in 1951: the Pakistan government formally recognised his princely status and awarded him a stipend.

Exile seems to have made little difference to Prince Aslam's outlook or his development as a spin bowler. Manavadar House offered a tile floor indoors for practice with spinning objects and a cement pitch just long enough for bowling without a run-up. His experiments continued. Like a later teenaged spin genius, Abdul Qadir, who grew up in a much humbler home, he would take a cricket ball with him to bed and spin himself to sleep. He was blessed with big hands and remarkably flexible fingers and thumbs. He loved to make a cricket ball hum in the air, and as a party piece he liked to bowl a ball close to the garden wall and make it stop dead with backspin. He played countless improvised games with his younger brothers and local children; he enjoyed announcing his deliveries to them and predicting their means of dismissal.

Still conditioned to be the heir to Manavadar, he made a series of short-lived visits to exclusive schools in Karachi, initially at Marie Colaco School, then for just one year, aged 15, at Karachi Grammar School, and then for an uncertain period at St Patrick's. He seems to have shown no interest in any subject except cricket. According to his admiring brother, Prince Idrees Khan, he helped all three schools win the prestigious Rubie Shield competition. Unfortunately, almost all records of the Rubie Shield have disappeared (as has the Shield itself).

His father, the Nawab, rejoiced in his son's cricket achievements but was so alarmed by the rest of his school performances that he made a different plan for his second son, Prince Mohammad Fateh-ud-Din Khan, eight years younger than Prince Aslam. He was sent away to prep school in England, and then to Millfield, a school of high sporting achievement. Also a fine cricketer, he spent three years as a leg-spinning all-rounder in the first team. As MF Khan he captained the side in 1962 and he played several seasons for Somerset Second XI. He was given many tips from his elder brother during the holidays and might have followed him into cricket. Instead he studied at Liverpool University, and had a distinguished medical career in England and Pakistan.

Whatever the facts about Prince Aslam's school cricket performances, he was recognised as a special talent in his late teens. He made his mark in club cricket in Karachi, which was then of a high standard, and was sought out as a net bowler for practice sessions with other promising players and established stars, including all five of the Mohammad brothers.

Qamar Ahmed was his contemporary, also a slow left-arm bowler. He recalls: 'Prince Aslam had a very good action. He was very steady and accurate, varied his flight and was difficult to play. He spun the ball sharply, both ways, on matting wickets.' In lesser matches, he often took the new ball and bowled five or six overs of seam, and would deploy some additional tricks, including bowling off the wrong foot, bowling from behind the stumps and even switching to his right hand.

At age 19, Prince Aslam was picked for a Karachi Combined Schools tour of Ceylon. Most records are missing, but he claimed a rich haul of wickets at low cost, including five for 24 (with a hat-trick) against Asgiriya. Not in the least nervous at his official selection, Prince Aslam indulged his habit of predicting dismissals. According to Prince Idrees Khan, he would invite half his fielders to go away and enjoy some sightseeing, since the remainder would be enough for him. It is not clear whether they accepted the invitation, and if so, what the other bowlers thought of it.

He did well enough to be picked for the longer and more important Eaglets tour of England in 1955, which followed the senior side's historic series-levelling victory at The Oval the previous year. There is a fine portrait of him in his Eaglets blazer, handsome, keen-eyed, a model cricketer representing his country – except for his tie, which must have been unofficial. It is a lurid number which PG Wodehouse's Jeeves would have burnt before Bertie could display it to the photographer.

On his return from England he made his first appearance in a major match. It was a four-day frolic in Karachi in aid of flood victims, between celebrity XIs for the prime minister, Chaudhry Mohammad Ali, and the governor-general, Iskander Mirza. (Pakistan was in its closing months as a monarchy.) He bowled 37 economical but wicketless overs for the prime minister against a batting line-up that included Imtiaz Ahmed, Raees Mohammad (the unlucky brother who never played a Test for Pakistan, see chapter 7), and Keith Miller. Prince Aslam's father, the Nawab of Manavadar, also played, aged 43. Raees and Miller scored centuries, and his father whacked a couple of sixes off him; some of the crowd accused Prince Aslam (wrongly) of bowling lollipops. He had some revenge in the second innings when he caught his father at mid-on. His bowling did enough to win Miller's lasting admiration.

Shortly afterwards he made his first-class debut, aged 20, for the Chief Commissioner's XI in the National stadium, Karachi, against the touring New Zealanders. Batting at number 9, he was dismissed for three runs, one of seven victims for New Zealand's star all-rounder John Reid, as his team subsided to 121. But Reid was the only New Zealander to master him in the reply, scoring 150 not out in a slow innings of 271 for nine declared. Prince Aslam bowled more overs than anyone else – 38 – taking four wickets for just 78.

Two months later, he was in action against MCC for Karachi. He bowled both openers, Brian Close and Peter Richardson, in the first innings, finishing with two for 80 off 30 overs. He took more punishment in MCC's second innings, but picked up the wicket of Jim Parks. His first seven first-class victims were all present or future Test players.

He got another chance against MCC as a superannuated schoolboy for Pakistan Combined Schools in a two-day match in Dacca (then in East Pakistan). The selectors made him a promise: 'Take five wickets and you'll play a Test match.' He was the most successful bowler but fell one short, taking four for 73 in 24 overs. The victims were the gifted Maurice Tompkin of Leicestershire (who would die tragically young),

Billy Sutcliffe (son of Herbert, as he was constantly reminded during a troubled spell as captain of Yorkshire), Ken Barrington, and Harold Stephenson, the Somerset wicketkeeper-batsman.

Besides these matches and club games, Prince Aslam continued to perfect his tricks in organised nets with top players and less organised sessions, outdoors and in, at his home. He still enjoyed playing with his brothers and local children. Although his stay there was brief, he was fond of his alma mater, Karachi Grammar School, and raised a team of leading Karachi cricketers to play the boys. His younger cousin, Nawabzada Abdul Khaliq Nasiruddin (heir of the princely house of Mangrol) has happy memories of these matches. 'Prince Aslam's team would always bat first. They murdered us gently. He would ask for me to be put on to bowl my medium pace, encourage me to keep it straight, and then hit me for six.' However, at the end of the over he would ostentatiously present his cousin with his wicket. 'I told him afterwards it would have been less embarrassing had he despatched me into the woods once again.' Prince Aslam would treat the boys to a few overs when they batted. 'When we got out he would tell us where we went wrong, demonstrate some better strokes and tell us to watch the bowler's hand.'

But cricket was only part of a hectic, happy life. Basalat Mirza was a long-term friend and former cricket pupil of Prince Aslam. He gave us a vivid portrait of a man who loved company. His apartment upstairs at Manavadar House was usually crammed with musicians and hangers-on. He was as happy talking to street beggars as to friends from Pakistan's elite, such as ZA Bhutto, the country's future leader. He was generous with his Scotch whisky (although he had a strong head he enjoyed pretending to be drunk to help the party mood) and even more generous with money, which he handed out freely to those he thought in need. If there was any left over, he enjoyed sleeping on wedges of banknotes; when these ran out he would touch his parents for more. He would also hand out Rolex watches and gold rings. He played a card game called Black Queen (which sounds very much like Hearts), but for fun, not for money.

When life in Karachi was too confining, he would pile people into his jeep for impromptu beach picnics, or take off into the forest to hunt boar and partridge. He also had a sporty Dodge Dart convertible, in which he was regularly sighted with a series of glamorous girlfriends, and an Opel Record.

Prince Aslam made his first competitive appearance in October 1956 for Karachi Whites against Karachi Greens in the Quaid-e-Azam trophy. In those days Pakistan's big cities, Karachi and Lahore, so dominated the country's cricket that they fielded two or three teams in the competition. His first captain was Hanif Mohammad, a serious man with little time for eccentrics, but Prince Aslam served him well in this match. He took three wickets for just 32 in 21 overs, as the Greens collapsed to 150. Then batting at number 10, he whacked 31 in a stand of 68 which built a big lead. He was wicketless in the Greens' second innings, but strangled one end with 22 overs for 34 runs while the experienced pace bowler Mahmood Hussain took eight for 95 at the other. Led by Hanif and Alimuddin, the Whites scored 111 for victory in quick time.

Perhaps more importantly, he renewed acquaintance with Keith Miller, who arrived in Pakistan with an Australian team still in the aftermath of their destruction by Jim Laker in their losing Ashes tour of England. It was their first visit to Pakistan and they badly needed practice. Miller asked about 'the young boy, the prince' with whom he had played in the charity game, and Prince Aslam was deputed to bowl at the Australians in the nets. He mesmerised a line-up that included Neil Harvey, Richie Benaud and Alan Davidson, as well as Miller. He bowled them out regularly and was invited to join them that evening at the Metropole Hotel. He rounded up some friends and they all enjoyed the beers that had been carefully packed by the Australian management, and Prince Aslam then bowled out the Australians all over again in the hotel lobby, using chairs as wickets. The Australians invited him as a guest to all their matches, including a historic win for Pakistan in an attritional Test, in which Fazal Mahmood took 13 wickets and his opening partner, Khan Mohammad, took the other seven. It was Miller's last Test but he was a regular visitor to Pakistan for some years afterwards, and he regularly inquired after Prince Aslam.

When informed that he was not in the Test team he said simply 'That is Pakistan's loss' and declared that he would have been better treated in Australia.

Miller, with his own rich social life and occasional conflicts with captains and selectors, may have identified Prince Aslam as a fellow victim of authority. He might usefully have advised him how to cope with it, and how to avoid provoking it gratuitously. In particular, he might have advised him to restrain his love of music, which twice got him into trouble.

When Prince Aslam was summoned to a training camp under the supervision of Pakistan's captain and stern godfather, AH Kardar, he played his music late into the night. Kardar asked him to stop, but Prince Aslam refused, saying he had not completed all the songs in his repertoire.

On another occasion, he was one of a Karachi team captained by Hanif Mohammad which was setting off by train to play an away fixture in the Quaid-e-Azam trophy. He was late. An irritated Hanif asked continuously: 'Where is Prince Aslam?' No one could answer. Hanif had the train delayed for a short time and then decided to set off without him. At the last moment Prince Aslam arrived – with a pick-up band. They played a short serenade before he boarded the train. Hanif gave him a dressing down, which Prince Aslam accepted in good part. When Hanif finished and turned away, Prince Aslam gave him an affectionate slap on the back, although perhaps the slightly built Hanif saw it differently.[2]

In general, Prince Aslam took such strictures calmly and was well behaved on the field – with one spectacular exception which has entered the record books as a mark of dissent. At a club match in Nazimabad, north of Karachi, he was incensed when the umpire gave him lbw. After arguing for some time, he marched off the pitch and headed for his parked convertible. He extracted the two revolvers he kept in the glove

2 However, Prince Aslam was a successful busker with his harmonium when the Eaglets mistakenly went to Geneva instead of Genoa on their way home from England – raising enough money for the team to buy train tickets to Genoa to catch their ship. Source: Majid Khan.

box, marched back on the field, and fired them in the air. The fielders from the National Sports Club and the umpires fled from the ground over the boundary fences and the match was abandoned.

In February 1957, Prince Aslam had one of his most memorable matches, a Quaid-e-Azam trophy semi-final for Karachi Whites against Karachi Blues. He was wicketless in the Blues' first innings of 314, but picked up two catches. The Whites' reply of 762 occupied a monumental 313.2 overs, of which 79 were bowled by a 15-year-old student on his debut, Nasim-ul-Ghani. Prince Aslam came in at number 10, at the crisis point of 568 for eight, following a double century from Hanif and a century from Hanif's older brother, Wazir. He proceeded to hit 112 not out, his only first-class century. Predictably, it was a free-hitting affair, with 13 fours, which occupied 210 minutes. The attack must have been tired but it was more than respectable, with four current or future Test players and the unlucky Raees Mohammad. He benefited from four missed catches (three before he had scored 20). In Blues' second innings he had three wickets, including Raees, the top scorer, and his young rival Nasim-ul-Ghani, and held two catches. His team won by an innings and 132 runs.

However, it was Nasim, not Prince Aslam, who was picked for Pakistan's inaugural tour of the West Indies shortly afterwards. AH Kardar liked picking very young, obedient spinners. In fact, Nasim was a strong character but he was certainly easier to control than Prince Aslam. Nasim had a fine tour of West Indies, in which he became the youngest Test player not long after his 16th birthday, only to lose the record a year later to the 15-year-old Mushtaq Mohammad.

Prince Aslam never again came into serious contention for a Test place. Several factors held him back. For one thing, Pakistan played few Test matches in this period – only 35 in the first ten years of his first-class career – and other spin bowling options were always available. Besides Nasim-ul-Ghani, there was another left-arm spinner, the calm and metronomic Pervez Sajjad. He was also competing with the leg-spinners, Intikhab Alam and Mushtaq Mohammad, who offered more with the bat. The selectors had doubts about the legality of some of his deliveries, a factor which became more important amid the anti-throwing crackdown during the early 1960s, which ended the short Test career of the off-spinner Haseeb Ahsan. However, most of the cricket public believed that Prince Aslam was excluded because of his lifestyle and his attitude to authority. Unfortunately, his father also came to that view, and he became more and more disappointed with his gifted son.

As his Test prospects slipped further and further away, Prince Aslam had to be content with his warm reception from the sparse crowds at Pakistan's domestic matches and the admiration of his contemporaries. He was still in demand for practice sessions with the Mohammad brothers and other established stars. He gave advice freely, even to rivals such as Intikhab Alam and Nasim-ul-Ghani, who remembers him as 'a great character and a good cricketer. He was a very positive person. He never hid his secrets. I learnt the doosra from him. But he was not popular with the selectors because he led his own life and was not a disciplined person.'

In both practice and real matches, he still enjoyed predicting the downfall of opposing batsmen. According to Basalat Mirza, his most illustrious victim was a young Zaheer Abbas. Baited by the crowd (and Mushtaq Mohammad, who told him that he would never dismiss Zaheer), Prince Aslam promised to achieve this on the fourth ball of his next over. He then bowled three from normal length and a fourth from behind the stumps. Zaheer missed it, and to his amazement was clean bowled. The scorebook confirms this – but also shows that Zaheer had already scored 202.

Prince Aslam continued to play pick-up matches with local children and to give practice and advice to promising young players. One important beneficiary was a teenaged Wasim Bari. Reading a left-arm mystery spinner was an excellent early training for Pakistan's greatest wicketkeeper. 'I played at his house as well as for City Gymkhana Club. He was a genius, with all the varieties up his sleeve. He could bowl the doosra, the arm ball and the googly. He did throw an odd delivery but no one cared.' The two combined to great effect for Karachi, when they beat the Lahore Education Board by an innings in the Ayub trophy final of 1964-65. Then 16 years old, Wasim Bari had nine victims in the match. Five were off Prince Aslam, then 29 and at the height of his powers. Prince Aslam had six other victims in the match, in which he took eleven wickets for 137 runs in 82 overs.

This was his best performance in domestic cricket. His bowling average drifted upwards in subsequent seasons, apart from 1966-67 when he routed the Public Works Department, again with help from Wasim Bari. He was out of the reckoning for Test matches, and increasingly finding first-class cricket a treadmill. In 1970-71 he was still good enough to take four top-order wickets for 94 off 41 overs for Karachi Blues against the Pakistan National Airlines (PIA) team (including the surprised double centurion, Zaheer Abbas). He outbowled his captain, Intikhab Alam, as PIA made 512. The Blues set PIA 191 to win. Prince Aslam was the most economical bowler but he couldn't remove Zaheer Abbas a second time. Zaheer scored 81 not out as PIA won comfortably by eight wickets.

Prince Aslam then disappeared from the first-class scene for seven years. He was recalled in the colours of the National Security Printing Corporation, one of the employers' teams encouraged by AH Kardar, now running Pakistan cricket by appointment from Prince Aslam's old friend, ZA Bhutto. The Corporation team was run by its 'Colonel-captain' Pervez Akbar. Pervez's cricket record was dreadful (four first-class innings as a middle-order batsman for a total of seven runs) but he knew enough to recognise his need for a bowler of quality and a crowd-pleasing celebrity. At nearly 43, Prince Aslam was hired for both jobs.

He was tired and drinking more heavily than before. However, he had a fine last hurrah at Faisalabad against Sargodha. Defending a first innings of only 170 by the printers, he peeled off 47 overs and dismissed the top six Sargodha batsmen, although they cost him 154. He had to watch the colonel-captain put himself on as the tenth bowler, and yield 46 runs off five overs. The printers failed to make Sargodha bat again, and Prince Aslam was dismissed for a duck in his final innings, going for yet another big hit.

At this match, he performed a characteristic act of generosity. One of the opposition was a Christian named Joseph, who invited him to drinks. Prince Aslam accepted gratefully: alcohol had become harder to obtain for Muslims as both Bhutto and his military successor, General Zia-ul-Haq, courted clerical support. Joseph supplied the drink but was reluctant to let Prince Aslam into his house. Joseph's sister was gravely ill and the house was in disorder. Prince Aslam over-rode him and talked to his sister for some time at her bedside. After he left, Joseph discovered a big pile of banknotes under the pillow to help pay her medical bills.

This was money Prince Aslam could no longer afford. He was estranged from his disappointed father, who had turned away from his first wife and family to be with his second. His father now had eleven children, and his state stipend had been eroded by inflation and cut by General Zia. He could no longer support his son in the old way, even if he had wanted to. Prince Aslam was doing more and more desperate things to maintain his partying lifestyle and support the entourage of friends, musicians and leeches. He was selling off cars, and jewels and other valuable items. He had given up his favourite Johnnie Walker Black Label and was drinking dubious local gin.

He had never married. Although he'd had many female admirers, they had found it hard to get close to him emotionally, or even to share any private time with him when he was almost constantly surrounded by a male entourage. He had one deep relationship with a woman, but the social gulf between them was too wide to contemplate marriage, although he carried a torch for her ever after. She was the sister of a backing singer to a celebrated performer, and he couldn't listen to the performer's songs without tears in his eyes. He had hopes of an arranged marriage, with a lady from a 'suitable' family, but these foundered on money. He wanted an independent income and control of some capital before marrying: his father would not give him either, and kept him to his allowance.

Prince Aslam had only two unhappy years left after that last match for the printers. Undermined by cheap drink and depression, he died suddenly, and alone, aged only 45. His father outlived him by 23 years, his mother by 27.

In a later time, he might have been a different kind of cricketer and found another life after his playing career. Without those formative years as heir to a throne, he might have added a professional approach to his self-taught arts as a cricketer. Like other talented Pakistani players born after him, he might have found his way into English league or county cricket. With money and independence, he could have married and enjoyed the company of a family instead of a collection of strangers. Free of the conventions and expectations of princely status, he might have used his talents as a coach or a teacher, or tried his hand as a professional musician, or reinvented himself as a television personality (like another left-arm spinner, Phil Tufnell).

Instead, he was fated to become the Lost Prince of Pakistan cricket. It might seem a wasted life but it was still full of victories. He bowled thousands of magical deliveries. He tested the skills of some of the greatest players of his time and won their respect. He encouraged hundreds of children and young players, and brought them to a higher standard. He entertained people on and off the field. He helped hundreds of people whom he thought to be in need.

His ultimate victory was to be remembered 35 years after his death with pleasure and affection. We spoke to dozens of people who had known him, family, friends, fellow-players and spectators, without hearing a bad word about him.

2

INTIKHAB ALAM: THE GREAT
SURVIVOR OF PAKISTAN CRICKET

When the Abbé Sieyès was asked what he did during the French Revolution, the veteran politician replied simply: 'I survived.'

Intikhab Alam is the Abbé Sieyès of Pakistan cricket. His service to it began in 1959, when in front of his home crowd in Karachi, he became the only Pakistani to join the select club of bowlers who have captured a wicket with their first ball in Test cricket. He still loves to demonstrate the quickish leg-break which bowled Australia's opener Colin McDonald. In each decade since then he has served Pakistan cricket in multiple capacities: player, captain, first-ever team manager, coach, senior administrator.[1] He has been at the heights and the depths. He has faced fierce personal criticisms and public dismissals. But he has also had multiple recalls.

Since 1959, he has seen off four military rulers of Pakistan, eight civilian governments, over 20 heads of the Pakistan Cricket Board[2] and 28 Pakistan Test match captains (not including himself). In 2015, aged 73, he was back in his fourth spell as team manager.

---

1 When we interviewed him in the summer of 2013, he was delayed by a long telephone discussion: subordinates were asking him to decide the depth of the water in the swimming pool at the National Cricket Academy.
2 The exact tally is difficult to establish because of ad hoc appointments and temporary changes imposed by court proceedings.

Throughout his career he has been attacked for being too diplomatic and too conciliatory to those in authority. However, it is easy to understand that approach to life when he shares his memories of Partition. He has done this frequently for the Pakistan teams he has managed, to give a sense of the risk and sacrifice that past generations faced in joining the new state. 'I would tell the young players about how the older ones got into Pakistan, and about the massacres and murders. My mother's family lost seven members at Partition, three murdered and four women who threw themselves into a well to avoid rape.'[3]

More than 15 million people were uprooted amid savage intercommunal violence, particularly in the Punjab, which was divided hastily and artificially between the two nations by the Radcliffe Commission in the final weeks before independence on 14 August 1947. The historian Nisid Hajari wrote that some British soldiers and journalists who had witnessed the Nazi death camps saw worse scenes at Partition. 'Pregnant women had their breasts cut off and babies hacked out of their bellies; infants were found literally roasted on spits.' He added: 'Foot caravans of destitute refugees fleeing the violence stretched for fifty miles and more. As the peasants trudged along wearily, mounted guerrillas burst out of the tall crops that lined the road and culled them like sheep. Special refugee trains, filled to bursting when they set out, suffered repeated ambushes along the way. All too often they crossed the border in funereal silence, blood seeping from under their carriage doors.' The final death tally was between one and two million.[4]

Many of Pakistan's early cricketers suffered at Partition. Hanif Mohammad and his family fled from a prosperous and settled life in the princely state of Junagadh when it was forcibly taken over by India, reaching Karachi virtually destitute and making a temporary home in an abandoned Hindu temple. Fazal Mahmood was saved on a train journey from a Hindu lynch-mob by a fellow passenger, the Indian Test cricketer, CK Nayudu, who defended him with his cricket bat. Waqar

---

3 Intikhab Alam: personal interview.
4 Nisid Hajari, *Midnight's Furies* (Amberley Publishing, 2015), cited in William Dalrymple, 'The Great Divide,' *The New Yorker*, 29 June 2015.

Hasan lost his grandparents in a particularly horrible death by being burnt alive in their home.

Intikhab Alam's account of Partition is especially searing as he remembers what it meant to him as a five-year-old boy, conveying not only the terror but the collapse of a secure and familiar world. 'At Partition, my family was living in Simla. My father was an electrical engineer in government service, in charge of the local power station. I was only five, but I knew that the situation was very dangerous. Although there were more and more clashes and threats to Muslims, my father thought it was his duty to stay with his job even though others were leaving.

'His number two was a Mr Bedi. I don't think he was any relation of Bishan. He was also our neighbour. He came to our house and told our family to leave home at once. He hid our whole family in one small room in his house: my parents and five children. I was the middle child, with two brothers[5] and two sisters.

'We stayed in that room for two to three days. Then Mr Bedi told us that a mob was on its way to search the house and we must leave.

'It was one in the morning and we headed off on a dark road to the power station. We just had one torch and it took us forty-five minutes. I was terrified of meeting leopards and snakes.

'When we arrived there was a man in charge sitting by a telephone but he was not allowed to use it. We sat down on the platform of some kind of engine. It made a huge noise. My father decided to get rid of the man sitting by the telephone, and asked him to go out and find him some cigarettes. He did, and my father was able to use the phone himself. He got through to a family friend, Brigadier James. My father, who was a fast bowler, had played cricket with him for the Maharaja of Patiala. He asked him for help, and Brigadier James arrived with a truckload of army personnel. They took us back to our old house to collect any possessions. My elder brother picked up a Holy Qu'ran and a little cash. That was all we took.

5 One brother, Aftab, four years older, had a first-class career which spanned 14 years, primarily as a batsman.

'My family was taken to relatives in Ludhiana. We stayed with them for a week, and my father resigned his government job. We were in real danger and we had to leave the country. We were told there was a train leaving from a place called Kalka [a small town in the foothills of the Himalayas, about 70 miles distance from Ludhiana, but further away from Pakistan].

'We headed out there. Our family were dumped in a field with an improvised tent, during the monsoon. There were mobs about, and some opened fire with weapons. I saw bullets flying through our tent. We had to wait all day and all night for the last train, which set off at about five or six in the morning. My family got on and hid my father. The train could easily have been attacked, but luckily the mob made a mistake with the train schedule and thought it was a goods train and not the passenger service.

'We made it to Lahore and stayed in the Walton refugee camp.' Intikhab gave no account of this, but an article in *Dawn*, Pakistan's oldest and most widely read English-language newspaper, some years ago described it as 'a nightmarish place, with sometimes two million destitute people milling about in abject misery and a state of shock, not knowing what fate awaited them next'.[6]

The family survived there for about six weeks, until Intikhab's father was able to contact his brother, a detective inspector in the Karachi police. They moved to Karachi and Intikhab's life slowly returned to normal. Within a few years he would be riding a bicycle for two miles each day to play cricket at Jahangir Park. He joined a club called Blackhawk which, unusually, was formed and run by boys. The leading light was a leg-spinning all-rounder with a famous brother. For over twenty years this boy would become his friend, colleague and rival: Mushtaq Mohammad.[7]

6 'The camp at Walton,' *Dawn*, 8 January 2009.
7 Mushtaq Mohammad, *Inside Out* (Karachi: 2006) pp.28-29.

3

THE MANY SONS OF MASTER AZIZ

Among the millions of families divided between India and Pakistan at Partition, one separation would have a lasting impact on cricket in both countries. The cricket coach Abdul Aziz Durani lost Salim, the 12-year-old son he adored and was grooming to be a Test player. When he fled to Karachi, the boy remained with relatives in India. Other people took over his cricket education and he did indeed become a Test player – a flamboyant, crowd-pleasing all-rounder with 29 caps for India.

In place of his lost son, Abdul Aziz Durani coached and mentored dozens of boys in his new country of Pakistan, earning the title of Master Aziz. His most important pupil would also earn the title of Master: Hanif Mohammad.

Hanif played nearly twice as many Test matches as Salim Durani – 55 – and in a completely different style, as a specialist batsman with unflinching concentration. Hanif and Salim never encountered each other on the cricket field, so Master Aziz was never able to watch his natural son and his adoptive one at the same time.

We were not able to reach Salim Durani (who is now 80) to discover what relationship he had in adult life with his father. They had only one meeting after Partition – at the Calcutta Test of 1960-61, when Salim Durani's left-arm spin took eight English wickets in the match, helping India to a big victory. Under instruction from his father, Salim produced a baffling delivery which took the crucial wicket of Ken Barrington. What might have happened if they had stayed together? For the rest of his life, Master Aziz could not talk about his son Salim without tears.[1]

Their separation may have had a deep psychological influence on Master Aziz. He was a superb cricket coach, who spent every possible waking moment with cricketers as coach, umpire or simply spectator, but outside of cricket some of his behaviour was decidedly eccentric and almost self-destructive.

Materials about the life of Abdul Aziz Durani are scanty. He was born in 1905, say standard reference sources (1910 says Najum Latif). Assuming that his birthdate of 15 August is reliable, he shared it with Napoleon. The sources give his birthplace simply as India, but he bore the clan name of the ruling dynasty in Afghanistan. He took his wife to Kabul to give birth to their child in the midst of the clan. Salim Durani is to date the only Test cricketer from Afghanistan.

Two years earlier, Abdul Aziz had settled in Jamnagar, the capital of Ranjitsinhji's princely state of Nawanagar. Ranji had recently died but his successor was hoping to build a strong cricket team to win the new Indian national trophy named after him.

Abdul Aziz was a burly wicketkeeper, over six feet tall who weighed over 220 lbs and had immense feet.[2] He made an impression by standing up to the pace bowling trio signed by Ranji's heir: Amar Singh, Mubarak Ali and Shute Banerjee. He became recognised as one of the finest wicketkeepers in pre-Partition India. He helped Nawanagar win the Ranji trophy in 1936-37, when he had to keep wicket to Vinoo Mankad as well as the pace trio and also made three appearances in unofficial Tests for India against Jack Ryder's visiting Australians and Lord Tennyson's visiting English.[3] Thanks to police inspector Amiruddin (uncle of Intikhab Alam) he acquired a nominal job in the Nawanagar police.[4]

1 Source: Najum Latif.
2 Source: Najum Latif.
3 See 'A Man From Kabul,' *The Hindu*, 2 September 2001.
4 Source: Najum Latif.

Salim was his first son and at his birth Abdul Aziz Durani passed a new cricket ball in front of the baby's eyes to get him used to the moving ball. He announced solemnly to the company that he had become the father of a Test cricketer.[5] He took this ambition seriously. Wazir Mohammad remembered seeing them when his school was playing an away match in Jamnagar before Partition. 'Salim Durani was then about seven or eight. His father was trying to give him catching practice, especially in the slips. He had put cushions on the ground on both sides of him to stop him getting hurt, and then started to give him diving catches. First they were easy but then he had to catch ten to twelve hard ones in a row, diving full length right and left.'

Abdul Aziz Durani took the decisive step of turning Salim from a right-hander to a left-hander in both batting and bowling. He thought it would improve the boy's chances of future selection.[6] Around ten years later, the Mohammad brothers did the same to the youngest, Sadiq, and for the same reason, but only in batting.

By then Abdul Aziz had finished his first-class career, and was coaching and umpiring. He lost his wife after ten years of marriage and four children. In 1947, he migrated to Karachi and attached himself to the well-known Sind Madrassa school, where Mohammad Ali Jinnah, founder of Pakistan, had been educated. To his lasting sorrow, his children remained in Jamnagar, on the other side of the new frontier. We cannot say why they did not follow.[7]

Thereafter Abdul Aziz filled his life with cricket. When not coaching the Sind Madrassa pupils, he went about Karachi searching out other talented youngsters. One of these was Hanif Mohammad, aged 15. 'He watched me in a club match where I scored a fifty and kept wicket. He came up to me, told me I had batted very well and asked my name. He said, "Why not join our school?" and promised to introduce me to the

---

5 Source: Qamar Ahmed.
6 Source: Najum Latif.
7 According to Mushtaq Mohammad two daughters came to live with him in Karachi, but Hanif and Raees remembered only one daughter, Amina, and that she lived in Jamnagar.

principal. Then he talked to my mother.' She agreed to transfer him to the Sind Madrassa from the City school.

Hanif now had daily sessions with his demanding but innovative coach. Abdul Aziz induced him to cut the last school lesson regularly, telling him to 'bowl a googly at the teacher'. Before long he was also helping his elder brothers, Wazir and Raees. The younger ones, Mushtaq and Sadiq, would tag along at net sessions and act as ball boys. In time they would also become his pupils. So Abdul Aziz became the guiding light for all the five Mohammad brothers.

Outside the family, he guided other future first-class and Test performers including the all-rounder Ikram Elahi, his brother Anwar Elahi, the fast bowler Mohammad Munaf, and Abdul Rashid. After Abdul Aziz's successful association with Hanif, he was sought out by almost every would-be cricketer in Karachi, and known reverentially as Master Aziz.

His innovations included suspending a ball from a string and making his pupils hit it repeatedly (to encourage them to play straight)[8] and bowling short-pitched high-bouncing golf balls at them, to teach them to hook. Another priceless service was to umpire – and then abuse his position to refuse lbws and caught-behinds against his best pupils. When the bowlers complained, he would reply genially, 'Son, what's this arm?' – which would be extended to show a somewhat retrospective no-ball. He would also explain unashamedly that he knew his best pupils were headed for greatness and wanted them to have the experience of playing a long innings.[9]

There was another motive for his umpiring. He was regularly out of money, although he lived modestly in a small room at the Sind Madrassa school. He would spend it impulsively, buying kit and clothing for young players who needed it – and would regularly have

8 A Western children's game of the same period, *Jokari*, worked on the same general principle. The tethered ball became unhittable unless you hit it straight.
9 Hanif, who was the source of this story, was at pains to point out that Master Aziz did *not* umpire during the triple century he scored for the Sind Madrassa against the Christian Mission school. 'That was the final of the Rubie Shield. He did his umpiring only in tours of Lahore.'

to borrow money from his pupils to get a cup of tea and something to eat. Outside of cricket, he often seemed disorganised and disconnected. He would lose the thread of conversations, recalled Wazir Mohammad, while Qamar Ahmed revealed that as a dresser, he would spoil the effect of his dapper blazer, tie and floppy hat by forgetting to do up his flies.

Meanwhile his natural son, Salim Durani, made a spectacular entry into first-class cricket, aged 19, playing for Saurashtra against Gujarat in the Ranji trophy. He scored 108 in the first innings in just 150 minutes, and also top-scored in the second innings with 41.

Initially they tried to groom him as a wicketkeeper, like his absent father, but under the influence of Vinoo Mankad, he developed instead into a slow left-arm bowler. He would become an idol of Indian crowds, with a reputation for hitting sixes on demand and suddenly producing unplayable deliveries, but also for a generous, open-hearted character. But his stop-start career of 29 Tests suggests an unfulfilled talent: 1202 runs at an average of 25, 75 wickets at an average of 35. Who knows whether his absent father's influence might have produced a longer career and a higher return?

Apart from their lone meeting at India's Test match against England, it is not clear whether Master Aziz kept up with his son's career. He concentrated on developing Pakistan's talent, and his status was recognised when he was appointed one of four national coaches to supervise a month-long coaching camp in Karachi in 1957. Qamar Ahmed attended as a well-regarded slow left-arm bowler. He remembered Master Aziz as the only coach who lived in the camp permanently. By now Master Aziz was supplying articles with coaching tips to the *Leader* newspaper, ghosted for him by Qamar.

As the years went on, Master Aziz continued to seek out new talent. Wazir Mohammad recalled meeting him in Dacca in 1961, where he would collect dozens of local children to help him at net practice. He was also an expert adviser to established stars. Mushtaq remembered a ten-minute session in which Master Aziz corrected his stance and enabled him to hook the fearsome West Indian Charlie Griffith.

In December 1960, on Pakistan's draw-infested tour of India, Mushtaq had a significant encounter. He played opposite Salim Durani in the side match against Central Zone. (Hanif was also on the tour but rested.) Neither did much in the game but they spent some time together. Mushtaq said, 'I had a great regard for him, and he was like a family member.'

However, this encounter does not seem to have led Salim Durani back to his father. In 2007, Qamar Ahmed met Salim Durani in a long coach trip in Rajasthan. He introduced himself and said that he had stayed with Master Aziz for a month in the coaching camp 50 years earlier. Salim Durani was fascinated and plied him with questions about his father.

By then Master Aziz had been dead for 38 years. Shortly before his death Qamar Ahmed arranged for Patrick Eagar to take a now celebrated photograph of him with three of his great pupils, Hanif, Mushtaq and Sadiq. However, according to Najum Latif, he died poor and forgotten, except by Omar Kureishi, who had him transferred at his own expense to a private hospital ward. In the Karachi Test of 1978-79, when Mushtaq Mohammad led Pakistan to a thrilling victory over India, Master Aziz sat alone and unrecognised in the stands, eating an omelette wrapped in an old newspaper.

It is happier to remember the uplifting article, 'What Is Cricket?', which he wrote in 1959 with the help of Qamar Ahmed for the brochure for the Test series against Richie Benaud's Australians.

It opened with a fine statement which expresses the values that Master Aziz transmitted to all his pupils: 'Cricket is not a game meant only for amusement or physical exercise as many people seem to think. It is also a great education for both young and old. Physically, it develops every muscle of the body. Mentally, it teaches cheerfulness in defeat and modesty in victory. It checks the growth of selfishness and creates a spirit of comradeship. It is perhaps the only game that builds up a sound character and adaptable temperament, not only on the cricket field but also in the wider field where the struggle for existence goes on.'

4

THE MAN WHO GOT AWAY: BILLY IBADULLA

For about 15 seasons from the mid-1950s, English cricket lovers grew familiar with the sight of a certain 'K Ibadulla' on the scorecard for Warwickshire. He came into the category of a 'utility' player – dependable opening batsman, dependable change bowler of off-spin or seam, dependable close catcher. His name was unusual, but his cricket profile was not.

Few supporters would have guessed from his figures that he was a history-maker. As a young man, cruelly disappointed by his country's selectors, he had pursued – and achieved – a daring ambition, to become the first Pakistani to play county cricket. He blazed a trail for a generation of Pakistani superstars to follow more than a decade later. When belatedly called up for his native country, he showed them what they had missed, scoring a big century on debut. But his Test career was short and sporadic – so he moved to a third country and coached some of their finest players.

Khalid Ibadulla was born in Lahore in December 1935. There was no cricket background in his family, but his father, Masood Ibadulla, had been a fine hockey player and their home had many inspiring photographs of his college team. His elder brother introduced him to cricket and took him to matches at the Lahore Gymkhana club played by leading local notables. 'The beauty of the game deeply impressed me, with the white figures moving on the green grass.'

With his brother he joined the Pioneer Cricket Club and started to play Sunday matches. Although a relatively minor club in the pre-Partition Lahore scene, it had a fine ground and the standard was high.

As a very young boy, he acquired the nickname Billy from an English teacher, Miss Nixon. Years later, he volunteered that name to his English county, Warwickshire, because they would find it easier than his Pakistani one. It stuck, and has led some sources to identify him as one of the Christians to play for Pakistan. Not so: he is a Muslim from a Muslim family.

He went to Mozang High School, where there was no cricket master, but the principal encouraged boys to practise under Nissar Ahmed, a fine coach who had been a first-class wicketkeeper. His guidance helped 12 other boys who gained representative honours, including Waqar Younis and fellow fast bowler, Mahmood Hussain.

As a seam-bowling all-rounder, Khalid Ibadulla was considered the finest schoolboy cricketer in Lahore. He was due to go to Islamia College, a great nursery of cricket talent before and after Partition, but he failed his matriculation. Instead he joined Universal CC (Fazal Mahmood's club) and Mamdot CC (Nazar Mohammad's).

He made his first-class debut at 16 for the Punjab Governor's XI in the traditional fixture against Punjab University. Batting at number 6, he made a fluent 38 before misreading a googly from another 16-year-old, SF Rahman, and shared the new ball with Dr Jahangir Khan. He took part in the trials in Lahore for Pakistan's inaugural Test tour of India in 1952-53 and did almost enough to earn selection as a swing bowler. Instead, under the patronage of Justice Cornelius (a brilliant man who would later become Chief Justice of Pakistan), he went to the Lahore Gymkhana club, bowling at lawyers and judges in the nets, filling in as a player or substitute when needed, and supervising ground preparations.

However, he came tantalisingly close to a Test call-up before his 17th birthday. On Pakistan's inaugural tour, the opening bowler Khan Mohammad was injured before the third Test in Bombay. The selectors sent him out as a replacement, annoying AH Kardar, the captain, who had strangely asked for a batsman, Ashgar Ali. Kardar reportedly complained that he did not want 'another baby' in his team. Khalid Ibadulla was unaware of this ('I think Kardar treated me as well as he could') and was glad to be 12th man in the remaining three Tests, as the best all-round fielder in a generally poor team. At net practice, he bowled tirelessly at other players but never got a bat himself.

Kardar gave him one first-class appearance in the side match against South Zone. He produced 22 cheap but wicketless overs of seam (with a dropped catch) and scored 2 not out in the second innings. Although unproductive, this match made him a Pakistan international – with a fatal effect on his future status in England.

His prospects brightened when he was selected for the second Pakistan Eaglets tour of England in 1953, under the leadership of Fazal Mahmood. Other members were Alimuddin and Ikram Elahi. He was coached by Alf Gover and Andy Sandham and mentored by Fazal. His all-round game improved – and he enjoyed the taste of English life. The final three-day match against Combined Services led him to meet Fred Trueman, Ray Illingworth and a Warwickshire opening bowler, Roly Thompson, who encouraged him to think about a future with the county.

Then came another bitter disappointment: missing the tour of England in 1954. 'I was named in the original party of eighteen, but then the selectors decided to hold trials in four provinces with forty-four players, and I was omitted from them. It was a big blow emotionally and psychologically.' Still only 18, and with almost no first-class record, he decided to seek his fortune with an English county.

'I landed in England with four pounds in my pocket and decided to seek a trial at Warwickshire. I stayed in Birmingham with a friend who was a student. I had offers from the Staffordshire League but I was determined to become a county professional.' He secured a trial of one week, watched by Warwickshire's famous coach, Tiger Smith, who had kept wicket, standing up, to Frank Foster and SF Barnes. It was Smith who latched onto his name as Billy. He impressed Smith enough to extend the trial to one month, including some 'club and ground' matches. There too he impressed enough to extend the trial to the rest of the summer – and to get paid for it. He was a county professional.

His status as a Pakistan international (for that solitary South Zone match) forced him to wait three years before playing a County Championship match for Warwickshire, or even a Second XI or Minor County match. Nor could he return home to Pakistan in that period and play any first-class cricket there. He could play a few non-championship first-class games, against Oxford or Cambridge Universities, or Combined Services and teams of similar status. He played the first of these at Edgbaston in June 1954 against Oxford. He had 13 wicketless overs against a powerful batting line-up led by Colin Cowdrey and Mike Smith, but made 35 and 40 as opening batsman, helping the county gain a thrilling one-wicket win.

He was made 12th man against the visiting Pakistanis, but the match was a casualty of a dismal wet summer. Otherwise he had no contact with the touring team that had rejected him, although he still knew many of their players.

Warwickshire were a rich county (based on a successful football pool scheme whose rules were periodically amended to frustrate HM Customs and Excise) and a generous employer. He earned enough to adapt to life in a Birmingham still heavily scarred by the wartime blitz. He boarded with a kindly English couple in Solihull. 'I think I was the first Pakistani anyone there had ever seen.'

Like all cricket professionals of the time, he needed a winter job. In his first winter, he worked at Rover Motors, as an electrician's mate. The following winter he worked in the stock room of Lewis's department store, where he was promoted to the sales floor. He also worked as a salesman for the Beehive department store, and demonstrated washing machines and kitchen furniture for them at the annual Ideal Home Exhibition. 'That became my line.'[1]

---

1 The Beehive closed in 1972. Comedian Jasper Carrott was employed there for a time, as a trainee buyer.

He impressed Warwickshire with his dedication during the long apprenticeship and the dressing room applauded him when it was ended in 1957 and he played against Surrey Second XI.

Originally a swing bowler, he had impressed Tiger Smith in the nets with some off-spinners. He converted to that style because the county needed a spin partner to their veteran leg-break bowler, Eric Hollies. He made his Championship debut, captained by Mike Smith, against Yorkshire in May 1957 at number 8. The first day was lost and he made little impression. However, by mid-season he had made 600 runs and taken 57 wickets so cheaply that he was third in the first-class averages. (He credits Eric Hollies at the other end: 'He was out of this world.') He was on course for the first Warwickshire double since Frank Foster in 1911, and earned a county cap. But then his season was ended by a cartilage problem that needed an operation. He went home to Lahore for the first time in over three years to recuperate, and then returned to the winter job at the Beehive.

His second season, in another wet, dismal summer, was less successful and he was in and out of the side as an off-spinner, but he was valued as a fielder, initially at cover or in the slips. Then Mike Smith had the inspiration to station him at forward short leg, where he gobbled catches off the precision in-swingers of Tom Cartwright.

Much more importantly, he met his wife Gertrude. 'She was German, on a working holiday, staying with family friends in Birmingham. We were introduced by a non-cricketing Pakistani whom I knew and her friends knew. She came from a small country town near Flensburg on the Danish border. When we married and I met her family, they too had never seen a Pakistani before. They were fascinated by me. She did not meet my family until we stopped in Pakistan in 1965 on our way to Otago, where I was playing and coaching. By then we had already had two children.'

Over the next few English seasons, he established himself for the county as an opening batsman, as a utility bowler of seam or off-spin and as an outstanding close catcher. In 1960, he and Norman Horner set a new record of 377 for an opening partnership for Warwickshire. When Ossie Wheatley declared, he had made 170 not out and Horner

203 not out. He then bowled 23 wicketless overs for 24 runs as Surrey ground out a lead.[2]

He had his best batting season in 1962 with over 2,000 runs. This included 62 as opening batsman against the visiting Pakistanis, whose attack was led by the restored Fazal Mahmood. Khalid Ibadulla added two smart catches and the wicket of Pakistan's captain Javed Burki as the tourists followed on. Pakistan's 1962 tour was one long disaster. Was he never considered as an SOS reinforcement? 'I don't think so. By then I was a case of out of sight, out of mind.' He had not played in Pakistan since January 1954.

He eventually returned as a 'foreigner' in November 1963, playing five unofficial Test matches in a Commonwealth XI which also included Rohan Kanhai, Tom Graveney and Basil D'Oliveira. In his native Lahore, he scored a not-out century *against* Pakistan.

In October 1964, the selectors finally noticed him. He opened the batting for a Pakistan XI against the powerful Railways team (who in their next match would gorge themselves against Dera Ismail Khan, see chapter 14). He scored 58 and 0, enough to earn his first Test cap aged 28 in the one-off Test in Karachi against Australia. He made up for lost time, becoming the first Pakistani to score a century on debut. Against an attack led by McKenzie and Hawke, he scored 166 in five and a half hours, with 20 fours. He shared a record stand of 249 with another debutant, Abdul Kadir. It was a fine way to celebrate the birth of his son, Kassem, far away in Birmingham.

Unfortunately, he was already committed to play and coach for Otago in South Island, New Zealand. He could not afford to abandon this engagement and join Pakistan's touring party to Australia and New Zealand. So he ended up playing *against* Pakistan yet again – for Otago. He took four cheap wickets and scored 43 and 102 not out. So they drafted him into the side for the third Test against New Zealand, where he contributed 28 and 9 as an opening batsman.

In 1967, he played against Pakistan one more time for Warwickshire,

2 Dennis Amiss made his first-class debut in this match. He did not bat but captured the first of his 18 wickets in a 27-year career.

scoring just 5 before being run out but most importantly dismissing
Hanif Mohammad for a duck when Pakistan collapsed in a follow-
on. Although the Pakistan touring party was already overloaded with
players, this led Hanif to restore him for the Lord's Test – the very next
match. He opened the batting and was bowled by Ken Higgs for 8.
Hanif made a monumental 187 not out to put Pakistan on level terms.
Brian Close set Pakistan a conceivable target, but Hanif was not interested. On instructions to save the game, Khalid Ibadulla made 32 off
155 balls (surprisingly, these had five boundaries, so the remaining 150
balls, yielding just 12 runs, were an ordeal for spectators).

He kept his place for Trent Bridge. Pakistan collapsed twice on a
rain-affected wicket, and he scored only 2 and 5, but he bowled 32 overs
for only 42 runs and the wicket of Tom Graveney.

That was the end of his Test career. There were other successes – above
all a partnership of 402 with Rohan Kanhai for Warwickshire – but he
never played another major match for any Pakistani team. Remarkably,
he played more matches, and scored more centuries, *against* Pakistan
than for them.

Warwickshire gave him a benefit season in 1969 which raised
£7,800 – a deserved tribute to the teenager who made the daring trip
to Birmingham in 1954. He added a good season in Tasmania to his
record, before leaving the first-class scene in 1972.

He settled in Dunedin, Otago, and lives there today with Gertrude.
They raised three children: one son, Kassem, had a short first-class
career as an all-rounder for Otago and Gloucestershire. Khalid Ibadulla
returned for two summers in England in the early 1980s as an umpire,
but his main commitment was as a coach in Dunedin, where he set up a
private academy. He worked with some of New Zealand's finest modern
players, including Glenn Turner, Ken Rutherford, Chris Cairns and,
latterly, Brendon McCullum. Glenn Turner's father introduced him to
fly-fishing, which is still his passion.

After a disappearance of nearly 30 years, Pakistan remembered him
again when he was asked to manage the Pakistan Under-19 tour of New
Zealand in 1993-94. Saqlain Mushtaq was a major beneficiary. Khalid
Ibadulla was set to become a national coach for the 1996 World Cup,

but by then he no longer understood how the PCB – or any Pakistani organisation – actually operated. 'I simply was not used to their way of communicating. So I thought it best to resign.' He resumed coaching in New Zealand and in 2004 received the New Zealand Order of Merit for services to cricket there.

As he approaches his 80th birthday, his private coaching academy is packed with teenaged pupils. He works there full time. If the PCB could establish some communication with him, he could still offer a great deal to Pakistani cricketers, whether teenagers or misfiring stars. But it would have to guarantee him a good supply of river trout.

5

SWINGING INTO HISTORY
WITH ISRAR ALI

In 2011, after the death aged 91 of Mohammad Aslam Khokhar,[1] Israr Ali became Pakistan's oldest living Test cricketer. He was 25 when he played in Pakistan's first-ever Test match, in October 1952, against India at the Feroz Shah Kotla ground in Delhi, for which he was paid a total of 60 rupees (equivalent to £5).

If Pakistani Test players wore numbered shirts, like England's, Israr Ali would be on the list as number 3. He was a bridge to history, one of those at the birth of Pakistan as a Test nation, who helped launch a contest between India and Pakistan which had all the drama and resonance of the Ashes.

The Indian side had some resonant names: Vinoo Mankad, Vijay Hazare, Vijay Manjrekar, Lala Amarnath, Polly Umrigar and Ghulam Ahmed. It has no survivors (the last was Umrigar, who died in 2006) but at the time of writing there are three living Pakistanis who took part in the match. They are the wicketkeeper-batsman, Imtiaz Ahmed (now 88), Waqar Hasan, the stylish batsman who became a major industrialist (now 83), and Hanif Mohammad (now 81).

---

1 Aslam Khokhar's one Test appearance was in Pakistan's innings defeat at Trent Bridge in 1954. He batted at number 9, scoring 16 and 18, but did not bowl. His long first-class career extended from 1938 to 1964.

We had wanted to meet Israr Ali for two years, but he had always made an excuse for evading appointments over the telephone: illness, fatigue, too busy with his family or his farm. Eventually, on the always-reliable advice of Lahore's pre-eminent cricket historian, Najum Latif, we descended on him unannounced. We took a bus to his nearest town, Okara, some 75 miles south-west of Lahore. Once a sleepy backwater, Okara has become a bustling place of nearly two million, a district capital with an economy based on agriculture and (on visual evidence) repair shops. On learning that we had come that far, Israr Ali despatched his jeep with his farm assistant Mohammed Farooq and we were soon bouncing along the road to his farm. The land seemed fertile and well managed. We passed through a small village with a number Chak 21-GD rather than a name and turned into his farmyard.

Israr Ali was lying there on a *charpoy* (simple bed), sheltered by a tall tree from the noonday heat, having his legs massaged. He quickly sat up to greet his visitors and listened to Najum's explanation of the forthcoming book. He was delighted to be included and immediately despatched the masseur to fetch a framed photograph of himself receiving a gold medal from President Musharraf in 2004, along with the other survivors of the inaugural match, who then also included Pakistan's early pace bowlers, Khan Mohammad and Fazal Mahmood. (The gold medal turned out to be plated, and a promised payment of 200,000 rupees to all the players was never made.)

Could we take more photographs? By all means, once he had put on his elegant striped *kameez* (long shirt). He hoped that there would be plenty in the book. He had a right to be vain. At 88, he still had magnificent features, reminiscent of the chief of some great tribe in pre-colonial America. Images of him in his playing days, as a left-handed all-rounder, show a tall, imposing figure with a shock of dark hair. He was primarily a seam bowler, with a gift for late swing, praised by contemporaries for his easy high action and aggressive follow-through.

Israr Ali played just four Tests: two in the inaugural series against India and then two more in a comeback at home seven years later against Richie Benaud's Australians. His Test career was blighted by misunderstandings with Pakistan's autocratic first captain, AH Kardar, and then terminated by a serious road accident.

Israr Ali was born in 1927 in Jullundur, in the undivided Punjab in pre-Partition India, and played at Islamia High School. He made his first-class debut, aged 19, for Southern Punjab, in one of the last Ranji trophy matches in an undivided India still, just, under British rule. His team contained Hindus, Sikhs and Muslims. He opened the bowling against Northern India with Lala Amarnath, who would later captain India against him in that inaugural Test. His three victims included two future team-mates, Nazar Mohammad and Khan Mohammad, and he added three more in the second innings, including Imtiaz Ahmed.[2]

At Partition, he made a hazardous journey to Pakistan, settling in Lahore. He does not like to talk about this, but like many other early Pakistan cricketers he was a participant in one of the biggest human tragedies of the 20th century.

Pakistan's first-class matches were initially very rare. Israr Ali played in two without distinction, but in November 1951 he had a fine performance for Bahawalpur and Karachi against the powerful visiting MCC side led by Nigel Howard. Opening the batting with Hanif Mohammad, he contributed 19 to a stand of 65 against an attack containing five frontline Test bowlers, before being run out (if he was a Hanif victim he would be in good company). Opening the bowling with Khan Mohammad, he had Tom Graveney caught by Hanif, then a specialist wicketkeeper, followed by the wickets of Donald Carr and Roy Tattersall, and took two sharp catches off the leg-spinner Amir Elahi.

MCC were made to follow on, and although there were no further

2 Northern India won but were unable to fulfil their semi-final match against Holkar, who progressed to the final by a walkover. In the final Baroda beat Holkar by an innings, thanks to a record stand of 577 between VS Hazare and Gul Mohammad. The next batsman, who waited with his pads on until Gul Mohammad was at last dismissed for 288, was the Maharajah of Baroda – who was promptly dismissed for 1.

wickets for him in the second innings, he had caught the eye of the founding father of Pakistan cricket. 'Cornelius picked me,' he said laconically of his selection for the tour of India.[3]

Unfortunately, the tour captain, AH Kardar, knew very little about Israr Ali, in spite of a long pre-tour practice session in Minto Park. In the opening tour match, against North Zone, he batted at number 4 and made 73, outscoring Hanif in a partnership of 134. It persuaded Kardar that he was a specialist batsman, and that as a left-hander he could counter the left-arm spin of Vinoo Mankad. 'Kardar did not know that I was a bowler. He did not bowl me in that game and made me number three in the Test.' Kardar's qualities as Pakistan's first captain are beyond dispute, but it seems remarkably casual and capricious to have known so little about a player selected for Pakistan's very first Test match.

Kardar also ignored his bowling in India's innings of 372, even during an irritating last-wicket stand of 109 between Adikhari and Ghulam Ahmed. In Pakistan's reply, Hanif and Nazar Mohammad had an opening stand of 64 when Nazar was run out. Israr Ali came in, managed a single and was bowled by Mankad. 'I had little experience of turf wickets and could not judge the ball. I went on the back foot and was completely beaten.' None of the other batsmen could cope with him either, as he achieved his best Test figures of eight for 52. Mankad claimed him again, this time for 9, as Pakistan followed on and lost by an innings and 70 runs. Israr was discarded for the second Test at Lucknow, in which Fazal took 12 wickets and Pakistan won by an innings, although he had the minor satisfaction of being the first Pakistani to take a catch as a substitute fielder.[4] He was back for the third Test, a ten-wicket win for India at Bombay, but this time Kardar parked him down the order at number 9. He scored 10 and 5 and was given just three overs at the end of India's innings of 387 for four declared.

---

3 Justice AR Cornelius, founding father of Pakistan cricket, leading administrator at the new Board of Control, chief selector.
4 The victim was Ghulam Ahmed, the bowler Amir Elahi.

Kardar had never discovered his ability as a left-arm opening bowler, and worse still, he believed that Israr Ali was part of a clique of players opposed to him led by Fazal Mahmood. Israr Ali certainly worshipped Fazal, and told us: 'He will never be born again. I have never seen a bowler like that.' But he insisted that he was never part of any clique.

He was not picked for the tour of England in 1954, although several less talented players were included as Kardar's choices. He thought he would be overlooked again for Pakistan's next series, at home to New Zealand, and decided to clear the air with Kardar. 'I went to his hotel alone. He was walking early in the morning. He took me to his room. He said, "I am playing a match in Bahawalpur against the New Zealanders. You will be asked to play. I will then announce the team for the second Test."' He duly appeared and took three for 43 in the visitors' first innings and five for 21 in the second. But he was not recalled for the next Test in Lahore or the last in Dacca, in which Pakistan gave a Test cap instead to a player, Agha Saadat Ali, for the sake of his fielding.

'Kardar was not sincere to me,' he recalled. He still marked down Israr Ali as one of the Fazal faction. Then the two almost came to blows in the Lahore Gymkhana ground. 'He called me over, "hey, hey, hey!" Very rude.' Israr added that others to suffer this imperious treatment were Maqsood Ahmed ('Merry Max') and Shakoor Ahmed. Israr missed Pakistan's inaugural tour of the West Indies in 1957-58, led by Kardar, and had no better fortune when Kardar was replaced by Fazal for the West Indies' return visit in 1958-59.

However, he produced some huge domestic performances in 1957-58. 'I had nine for fifty-eight for Bahawalpur against Punjab A.' It was in the second innings as Punjab A followed on. He was on course for all ten, and it would have been especially satisfying to have cleaned up the inexperienced number 11, Farooq Kardar, cousin of the retired Pakistan captain. Unfortunately, the young man succumbed first to another Kardar relative, Zulfiqar Ahmed, AH Kardar's brother-in-law. Later that season, against Dacca University Israr took six wickets for just 1 run. He had no memory of this at our meeting (perhaps he did not rate the opposition) and was unable to explain the single which blotted his figures.[5]

He could no longer be ignored and was selected for the first two Tests against Australia in 1959-60 at Dacca and Lahore. He remembered that the match fee was unchanged at 60 rupees (still equivalent to £5). He took six wickets in the two matches, and remarkably four of them were Les Favell, and without the assistance of a fielder.

At Dacca, he bowled the hard-hitting South Australian in the first innings before a single run had been scored, and in the second he had him caught and bowled. For the second Test in Lahore, Favell was moved down the order to number 5 to protect him. 'But Imtiaz gave me the second new ball. I clean bowled him and broke a stump. They gave me the pieces and I gave them to the City Museum at Lahore.' (They are no longer on public view there. If the museum no longer wants them, it should return them to their perpetrator's heirs.) Favell was restored to open the batting in the second innings – and he promptly bowled him once again, for 4 runs. 'He could not play my inswinger.' We asked whether it might have reversed but he was not impressed. He claimed that he could achieve reverse swing routinely – and at the same pace as Wasim Akram. With a hastily borrowed tennis ball, he demonstrated his grip. It looked like an orthodox left-arm seamer's grip, but there may have been some hidden magic.

Apart from Favell, he dismissed the left-handed Alan Davidson twice, lbw and caught behind. But he failed to score a run at Lahore, and in three completed innings he was dismissed cheaply by Richie Benaud. Pakistan lost both Tests after funereal batting (their 134 in the second innings at Dacca took more than 100 overs). He was dropped for the third Test at Karachi, and thereby missed his chance of shaking hands with US president Eisenhower.[6]

His Test return followed an enjoyable season in the Lancashire

5 Unlike the Indian slow left-arm bowler, Bapu Nadkarni, who completed a record-breaking sequence of 132 dot balls against England at Madras in 1963-64. When Richard met him over 40 years later, he was still furious that it was ended by a misfield at mid-off which allowed a single.

6 See chapter 12.

League as professional for Bacup. He made a one-off appearance for them in 1957 as a replacement for Khan Mohammad who was himself replacing Everton Weekes, on Test duty with the touring West Indians. Opening the bowling, he took five for 44 against league rivals Church, and clearly made an impression when Bacup were seeking a professional in 1959.

He gave an entertaining account of the negotiations, conducted by Fazal Mahmood, established at East Lancashire, as his self-appointed agent. 'The captain of the Bacup team came to the place where I was staying with Fazal Mahmood and Hanif Mohammad. Fazal offered them Hanif, as a world-class batsman, but they thought he was too slow and would bat for too many draws. So the captain said, "We want Israr." They offered £700 for the season. I asked for £1,000. Fazal said £900. Then we all agreed on £800 for a one-year contract.'

In the fine summer of 1959, he produced excellent all-round figures for Bacup: over 900 runs at an average of 51, 47 wickets at 22. One highlight was top-scoring in a low-scoring match against Fazal's team, East Lancashire, and then bowling Bacup to victory with five wickets. He was snatched up by Ashton in the Central Lancashire League in 1960, and topped the league batting averages for almost the whole season. But that is not his main memory. 'I bowled Garry Sobers. Ashton came up to me and said we're giving you a contract for two years.' But fate decided otherwise.

He was travelling on a bus from Montgomery (later Sahiwal) to Pakpattan and it was hit by another bus. Three fellow passengers were killed and he was badly injured. 'I had fourteen inches of intestine damaged,' he told us, and showed me the deep network of operation scars to prove it. Through the good offices of his old Jullundur school friend, Masood Nabi Nur, Deputy Commissioner of Montgomery, he was rushed to hospital and underwent a five-hour operation by one of Lahore's finest surgeons. He remained in hospital for 20 days, coming to terms with the end of his cricket career. The Commissioner for Multan secured him the franchise for two local bus routes. If he thought there was any irony in this gesture, after his near-fatal bus

The non-conformist Prince Aslam Khan, often credited as the true inventor of the doosra in the 1950s. (*Nawabzada Muhammad Idrees Khan*)

Intikhab Alam began his service to Pakistan cricket in 1959, and in 2015 he took up the role of team manager for the fourth time. Here, he and Shahid Afridi discuss tactics in Sri Lanka in 2011. (*Getty Images*)

The last known picture of 'Master Aziz', the cricket coach who inspired so many – among them Hanif Mohammad – but who died in obscurity. (*Najum Latif*)

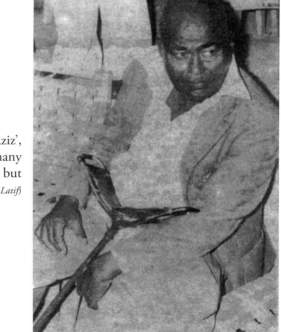

In his later years, Billy Ibadulla became involved in coaching at junior level. Here he talks with Haroon Lorgat (right) at the launch of the ICC Under-19 World Cup in New Zealand in 2009. (*Getty Images*)

Israr Ali, who played in Pakistan's first-ever Test match in 1952, demonstrates the grip he used to get reverse swing. (*Richard Heller*)

A young Raees Mohammad – one of five brothers, he was unlucky to be the only one not to play Test cricket.
(*Raees Mohammad*)

Malik Miran Bux (furthest left, behind Maqsood Ahmed, Fazal Mahmood and AH Kardar) takes to the field for Lahore Test against India in January 1955 – at 47 years and 284 days, he is the oldest Test debutant since James Southerton in 1877. (*Najum Latif*)

SF Rahman, former Pakistan leg-spin bowler and fine ballroom dancer, in his study. Now aged 80, he has become an influential Islamic scholar and preacher. (*Richard Heller*)

Presidents Eisenhower and Ayub Khan watch one of the dullest days of Test cricket, as Pakistan took on Australia in Karachi in December 1959. (*Najum Latif*)

Duncan Sharpe (batsman), the only Anglo-Indian to play for Pakistan, had three Tests before moving to South Australia, where he had a second successful cricket career. (*Yahya Ghaznavi*)

The Dera Ismail Khan team line-up, who went on to suffer the heaviest defeat in all of first-class cricket, losing to Railways by an innings and 851 runs. (*Brigadier MAK Dotani*)

Wasim Bari, whose successful career as Pakistan's wicketkeeper grew out of an insatiable work ethic, and lots of practice. (*Getty Images*)

Jawed Iqbal's cartoon of fast bowler Sarfraz Nawaz shows his great affection for his cricketing subjects.

Aftab Gul, former radical student agitator, still a radical lawyer, leaving court with Salman Butt, during the latter's hearing in Dubai in 2010 over allegations of spot-fixing. (*Getty Images*)

Zaheer Abbas, 'the Asian Bradman', meets the real Bradman at Adelaide in 1972. (*Zaheer Abbas*)

Abdul Qadir, who set up his own cricket academy after retiring, advises Imran Tahir of South Africa in Lahore in May 2012. (*Getty Images*)

Mohsin Khan, 45 Test caps, 53 movie roles, in a poster for the thriller *Raaz*, with co-star Babra Sharif, Pakistan's leading actress. (*Najum Latif*)

Tauseef Ahmed, the net bowler who got called up into the Test side in February 1980. (*Getty Images*)

Television did much to spread the love of cricket throughout Pakistan. Viewing is still frequently a shared outdoor activity, as here in Quetta in 2005. (*Getty Images*)

accident, he put it out of his mind and built up a successful transport business.

Later he was able to buy his farm, 100 acres of well-irrigated land, on the Okara–Faisalabad road, which produces sugar cane, rice, wheat, potatoes and maize. He raised a family of three sons, who played cricket but not at first-class level.

He severed his links with the game, apart from one spell as a national selector in 1982. This was a difficult assignment because the national side was convulsed by a players' revolt against the captain Javed Miandad.

Israr Ali gave an account of the key episode in the revolt – the return of Imran Khan to the side – which varies from the usual history (in which the rebel players returned after Javed's decision to resign the captaincy). He suggested instead that Imran returned under pressure from the powerful chairman of the Board of Control for Cricket in Pakistan, Air Marshal Nur Khan. 'We picked a team for the Lahore Test against Sri Lanka and included Imran Khan. I asked him if he would play in the Test and he said no. We made up a team without him and I took the paper to Air Marshal Nur Khan. When he saw it, he said, "You are against me. I will select him." He sent someone to meet Imran at Lahore airport and he changed his mind. So he played in the Test but he did not do anything.' (Here Israr Ali's memory was faulty: Imran in fact took fourteen wickets for 116.)

In general, he does not rate the Pakistan cricketers after his time, although he conceded tersely that Misbah-ul-Haq and Younus Khan were good batsmen. However, he was a mentor to a local boy, Pakistan's current left-arm spinner, Zulfiqar Babar, born and raised in Okara. 'When he was chosen for the national team he came to me and touched my knees out of respect.'

That was a good note on which to take our leave. We snapped a few more pictures of his magnificent profile and we bounced off again in the jeep. On returning to Okara, we saw people being hurriedly evacuated from buildings, shaken by the earthquake which had killed hundreds of people in the north-west of the country and Afghanistan.

It confirmed a message from Israr Ali's long life: Pakistan cricketers play constantly on the boundary of fate.

Israr Ali died a few weeks later, peacefully at his farm.

6

HITTING AGAINST THE SPHINX:
WHEN PAKISTAN PLAYED EGYPT

On their way to England in 1954, the Pakistanis under AH Kardar stopped to play a match in Egypt against the Gezira Sporting Club.

Before the war, the elite club was at the centre of a small but lively Egyptian cricket scene. It received annual tours from the Free Foresters and teams raised by the well-known amateur and cricket patron Hubert Martineau. In 1939, he managed to recruit RES Wyatt, FR Brown and TN Pearce. Cricket became unpopular in Egypt after the war, because it was associated with the country's privileged classes under the obese, luxury-loving monarch, King Farouk, and with the British army, which most Egyptians regarded as an occupying force. However, it was still the main sport at Egypt's most expensive school, Victoria College, and one of its old boys, Fares Sarofeem Bey, organised an Egyptian tour of England in June 1951, playing matches against English public schools, the Lords and Commons and MCC. Among his star performers was a former captain of the school team, an all-rounder of Lebanese origin called Michel Chaloub. He would be better known as the actor, Omar Sharif.

By 1954, Egyptian cricket was in serious eclipse. The monarchy was overthrown in 1952, while British forces were reduced and kept a lower profile. Influenced by the new nationalist regime led by Colonel

Nasser, Egyptian schools gave less time to cricket or stopped playing it altogether. In January 1952, the hitherto private Gezira Club was nationalised, and Nasser seized half of the 18-hole golf course to set up a new youth club to serve poorer families.[1]

The Pakistanis played their match at the club on 23 April. As in the days of WG Grace, it was played against odds. The club were allowed 15 players but only three had Egyptian names.[2]

The Pakistanis batted first and progressed with little difficulty to 218 off 45 overs. Today that scoring rate would seem sedate, but by current standards it was fierce. They lost only four wickets and those included Alimuddin, 'retired out' on 52. MEZ Ghazali made 52 not out, Hanif 37, Aslam Khokar 29 not out, Maqsood Ahmed 29. Only Imtiaz Ahmed failed – dismissed for 14 by one of the Egyptians, listed on the scorecard simply as Narriman. Even with 15 batsmen the club was no match for the Pakistan attack. Fazal Mahmood took seven for 28 and the 16-year-old leg-spinner, Khalid Hasan, took five for 11. He would find it much harder to dismiss first-class batsmen on the English tour, on wet wickets in a miserable summer.

The Pakistanis had 13 Gezira wickets down for 52 in 25 overs. They did not bother to claim the last, leaving the former Somerset amateur, RVM Stanbury, undefeated on 13.

Imtiaz Ahmed, one of the survivors of the match, gave the reason for the early finish. 'We went off to see the Pyramids and the Sphinx. It was a famous club, with plenty of grass on the pitch, which I liked. After the sights there was no time for shopping and we went straight to Port Said.'

Sadly, the match did nothing to revive local cricket. According to *CricketArchive*, no Egyptian team has played an international match

---

1 See under Egypt in ed R Morgan, *The Encyclopedia of World Cricket* (Sportsbooks, 2007), and 'Is the Gezira Club still the "in" place in Cairo?' *Huffington Post*, 10 July 2014.
2 One name on the club team was intriguing, listed simply as 'de Botton'. Might this have been Gilbert de Botton, the financier and father of the philosopher, Alain? Gilbert was born and educated in Alexandria and he would have been 19 when the match was played. Alain de Botton said no, but thought it might have been one of his relatives, Claude or Ben. Against the Pakistanis, the initial-less de Botton caught Maqsood Ahmed off the experienced Abdou Hassanein and scored 3 before being bowled by Fazal Mahmood.

since, apart from a Cairo International XI, which hosted two matches on the same day in May 1983 on a world tour by the New Zealand Ambassadors. Egypt is not a member of the ICC, but there is a Cairo Cricket League with a Pakistan Expatriates team. In April 2008, they won a memorable victory against the Indian Cricket Club of Egypt beside the Pyramid of Cheops.[3]

3 See 'A Khawaga's Tale: A day of cricket,' *Daily News* (Egypt), 20 April 2008.

7

THE BROTHER WHO HAD NO LUCK

From its inaugural Test in 1952 to 1978, Pakistan never played a Test match without at least one of the five Mohammad brothers in the team. In total, Wazir, Hanif, Mushtaq and Sadiq Mohammad collected 173 Test caps in 100 Test matches. But there should have been more. A fifth brother, Raees, never received the reward that his talents merited.

Raees was the second son of Sheikh Ismail, a former captain in the Indian army and a club cricketer, and Amir Bee, a champion at badminton and the skilful indoor flicking-counter game of carom. He was born on Christmas Day 1932, almost exactly three years after the eldest brother, Wazir, and was almost exactly two years older than the next brother, Hanif. (Mushtaq broke the sequence of late December babies on 22 November 1943 and Sadiq on 3 May 1945.)[1]

The brothers were all born in the princely state of Junagadh, in Gujarat, in pre-Partition India. They enjoyed a prosperous, peaceful life. The two eldest played for the Madrassa High School team and were talent-spotted by the cricket-loving Maharajah. 'He was at Cambridge,' recalled Raees, 'but when he came back to Junagadh he raised his own team. I was one of his players.' Younger brother Hanif watched him and Wazir in the Maharajah's nets. Wazir was heading to be a specialist batsman with a sound technique, but Raees was

1 According to Mushtaq, there are no birth certificates for any of the brothers.

already a genuine all-rounder, a stroke-making batsman and a right-arm leg-spinner.

The family had time for long imaginary cricket matches – 'county matches' on the balcony of their home and 'Test matches' in the big space in front of the neighbouring guest house. Raees was an imaginative teacher for Hanif, as he later would be for Mushtaq and Sadiq in a much smaller space in Karachi. 'I used to bowl at him with a tennis ball and we invented rules for scoring on different sides of the wicket. If the ball hit any part of the body – that was out.' (A tougher version of French cricket, where 'out' is limited to below the knees.)

When Raees was 14, two traumatic events occurred. The boys' father was diagnosed with cancer, and the whole family had to flee Junagadh at Partition, leaving behind all of their property and nearly all of their money. The family settled in an abandoned Hindu temple in Karachi. Sheikh Ismail was now desperately ill, and Wazir and Raees became breadwinners by taking jobs at the Habib Bank. In 1949 their father died, and they had to support their mother, Amir Bee, as she took full responsibility for the youngest brothers. They were able to continue playing cricket for the Bank and at the Pak Moghul Club and in dozens of pick-up matches at the Polo Ground next to the Karachi Gymkhana.[2]

A few years later, Wazir and Hanif, still only 17, were selected for Pakistan's first Test tour, of India in 1952-53, but Raees missed out. 'I was in a trial match at the Bagh-e-Jinnah ground in Lahore. The selectors promised that the best performers would go to India. I scored ninety-three not out and took four for forty-two. I was very happy about my performance. But when the team was announced I was not in it. That was because of politics. Amir Elahi went in my place.' Elahi had been a fine leg-spinner – but he was then 44 years old. At 19, Raees offered much more as a batsman and a fielder in a generally poor fielding side. Amir Elahi played in all five Tests (joining Kardar in representing both India and Pakistan). He played one important innings of 47 but made only 18 runs in his other six innings. He took seven expensive wickets and no catches.

2 H Mohammad, *Playing For Pakistan* (Pakistan: 1999), pp.17, 22.

Amir Elahi retired after the tour and was given a benefit match. Raees was selected for it and had a point to prove. He top-scored with 66 in the second innings (for The Rest, captained by Amir Elahi himself). The following season he repeated his 66 in a benefit match for the veteran Nazir Ali. Early in 1954, he was invited to the trial match in Bahawalpur (on one of Pakistan's then rare turf wickets) for Pakistan's tour of England in 1954. 'I batted and scored forty-eight. Then the selectors called me back. I was really surprised. I could have got fifty – and that is *why* they called me back.'

Once again, Wazir and Hanif made the tour party but Raees was left out. Looking at the first-class tour averages for 1954, one sees several players who seem lucky to have been selected ahead of him. Raees got a consolation prize of touring England with the Pakistan Eaglets. In unhelpful conditions during a very wet summer, he took 49 wickets with his leg-spinners and googlies. At Brecon, he played against a powerful Combined Services team and took three wickets. One of his opponents asked, 'Why are you not in the Pakistan team? Khalid Hasan is nowhere near you.'

Khalid Hasan was picked at 16 after two first-class matches. Most sources suggest that he was handpicked by Kardar (who liked to be a mentor to young players) but Raees claimed that he was also the nephew of the tour manager, Fida Hasan.[3] The young leg-spinner played one Test at Trent Bridge. It made him then the youngest Test player, just short of his 17th birthday, but he was battered by Denis Compton after missing a chance to run him out. He eventually bowled Compton for 278 and finished with two for 116. This was Khalid Hasan's only Test. He took 23 wickets on the whole tour for nearly 40 apiece, and scored 76 runs in six completed innings. That completed his first-class career, except for one wicketless reappearance for Lahore against Railways in December 1958. Reasonably enough, Raees still believes that he might have contributed more on the England tour than Khalid Hasan.

When India toured Pakistan in 1954-55, Raees performed brilliantly in domestic matches, scoring two centuries and taking 14 wickets.

3 We have found no corroboration of this, but the belief clearly still haunted Raees.

The selectors had to take notice and he was picked for the squad in the first Test at Dacca. 'AH Kardar, the skipper, told me to go to bed early because I would be playing the next day. I was very happy, but somehow Maqsood Ahmed arrived in Dacca early in the morning. How he got a flight there I don't know, but he was in the team and I was twelfth man.' Maqsood was a Kardar favourite, and regular nocturnal companion. When he declared himself fit, Kardar put him back in the side. Maqsood kept Raees out for the rest of the series. Raees was 12th man in the next Test at Bahawalpur and watched Hanif make his first Test century. Then he dropped out of the squad altogether, but had the consolation of a spectacular performance for Karachi against Combined Services in the Quaid-e-Azam trophy final. He and Wazir and Hanif each scored a century (his was much the fastest): it was the only time that three brothers achieved this in a first-class match. Then Raees took four wickets in the second innings and helped Karachi win by nine wickets.

In October 1955, he nudged the selectors again, in a special flood-relief match, which included two visiting celebrities, Keith Miller and Mushtaq Ali. He scored 129 not out (repelling a long spell of left-arm mystery spin by Prince Aslam, see chapter 1) and won the admiration of his partner, Miller, who also scored a century. Miller later wrote: 'Raees made one of the finest centuries imaginable. Had I been asked to name a potential Test player, it would most certainly have been this one member of the family who just missed out.'[4] Raees also took two wickets. But the selectors ignored him for the home series against New Zealand: they gave a cap to one player, Agha Saadat Ali, as a fieldsman.

Meanwhile Raees continued to work at the bank, and on returning home would devote long sessions to coaching his younger brothers Mushtaq and Sadiq. His rules had to be slightly adapted for indoor play, but the basic premise remained. The younger boys had to hit the ball and prevent it touching any part of their body. Mushtaq has warm memories of him as a teacher and a father figure, turning the ball sideways for hour after hour. 'From a very early age I was taught

4 *Wisden 1976*, p.127.

by a very fine spin bowler. He taught me how to read bowlers and play spin.' He turned Mushtaq into a leg-spinner himself – after rejecting his bent-arm attempts to bowl off-spin.

When still only 15 (officially), Mushtaq made his Test debut for Pakistan against the West Indies. It would have been human to resent being overtaken by his younger brother and pupil and never getting a chance himself. But Raees did not express this at all.

He finally pulled stumps on his first-class career in 1962, just after his 30th birthday. In 30 matches he had scored 1344 runs at an average of nearly 33 and taken 33 wickets at 31 apiece. He also took 21 catches. The figures understate the impression he made as an attacking batsman and as a bowler with an unusually potent googly.

All his family, especially his mother, were disappointed at his near-miss as a Test player – and that he never got another chance. All his brothers believe that inferior players were selected instead of him because they were Lahorites, or favourites of Kardar – or simply because Wazir and Hanif were established in the side and the selectors did not want a third Mohammad brother.

Raees himself gave an impression of melancholy rather than resentment over his unlucky career. 'When I see some youngster playing I look back to my past. I regret it very much. I was very unlucky. There were politics against me.' He had one particular regret. 'I had a chance to play league cricket in England. Alf Gover offered me the opportunity, with accommodation and the prospect of a job afterwards. But I had just married. I could not take the risk of giving up my job at the bank.'

His life outside cricket also had its setbacks, over money and health, and in 1987 he lost his wife of 33 years. However, he was proud of maintaining his habit of playing two games of snooker each day, to keep fit. He urged Hanif, still recovering from treatment for liver cancer, to move about more. It was quite poignant to see Hanif, so much more successful in cricket and personal finances, taking advice from the elder brother who had taught him so many years ago.

One other discovery was even more poignant. Raees had prepared with great care for the meeting for this book, handing over notes, extracts from Mushtaq's book, and a fine photograph of himself in his prime. He was the tallest Mohammad brother and the most dashing in appearance. In modern times, he would have attracted groupies.

Why had he prepared so carefully? Because, at the age of 82, it was the first time this fine but luckless cricketer had been interviewed in his own right.

8

A TEST MATCH
SUMMONS AT 47

Pakistan cricket is famous for teenage prodigies. Mushtaq Mohammad was the youngest player to play Test cricket, aged 15 years and 124 days on debut.[1] Twelve other Pakistanis made their debut before their 18th birthday.

But the record of Malik Miran Bux[2] was more startling than any of these. He was picked for Pakistan's Test team against India at Lahore in 1955 at the age of 47 years 284 days. That made him the oldest Test debutant in the 20th century. In the all-time list, only James Southerton of England was older on his first appearance, against Australia in the first Test match of all in 1877.

Malik Miran Bux is a poster boy for ageing cricketers who still dream of international recognition – all the more, because his selection was based on performances in club cricket. His lone first-class match, five years previously, was ruined by rain after he had bowled seven cheap but wicketless overs. His captain, AH Kardar, was strongly

---

1 Mushtaq was briefly displaced by Hasan Raza, but later medical evidence led to the rejection of his claim to have made his Test debut at 14 years 227 days. According to official figures, Aaqib Javed was 16 years 189 days on Test debut – and only *12 years 82 days* when he opened the bowling in a first-class match.
2 He spelt his name thus, as used by the British in his birthplace of Rawalpindi, but some sources spell it Bakhsh, as it was pronounced.

criticised for bringing an old man into the side – but it nearly proved to be Kardar's most inspired decision.

Malik Miran Bux was born in Rawalpindi on 20 April 1907. In his 81st year, he told the historian Najum Latif about his early cricket days. 'I got interested in cricket in 1914 when the British ruled the subcontinent. Rawalpindi was a military cantonment of the British then. The British soldiers brought cricket here from England. It was my father who started my cricket coaching. I was a student at Daniel School and he was a cricket coach there. His love for cricket got rubbed on me. There was no end to my madness for cricket. After school I used to go straight to the Pindi Club ground. When the school was closed I spent all my day at the ground bowling, batting and fielding. During my childhood and youth my father guided and encouraged me at every step.

'My father would take me along to Sialkot where he would buy me a bat and a ball. I think I started to play cricket in 1916. In fact, like hockey, cricket was brought to India by the British. The British played cricket here with great gusto. My father used to give them practice and I used to go to the ground with him and would join the practice sessions. I was a good bowler from the very beginning and whenever the British would go to play cricket in other cities they would take me along and I would take many wickets. Seeing my talent, my father kept encouraging and guiding me.'

Some sources say that he never went to school but Malik Miran Bux denied this. 'I studied till the eighth class, though people like to assume that I never went to school. It was my love for cricket that prevented me from going any further in education. After I finished the eighth class, I joined the army (Royal Artillery) as a Sepoy and a gunner because with that kind of an education I could not become a commissioned officer. When the English officers came to know that I could bowl very well, they started respecting me more despite my being just an ordinary Sepoy. In fact, the British thought that it was hockey and not cricket that interested the Indians. I reached the rank of a Havildar [sergeant in the Indian army] not because of cricket but because of the normal course of promotions.'

Malik Miran Bux grew to be six feet tall. He taught himself to bowl quickish off-spinners from a high action and a 12-pace run-up. The

British club members were so impressed with his talent and application that they began to include him in the first XI – a remarkable achievement at the time for a local youngster from a modest background.

His exploits at the Pindi ground earned wider recognition. In 1932, he was selected for a four-and-half-month tour of the whole of pre-Partition India, playing matches in Bombay, Calcutta, Karachi and a number of princely states. He took over 125 wickets. He told Najum Latif: 'During the Second World War there used to be a cricket tournament at Lahore on Christmas Day and I played the first important match of my life in this tournament. I took three wickets for thirty-two runs and my performance was lauded all over.'

He was over 40 when he caught the eye at his beloved Pindi ground in November 1948, against the West Indians under John Goddard, the first international visitors to independent Pakistan. 'I played a two-day match for the C-in-C's XI under the captaincy of Dr Jahangir Khan. I got five for sixty-one in the first innings that included the wickets of George Carew, George Headley, Clyde Walcott, John Goddard and Robert Christiani.' They were all frontline batsmen with Test match experience, especially the magisterial Headley.

'After that I played against the Commonwealth team that toured Pakistan in 1949 under Jock Livingston.[3] I was simply unplayable. The tourists were shot out for eighty-one runs before lunch. I got five wickets for sixteen runs in the first innings and again five wickets for sixty-five runs in the second innings. We almost won the match!'

In the same year, he played his first first-class match in Pakistan, again at the Pindi ground, for the Commander-in-Chief's XI against Ceylon. He was 12 days short of his 43rd birthday. Rain limited him to seven overs which were wicketless but cost only eight runs.

He then returned to club cricket. He was not considered for Pakistan's first Test tours, to India and England, and he did not appear

---

3 Livingston did not play in this two-day match. The Commonwealth side was predominantly Australian. They were led at Rawalpindi by Fred Freer (one Test cap for Australia as a seam-bowling all-rounder). Miran Bux's victims included Jack Pettiford, Bill Alley, George Tribe, Winston Place and George Dawkes, who all went on to distinguished careers in English county cricket.

in Pakistan's new first-class competition, the Quaid-e-Azam trophy, when it was inaugurated in 1953.

So why was he selected for the third Test against India, in February 1955, in his 48th year?

It was at the Bagh-e-Jinnah ground in Lahore, not his happy hunting-ground at Pindi, where he replaced an injured fast bowler, Khan Mohammad. In the first two Tests, Pakistan's spin attack was in the hands of two slow left-arm bowlers, Shuja-ud-Din and Kardar. If they had wanted to add an off-spinner, why did they not restore Zulfiqar Ahmed – a hero of the recent victory over England at The Oval? He was over 20 years younger than Malik Miran Bux. He had taken 63 first-class wickets at only 17.46 apiece on the England tour and offered more than Malik Miran Bux as a batsman and a fielder.

However, Zulfiqar had had a sharp family quarrel with Kardar, who was his brother-in-law. He objected fiercely to Kardar's second marriage to an English bride, and had made certain that she went home when she joined Kardar at a festival match in Bombay before the Indian visit. The rift kept Zulfiqar out of the Pakistan team for all the India Tests. Malik Miran Bux was recommended as his replacement by Maqsood Ahmed, a strong influence on both Kardar and Justice Cornelius, and there was a strong lobby for him from the Rawalpindi Cricket Association.[4]

Pakistan batted first. At number 11, Malik Miran Bux contributed an undefeated single to their total of 328. Najum Latif remembers him waiting to bat – looking like an outsider in the team. 'He stood tall at six feet with a dark complexion and sporting a light moustache. He had a high forehead with black dyed hair. He was decent, aloof, and quiet and sat mostly by himself. Even his cricket kit was different from the others. Instead of the green blazer of Pakistan, he was wearing a blue-coloured blazer with a badge of a Rawalpindi team on it. The colour of his cricket kit was completely white, as against the rest of the team who wore cream-coloured kits as was the traditional colour of Test teams in those days.'

4 Source: Najum Latif.

He was in action early in the Indian reply. Kardar gave him an aggressive 'Carmody field' with seven close catchers, but he needed none of them when he clean-bowled the Indian opener, Punjabi, to the delight of the packed crowd. 'Caps and handkerchiefs were hurled in the air,' wrote Qamaruddin Butt in his account of the India tour.[5] Spectators were even more delighted shortly afterwards when Miran Bux clean bowled the stylish Manjrekar for a duck. His first two Test (and first-class wickets) had cost only 14 runs from 12 overs.

The 47-year-old bowled the most overs in India's innings – 48, including 20 maidens. He failed to take more wickets, but should have had Umrigar, India's top scorer, caught by Fazal. According to Qamaruddin Butt, Miran Bux 'kept an immaculate length' and 'beat the batsmen all ends up. He justified the confidence reposed in him.'[6]

Pakistan gained a lead of 77. But there was little time to attempt to force a win and Kardar took no risks with his second-innings decla-ration at 136 for five – in the 88th over. Miran Bux did not bowl in India's short second innings as the match limped to a draw.

The Indians played a side match against a Services XI at Pindi – but Malik Miran Bux was not selected. Did the selectors want to hide him? He might have tormented the Indians on his favourite pitch. Instead, they cruised to an innings victory.

He came back for the next Test at Peshawar. It was a low-scoring affair in which he was given only eight overs in India's first innings. They were wicketless and cost 30 runs (carnage by the standard of that series). Again at number 11, he failed to score in either Pakistan innings. He bowled two wicketless overs for 3 in India's meaningless second innings.[7] With this anti-climax, his Test career was over. He told Najum Latif: 'I never went boot-licking after anyone, making requests to be included in the Test team. Perhaps for this reason I was kept away.'

There were some further successes. He played for the Governor-General's XI at Peshawar against Henry Cave's New Zealand team.

5 Qamaruddin Butt, *Cricket Without Challenge* (Maliksons, 1955), p.135.
6 Ibid., pp.135, 137.
7 He gave way to Hanif Mohammad – who took his only Test wicket, bowling with his left hand.

In the first innings, he took three wickets for 89 runs in 59 overs of which 28 were maidens. His best bowling performance of six wickets for 15 runs came for the Services XI against East Pakistan Whites in the Quaid-e-Azam trophy at Dacca Stadium in 1956-57. He played his last first-class match at the age of 51 at his home ground. His aggregate of four wickets for 45 runs helped Rawalpindi beat Peshawar by 28 runs after being dismissed for 53 in their first innings. He finished with 48 first-class victims at 19.43 apiece. He coached college students at Faisalabad and Sargodha, followed his father as head groundsman at the Pindi Club, stood regularly as an umpire in club fixtures and enjoyed watching matches from his special seat beside the sight screen. He enjoyed the enduring respect of generations of Pakistani and visiting cricketers: Maqsood Ahmed always regarded him as 'the sweetest and gentlest soul of Pakistan cricket'.[8]

Malik Miran Bux had a benefit match in December 1986 which earned him 125,000 rupees (then equivalent to around £4,300). However, when Najum Latif met him in January 1988 he was living in modest one-room accommodation in a lower middle-class section of Dhok Rata in the old city of Rawalpindi. 'He was sitting on one of the two *charpoys* covered with white sheets wearing a white *shalwar kameez* (baggy trousers and loose shirt) with a black coat. There was no other furniture in the room.'

He talked to Najum Latif about his career and commented proudly: 'I had never thought of playing as a professional. I was just happy to know that I could bowl better than the other bowlers. This feeling made me crazy about cricket.' He added: 'I was born in Rawalpindi and spent all my childhood and youth here and I want to end the journey of my life here as well. I began my cricket at the Pindi Club ground and kept on playing till I could and finally ended it at the same ground. You can say I spent all my life at the Pindi Club ground.'

This remark became even more poignant on 8 February 1991, when during his regular early-morning walk he died along the roadside not far from his house. No one recognised his body. Loudspeakers of the

8 Source: Najum Latif.

mosques announced that a dead body of an unknown man was found along the road and asked the residents to come to identify it. Such was the tragic end of 'Babujee', the affectionate and respectful name given to Malik Miran Bux by the cricket-loving residents of Rawalpindi.

9

PRIVATE AND PUBLIC FAITH
IN PAKISTAN CRICKET

When Pakistan was founded almost 70 years ago in the aftermath of World War Two, it was beyond doubt an Islamic state. But its founders insisted it should be a tolerant place, open to all faiths.

Only days before independence, Mohammed Ali Jinnah, the country's first governor-general, presented his personal vision in his famous speech of 11 August 1947 to the Constituent Assembly of Pakistan: 'You may belong to any religion or caste or creed. That has nothing to do with the business of the state ... We are starting with this fundamental principle that we are all citizens and equal citizens of one state ... Now I think that we should keep that in front of us as our ideal and you will find that in the course of time Hindus would cease to be Hindus and Muslims would cease to be Muslims, not in the religious sense, because that is the personal faith of each individual, but the political sense as citizens of the state.'[1]

But even before independence, his vision of Pakistan had been strongly challenged by two clerical organisations, the JUI and the JI, which demanded that the new state should express the paramountcy of Islam and act as an agent for restoring an Islamic society. The intensity of this debate delayed for nearly a decade the formation of

1 Cited in C Jaffrelot, *The Pakistan Paradox* (London: C Hurst, 2015), pp.439-40.

a constitution for Pakistan, and was not resolved by the compromise adopted in 1956.[2]

Pakistan cricket suffered no immediate fallout from this debate. Indeed, its founding fathers were an advertisement for Jinnah's vision: Justice Cornelius, a Christian, Mr Collector, a Parsee, and Professor Aslam, a Muslim. Three Christians played Test cricket for Pakistan in the 1950s and one Parsee achieved representative honours before Pakistan had Test status.

In its early days, Pakistan's cricketers were generally drawn from small networks of people in the major cities of Karachi and Lahore, connected by membership of the same schools and colleges and clubs and often by family and marriage ties. This environment encouraged strong personal loyalties – and rivalries – and discouraged any sense of religious identity, even in those with strongly religious backgrounds. They all became a special group in Pakistan society – as cricketers. Through their specific cricket skills, they could aspire to higher living standards and social status and to the honour of representing their city or province – and, most importantly, their newly independent nation.

In the cricketing memoirs of Kardar, Fazal Mahmood and Hanif Mohammad there are virtually no references to any religious issue, other than Hanif's entertaining encounters with the cricket-mad Pir of Pagaro, spiritual leader of the Hurs (and the only acknowledged living saint to play the first-class game).[3]

After his retirement, Fazal Mahmood, once a celebrated partygoer, adopted a devout lifestyle. In 1970, he published a devotional work called *Urge To Faith*, which has a detailed blueprint for applying Islamic principles to Pakistan's economy, government and social system. But significantly, the book has no mention of cricket. He makes no suggestion that cricketers have any special obligations towards Islam. There is no sporting reference at all except in the dedication: 'To Muhammad Ali Clay, The World Boxing Champion and a zealous Teacher of Islam

2 Jaffrelot, ibid, ch 8, especially pp.439-54.
3 Hanif Mohammad, op. cit., pp.28-29.

for his sportsmanship and fearless expression of views and his refusal to be a party to massacre in Vietnam.'[4]

During the 1970s and 1980s, Jinnah's vision began to fade. Pakistan's leaders gave Islamic interests far more power. They did this largely out of political opportunism, but the effects were far-reaching. Prime Minister ZA Bhutto introduced a pro-Islamic constitution which discriminated against non-Muslims, moved the weekly holiday from Sunday to Friday, gave degree status to various Quranic qualifications and cracked down on alcohol, gambling and nightclubs. His successor, Zia-ul-Haq, promoted a working alliance between the Islamic Right and the armed forces, extended Islamic influence in education and introduced a virtually parallel Islamic legal system, including new laws on blasphemy enforceable by life imprisonment and even the death penalty.[5]

But even these developments had little influence on Pakistan men's cricket, although they had a terrible impact on the women's game.[6] For men's cricket there were more powerful influences of another kind. One was the enduring elitism of Pakistan cricket – the cricketers were still largely drawn from the same city-based networks which supplied them in the 1950s.

Another was the experience of English county cricket, which was shared by all of Pakistan's major Test cricketers in the 1970s, except for Wasim Bari.[7] It encouraged the players to regard themselves as part of a professional international cadre, and made them aware of their commercial value. Eventually this triggered the long dispute over touring pay and conditions which led to the end of AH Kardar's control over Pakistan cricket.[8] The sense of professional identity was deeply reinforced by the experience of playing for Kerry Packer's 'circus'. It is worth adding that by joining English county cricket, Pakistan's

---

4 Fazal Mahmood, *Urge To Faith* (Pakistan: 1970), p.iii. It was inaccurate of Fazal to include Clay in the dedication, a name which the great man had repudiated.
5 Jaffrelot, op. cit., pp.465-77.
6 See chapter 27.
7 There was no market for an overseas specialist wicketkeeper.
8 See Peter Oborne, *Wounded Tiger* (Simon & Schuster, 2014), pp.246-52.

cricketers became part of a very strong community with a distinctive social life. They were never expected to violate their religious principles, but they were expected to 'do their turn' at the bar, and to accept drinkers, gamblers and womanisers as friends and colleagues.[9]

Pakistan cricket also had strong leadership during this period with distinct and non-Islamic agendas. AH Kardar made Pakistan cricket an expression of ZA Bhutto's 'state socialist' project rather than his accommodation with Islamic interests. When Air Marshal Nur Khan became chairman of the Board of Control under General Zia-ul-Haq in 1980, he pursued a personal agenda. Assisted by his lieutenant Arif Abbasi, he focused relentlessly on improving the financial and administrative operations of Pakistan cricket, developing its infrastructure, and, above all, capturing all the opportunities to enhance its commercial value.

Of course, for most of this period Pakistan was led by two powerful captains, Javed Miandad and Imran Khan, who had learnt from English county cricket and Packer. Both of them judged other players by their professional cricketing standards and dedication to the Pakistan team. Religious matters and lifestyle choices were for the players' personal choice. Some players were more publicly observant of Islam than others (for example, Javed often performed the *wazu* (Muslim ablution) before going in to bat), but none ever suggested that religion should be part of a team ethic.[10]

In his book *Pakistan: A Personal History*, Imran Khan describes at some length his rediscovery of Islam and the values of Islam that inspired his political philosophy.[11] But as with Fazal before him, he makes no suggestion that cricket or cricketers should become special representatives of Islam.

Finally, it should be mentioned that cricket itself had become too

---

9 For a brilliant portrait of county cricket life in the 1960s, see Stephen Chalke, *Runs In The Memory* (Fairfield Books, 1997). Several Pakistan cricketers, notably Sarfraz Nawaz at Northamptonshire, thoroughly explored all the social opportunities of county cricket.
10 See Nadeem F Paracha, 'Pakistan cricket: a class, ethnic and sectarian history,' *Dawn*, 19 September 2013.
11 Imran Khan, *Pakistan: A Personal History* (Transworld, 1999), ch 3.

popular in Pakistan for Zia to risk subjecting it to an Islamic regime. He actually encouraged the state-run PTV, still a monopoly television network, to give extensive coverage to the international cricket team as a distraction from protests against his dictatorship. At the same time, he directed the network to give a regular weekly spot to an ultra-conservative Islamic lecturer, Dr Israr Ahmed. For several months, Dr Israr inveighed against immodesty among women actresses and newscasters and women in studio audiences for television programmes. He induced the PTV to impose a short-lived crackdown and a strict dress code. Zia was compelled to relax this after women's protests, but Dr Israr kept his slot.

It was a different story when Dr Israr suddenly announced that cricket should be banned from television because it was making Pakistanis forget their religious obligations, and that women should be banned from attending live matches. This particular broadcast was not aired at all. Officially, Dr Israr was ill. A few weeks later he denied this, and amplified his remarks, telling *Jang* newspaper that women had been corrupted by the sight of players, especially Imran Khan, polishing the ball on their groin area. This was too much for Zia, and his Information Ministry invited Dr Israr to stay away from cricket. He refused, and that ended his broadcasts on PTV.[12]

After reaching its zenith by winning the World Cup in 1992, Pakistan cricket collapsed vertiginously into the depths. There were eight years of poor results, factional fighting and outright scandal, and a succession of short-term captains and leadership regimes at the PCB. Meanwhile, the country itself endured a series of corrupt and incompetent governments, a worsening economy and increasing insecurity and violence.

Partly as a reaction to this era, religion became for the first time a major public influence on the Pakistan cricket team. The main agent for this change was the evangelistic Islamic movement, the Tableeghi-Jamaat.

12 See Nadeem F Paracha, 'The heart's filthy lesson,' *Dawn*, 14 Feb 2013.

Its name means simply 'society for spreading faith'. Tableeghi-Jamaat was founded in 1927 in the Mewat region, near Delhi, initially as a means of countering rising Hindu influence over the Meos, the main local ethnic group. It was an offshoot of the revivalist, anti-colonial Deobandi movement founded in the wake of the failed Indian uprising, but its founder, Mohammad Ilyas, soon broke free of the Deobandi's heavily scholastic approach. Instead, he offered his followers Six Principles to help them become better and purer Muslims. The most important was Dawah – leading a righteous life and evangelising others. Tableeghi-Jamaat gained many adherents in post-independence Pakistan, West and East (it retained them in independent Bangladesh, which now has its largest single chapter). In its absence of doctrine, hierarchy and ceremony and its emphasis on believers' personal relationship with God, Tableeghi-Jamaat's approach resembled many born-again Christian movements in the United States. Like them, it began to attract well-educated adherents and a number of celebrities, particularly in the 1990s.[13]

Its first major cricketing convert was Pakistan's former captain, Saeed Ahmed, a scintillating batsman and serious partygoer in his prime in the 1950s and 1960s. We heard Saeed describe for over an hour the extended mystical experience which led him to join the movement in 1978. Saeed was then at a low ebb. Banned and disgraced while AH Kardar ran Pakistan cricket under ZA Bhutto, he failed in an attempted comeback under the new regime of Zia-ul-Haq. His marriage to the socially prominent Salma[14] had failed, and with it the business ventures he had acquired through her connexions. He embraced his new Islamic life whole-heartedly, acquired a beard, replaced his Western wardrobe with a *shalwar kameez*, and became a fervent evangelist for Tableeghi-Jamaat. He made little headway among cricketers in the era of Javed Miandad and Imran Khan. But Saeed Ahmed persisted through the 1990s, visiting the players' dressing rooms, giving them

13 For analysis of the social appeal of Tableeghi-Jamaat, see Nadeem F Paracha, 'Reverse Sweeps: Pakistan's crazy cricket controversies,' *Dawn*, 19 June 2013.
14 She was the sister-in-law of Shaharyar Khan, scion of the princely house of Bhopal, future head of Pakistan's foreign service and chairman of the PCB (see chapter 36).

a religious lecture, and leaving behind cassettes of the movement's leading preachers.

His first convert was the brilliant opening batsman, Saeed Anwar. Once a happy-go-lucky personality and a party-lover, he joined Tableeghi-Jamaat after the heartbreaking death of his young daughter. He too grew a beard, prayed and observed Islam conspicuously in public, lectured other players, and took them to local Tableeghi-Jamaat meetings at home and abroad. He told Pakistan's World Cup team in 2003 that they were bound to win because Allah would send angels to help them. When Pakistan crashed out in the first round, he was asked why the angels had not appeared, and replied instantly 'because we were not good Muslims'.[15]

Meanwhile, the leg-spinner Mushtaq Ahmed joined the movement under the influence of the former Pakistan wicketkeeper Zulqarnian.[16] Saeed Anwar's prize capture was Inzamam-ul-Haq, who allowed him to continue his evangelism in the team even after his last match as a player in 2003.

Tableeghi-Jamaat also recruited Saqlain Mushtaq, Shahid Afridi and (temporarily) Waqar Younis. It played a role in the dramatic conversion of Yousuf Youhana, the only Christian to captain Pakistan, to Mohammad Yousuf. At the height of its influence, under the dominating captaincy of Inzamam, Tableeghi-Jamaat had captured almost the entire Pakistan team, who followed a highly demanding – and highly public – religious regime. There were a few major standouts from the movement: the all-rounders Azhar Mahmood and Abdur Razzaq, the batsmen Younus Khan and Misbah-ul-Haq (both highly devout men who kept their faith private) and the mercurial fast bowler, Shoaib Akhtar.[17]

15 For this and a history of Tableeghi-Jamaat's influence in the Pakistan cricket team, see S Khan and A Khan, *Cricket Cauldron* (IB Tauris, 2013), pp.166-75.

16 Mushtaq Ahmed, *Twenty20 Vision* (Methuen, 2006), ch 16. Zulqarnian should not be confused with Zulqarnian Haider, the Pakistan wicketkeeper who fled from the team in 2011 alleging that he and his family had been threatened by match-fixers.

17 For a scathing attack on the team's semi-compulsory religious regime, see Nadeem Paracha, article op. cit., and S Akhtar, *Controversially Yours* (Harper Sport India, 2011), pp.238-39.

After Mohammad Yousuf's conversion, the Hindu Danish Kaneria became the only non-Muslim in the team. But he too accepted the demands of the new public culture, at least in words. In the 2006 edition of *Wisden Cricketers' Almanack,* Osman Samiuddin wrote: 'Rare today in Pakistani cricket is the public soundbite, or even private utterance, not bracketed by *bismillah* (in the name of Allah) or *inshallah* (God willing). The team prays together fastidiously, recites *ayats* (Quranic verses) in its huddles, and celebrates personal and collective milestones with the *sajda* (the act of kneeling in Muslim prayer); they all fast during Ramadan, some even during games ... Even Danish Kaneria, a Hindu, peppers his talk with *inshallah*.'[18]

Tableeghi-Jamaat influence finally receded after Pakistan's dismal performance in the 2007 World Cup, followed by a swirl of speculation about its role after the death of Bob Woolmer. Under pressure from his tottering patron, President Musharraf, the PCB chairman, Nasim Ashraf, announced that the team would concentrate more on playing than piety.[19]

The team went through another terrible era, marked by the terrorist attack on the Sri Lankan tourists in 2009 and the new match-fixing scandal the following year. Younus Khan, Shahid Afridi and, above all, Misbah-ul-Haq were left to pick up the pieces and restore both the playing performance and the moral standards of a Pakistan team in international exile. In setting about this task, they turned their backs on the ostentatious religiosity of the Tableeghi-Jamaat regime. Faith again became a private matter.

All these developments were watched by a player from the early days of Pakistan cricket. He is far less familiar than those who joined Tableeghi-Jamaat, but he made a journey into faith which was longer and deeper than any of theirs.

18 O Samiuddin, 'With Allah on their side,' *Wisden 2006.*
19 'Pakistan trades pizzazz for piety,' *The Australian,* 24 March 2007.

10

THE SECOND INNINGS OF SF RAHMAN

By Richard Heller

T he preacher in the mosque in Lahore begins in a pleasant conver-
sational tone. His twinkling eyes and fulsome white beard make
him look like an indulgent grandfather to the men and boys attending
the Friday Prayer. But as the sermon gathers momentum, the eyes
harden, the phrases become more staccato and his whole demeanour
becomes admonitory. Soon he is acting out an intense drama, taking
on himself all the roles of those he cites for praise or condemnation. I
discover afterwards that he is delivering a passionate warning against
all the men and women of today who have forsaken the learning and
the standards of true Islam. They are wasting their lives on trivialities
such as television and movies and sport. One passage is especially fierce:
'Women have stopped covering themselves and men are interested only
in dancing.'

The dramatic preacher is Maulana Shiekh Fazal-ur-Rahman Bin
Mohammad Al-Azhari.[1] He is not to be confused with a religious
politician of a similar name, having resisted many invitations to enter
politics. He is a few days short of his 80th birthday. As SF Rahman,

---

1 The spelling Rehman which appears in *Wisden* and other reference sources is inaccurate. His own signature, in English characters, clearly says Rahman.

aged 22, he won a Test cap for Pakistan as a leg-spin bowler. He also won a reputation as a snappy dresser, a popular clubman and (piquantly, given his sermon) a ballroom dancer. Many Pakistan cricketers have turned to religion but none have committed themselves so deeply. He became an Islamic scholar of international repute, and a preacher who won a national following without the aid of radio or television.

He is a Wahhabist,[2] part of the school of Sunni Islam which originated in the 18th century in the remote province of Najd in the Arabian desert. It is often described as 'fundamentalist' but a more accurate term would be 'literalist' or 'puritanical'. The founder, Mohammad ibn Abd al-Wahhab, had something in common with the Puritan agenda for Christianity, in that he sought to purge Islam of superstitious and idolatrous practices, particularly the veneration of saints and shrines, and emphasised the individual relationship of every Muslim with God. He formed an early alliance with a local leader, Mohammad ibn Saud. The alliance deepened and endured under Saud's successors, such that Wahhabist Islam is the officially recognised form of Sunni Islam in the kingdom of Saudi Arabia. With Saudi resources, it has proselytised extensively in Pakistan, and endowed hundreds of mosques and madrassas. However, the Muhammadi mosque, in Sant Nagar, Outfall Road, where Maulana Rahman now preaches, has no such funding. Its expenses are met by its local worshippers in a far-from-wealthy area of Lahore. He pays a good portion of them himself.

Since Wahhabists are often identified as violent and fanatical in British media, and as supporters of Islamic terrorism, I want to emphasise at this stage the warmth and hospitality I received on three visits to hear Maulana Rahman preach. No religious congregation anywhere could have been more welcoming to a stranger and an infidel. Mr Rana Muhammed Arshad, the secretary, insisted on serving me tea and biscuits the day after he had suffered the heartbreak of losing his wife of

2 I have adopted this term as the easiest for British readers to follow, and the one which identifies the history of this branch of Islam. Many of its adherents reject it, and prefer to be known as Salafists.

36 years. Maulana Rahman himself repudiates terrorism. He told me: 'I have been talking according to the Holy Qu'ran, whatever the issue. It may be against the government, it may be against jihadi groups. A jihadi group tried to contact me. I said, "No, thank you very much, I will have nothing to do with you. If you want to preach, preach peacefully, go to the people, knock at their heads to be let inside, or hearts, give them a little tap." This is the teaching of all prophets.'

There would be other issues where we sharply disagreed, but not terrorism. I never had any doubt that he reached all of his views by independent thought, standing apart from politics and power and fashionable currents.

Before listening to his sermon, I had met him twice in his house in the Upper Mall Scheme of Lahore, in the company of his long-time friend, the historian Najum Latif. A few years ago he lost his wife after over 55 years together; he now shares the house with his younger son and his children. The rooms are spacious and well appointed. The largest serves as his bedroom and study; it looks smaller because its shelves are neatly arrayed with religious books and texts, not only Islamic ones because he is proud of his knowledge of many faiths. He has found nights unbearably lonely after his wife's death and he shares his bedroom with his youngest grandson. (This was a poignant echo of AH Kardar, who in his last years shared his bedroom with his youngest grandson.)

The house, in one of the most exclusive residential areas of Lahore, has a garden large enough for several cricket nets. It would fetch him a fortune if it ever went on the market. Apart from his income from a successful family business, he owns several commercial markets in Lahore. He has regularly waived rents from his tenants if they fall on hard times. He has never made any money from his religious life, and paid for publication of all of his books himself. He writes a regular column for the prestigious daily *Nawa-i-Waqt* without payment. He keeps none of his money in a bank, lest it accumulate interest. Every winter, he sets aside a sum of money to distribute 300 warm jackets to poor children.

Maulana Rahman talked freely about his remarkable twin life. The cricket part of it ended 50 years ago, in disappointment; the religious part has been dominant since then and full of achievement. But the cricket memories still bubbled through his conversation, with a clear sense of what might have been.

FIRST INNINGS

His life began in Amritsar, still part of British India, in 1935. He was the youngest of nine children in a family whose prosperity was built on a company that supplied safes and strongboxes. After Partition, the company switched to the import of industrial machinery and spare parts, and prospered even more. It is still in the family and he keeps an eye on it. This is mainly as a diversion after his wife died a few years ago, but I sensed that he might have run it successfully, if he had so chosen.

He was 12 at Partition when the family moved to Lahore, but his life then was strongly influenced by the army career of his elder brother (by 17 years), SA (Abdur) Rahman. He followed his older brother when he was assigned first to Karachi and then to Rawalpindi, where SF joined the prestigious Mission High School. When SF eventually returned to Lahore, he joined the even more prestigious Central Model School, where he set a Pakistan schools record for throwing the discus.

Abdur Rahman was a first-class cricketer before and after Partition and a friend of the leg-spinner Amir Elahi, one of the three Test players to represent both India and Pakistan. He became the youngest Rahman's cricket role model. Abdur Rahman went on Pakistan's first overseas tour, to Ceylon, and became an administrator after his playing days. As Major SA Rahman, he was assistant manager to Brigadier 'Gussie' Hyder on Pakistan's 1962 tour of England. He had his work cut out: a weak touring party, beset with factional rivalries under an inexperienced captain, was overwhelmed 4-0 in the Test series.

There was a powerful family counter to his brother's influence. 'My parents pulled me back from cricket with prayer. My father and mother were very religious, good, kind-hearted people. They called me from the cricket ground and had me sitting in the mosque, reading religious books.' But his cricket ambitions were fired by a move to Lahore in his teens. As a leg-spinning all-rounder, he played for two local clubs, Friends CC and the more prestigious Universal CC. He came into contact with some of Pakistan's early cricket stars: Nazar Mohammad, Imtiaz Ahmed, Waqar Hasan (cricketer turned business leader, still a great friend), and, an especially strong influence, Mian Mohammad Saeed, Pakistan's first captain. Under his leadership, SF Rahman went on the first Pakistan Eaglets tour of England, in 1952, aged only 16.

His first-class career had already begun with a bang in February that year, playing for Punjab University in the long-established fixture against the Punjab Governor's XI. He took five for 63 in the first innings, including three past or future Test players, Nazar Mohammad, Khalid Ibadulla and Jahangir Khan (who played for India in 1936). He then disappeared for two years (when Pakistan had few first-class fixtures) but produced some impressive performances afterwards, notably in 1956 for the Combined Universities side against a strong MCC touring party led by Donald Carr. Batting at number 8, he top-scored with 59 in the first innings and then removed two top-order batsmen, Maurice Tompkin and Jim Parks, in a tight spell of 30 overs.

Very much in the selectors' eyes as a future star, he was chosen for a second Pakistan Eaglets tour of England in 1957. Shuja-ud-Din and Hanif Mohammad, two heroes of the full tour in 1954, were captain and vice-captain, and the manager was Idris Baig (who had presumably forgiven the rough handling he received as an umpire from Carr's tourists the previous year). SF Rahman was the outstanding bowler, grabbing 104 wickets at only 8.60 apiece. The matches were not first-class but the wickets still had to be earned, and in conditions which gave little help to his leg-spin.

He might have been a candidate for Pakistan's first tour of the West Indies in 1957-58, but he was out of favour with the autocratic captain, AH Kardar. 'Somehow, I could never please my captains, Kardar or Fazal. Maybe it was because I was a member of a fortunate family. I had a car.' This certainly set him apart from most other Pakistan players. It might also have been a mistake to have an even better tailor than the immaculate Kardar. Two other young spinners were picked instead, the slow left-arm Nasim-ul-Ghani and the off-spinner, Haseeb Ahsan. He stayed in domestic cricket and in March 1958 his persistence was rewarded when he answered an SOS from the West Indies after injuries left Pakistan short of bowlers.

On arrival, he was immediately picked for the fourth Test at Georgetown, in what was still British Guyana. He had no match practice but Imtiaz worked with him for two days in the nets. It may not have helped his cause with Kardar that he was in favour with the manager, Saeed Ahmad Khan, and was invited to share his hotel room. Pakistan batted first and SF Rahman came in at 349 for seven when Saeed Ahmed was bowled by Gibbs for a superb 150; he made 8 before being bowled himself by Gibbs. In the West Indian reply to Pakistan's 408, his first day in the field went reasonably well. Kardar brought him on as fourth change. 'I bowled ten decent overs,' he recalled, although they were wicketless. Then came a terrible social faux pas. 'The manager included me, against Kardar's wishes, in a trip to a nightclub.' The next day, the captain gave him only seven more overs in three spells, which made it impossible to get into any rhythm. 'He kept Haseeb and Nasim going even though they were erratic.' His only satisfaction was a smart catch at mid-wicket to dismiss Everton Weekes off Nasim.

In the second innings, he was run out for 2. 'It was my fault, I called Wazir Mohammad for a run. I thought I was home. The West Indian umpiring was poor. I had a big appeal against Sobers in the second innings, plumb in front. The umpire refused it.' The reprieve enabled Sobers to complete a second hundred in the match as West Indies achieved a target of 317 with only two wickets down. When SF Rahman bowled Conrad Hunte with 'a perfect googly' it was far too late to influence the outcome. Over 50 years later, he told me that the umpiring was a sign: 'God wanted me to come to the religious side.' Yet clearly the decision on Sobers still rankles.

He bowled 17 overs in each innings on his debut: Hunte was the lone success at a cost of 99 runs. The amiable manager Saeed Ahmad Khan thought he deserved to keep his place. Kardar over-ruled him and he watched as Pakistan gained a consolation victory in the final Test, by an innings, with only four bowlers.

SF Rahman's prospects did not improve when Fazal took over as captain. He said that he was unfortunate in attracting the attention of a girl who had caught Fazal's eye. He put himself into strong contention for a Test recall on the return tour by the West Indians, in a trial match for the President's XI in Peshawar. Sympathetically handled by the captain, his friend Waqar Hasan, he took five wickets in the first innings, including Kanhai, Sobers and Butcher. But he was disappointed when Fazal Mahmood rejected him and he was made 12th man in the third Test. His place went to Mushtaq Mohammad, who became the youngest Test player with an official age 15 years and four months. Mushtaq had an illustrious career but it began poorly: six expensive wicketless overs, 14 in the first innings and (first victim of Wes Hall's hat-trick) 4 in the second.

SF Rahman resented Mushtaq's selection all the more when his elder brother Abdur, now a liaison officer for the tourists, told him that the West Indians expected him to play and had held a team meeting to discuss how to counter him. There was more disappointment for him on Australia's short visit the following year: although he amazed Australian reporters who watched him at practice, he missed selection in the side match for the President's XI, captained by Kardar in an ill-judged attempt at a comeback. Intikhab Alam took seven wickets in that match and was selected for the third Test. From that point, either he or Mushtaq Mohammad stood between SF Rahman and any Test recall as a leg-spinner.

He had a consolation prize in a happy Eaglets tour of Ceylon and Malaya. He showed me a well-preserved press report: 'Rahman as good as Benaud, say Singapore players.' He had a big domestic season in 1960-61, with 17 cheap wickets and his only first-class century. But he pulled up stumps on his first-class career two years later, still only 26. He had no trouble remembering his final tally of 96 wickets in 29 matches; statisticians later supplied his career bowling average of 21.32, his strike rate of 52.42 and his economy rate of 2.42.

INNINGS DECLARED

'I said, the hell with cricket,' SF Rahman told us, melodramatically, as we went into dinner. However, he did not abandon cricket entirely. He had joined the prestigious Lahore Gymkhana club in 1958 on the insistence of Justice Cornelius, and played for them on Sundays for fun, although he enjoyed putting one over on the Test captains who had rejected him, with a century against a high-quality invitation team led by Kardar and a bigger haul of wickets than Fazal Mahmood. In one match, when Fazal relieved him he announced cheekily: 'Now we're going to lose!'

He took up squash and promoted the game vigorously on behalf of the West Pakistan Squash Association in colleges and schools and among the armed forces, the police and government officials.

He also consolidated a reputation as a ballroom dancer, a sought-after partner who was the last to leave the floor, although he added quickly: 'I never allowed my married life to be disturbed.' He had married young, in 1955, and had three children, two boys and a girl. None was interested in cricket but his nephew, son of Abdur Rahman, was a fine batsman with a first-class record cut short by a medical career in the army. SF Rahman, clubman, was clearly a happy interlude. 'I was very popular. I enjoyed my life then very much. Those days are gone.' But he added quickly, 'Of course, I also enjoyed religious life.'

SECOND INNINGS BEGINS

That life began in 1968, when he was 33. When praying at his local mosque, he began to think that the congregation needed more educated guidance from their *khatib* (preacher) and that he might provide it. His father had supported the mosque for many years, and when he died in 1967 the son offered to assume his responsibilities. SF Rahman set out to acquire the religious knowledge which he felt necessary for a *khatib*. 'I took a teacher and studied the Holy Qu'ran for five years day and night. When I began, I knew very little. I was given one verse to study. I spoke it for two to three hours.' Finally, he preached for the first time. He had prepared thoroughly but had only eight listeners. He challenged them: why should he work so hard for such a small congregation? The next week there were 20 to 25 people, and he repeated the challenge. Gradually his reputation grew, almost entirely by word of mouth. Unlike other popular preachers, he turned away opportunities to broadcast.

He completed his religious education, gaining two master's degrees at Punjab University, in Islamic Studies (first class) and Arabic (gold medal), and added a course in sharia law at the ancient Al-Azhar University in Cairo. He published the first of his works of Islamic scholarship. By his estimate he has written 30,000 pages of religious study, all of them by hand. By my estimate, that is at least 20 times the length of *War and Peace*. They include eight volumes of the Translation and Tafseer (analysis) of the Holy Qu'ran, known as FAZAL-UR-QURAN. The best-known of his works is called, in translation, *Travelling to Mecca with a True Intention*. The last phrase is at the heart of his philosophy. He expressed deep scorn for all those who parade their observance of the forms of Islam without acting on them.

His growing reputation won many invitations to preach and lecture overseas, including London and Birmingham. In 1983, he became the first Pakistani to preach at the United Nations. He also had an extended visit to Duke University and preached to the Muslim inmates of a gaol. His knowledge of Christianity so impressed the prison governor that he was invited to come back and address the Christians. He takes pride in his understanding of other faiths: 'They have good people and good teachings in their books. I have read nineteen of the world's religions.' He showed me a King James Bible, whose blank spaces were covered in multi-coloured English notes in a fine handwriting. He gave me a cricketer's take on the Church of the Latter-Day Saints (Mormons). 'They have twelve prophets and when one dies they elect another. They know you should always have a twelfth man.'

On the American tour, the Reagan administration tried to entice him into politics. He rebuffed them, as he also rebuffed a direct appeal from Pakistan's military ruler, General Zia-ul-Haq. 'I could have been a judge of the sharia court. I said, nothing doing.' Recently, he received a handsome diary as a gesture of respect from the current prime minister, Nawaz Sharif. 'They gave me this – but I took out all the pictures of Nawaz Sharif,' he added with his gurgling laugh.

He has never hesitated to attack abuses by Pakistan governments or institutions. He was especially eloquent against Benazir Bhutto, since he did not believe that any woman should be a head of government, but was also outspoken against the corruption he saw in the regimes of her husband, AA Zardari, and her rival, Nawaz Sharif. He expressed pride in having collected five criminal charges for speaking out and one short gaol sentence.

ON THE PUBLIC RELIGION OF PAKISTAN CRICKETERS

Maulana Rahman was scathing about the era of ostentatious religion in Pakistan cricket. 'Those Tableeghi-Jamaat people ... They are just there to say "come to the mosque and pray," that is their only duty.' (This is somewhat unfair: the movement emphasises the need to lead a righteous life.) 'All the religions in the world, not only Islam but those of Jesus and Moses, all came to rectify their nations, to tell them they are on the wrong path. These people all say, come into the mosque and pray, but they do nothing against the bad things happening in Pakistan, so what is their use? I believe in action. There is a verse in the Holy Qu'ran: say nothing which you do not practise yourself. For God, it is the worst thing to say something you do not practise.'

RELIGIOUS PHILOSOPHY – AND
THE CASE OF SALMAN TASEER

I was invited into his study-bedroom to admire the books and the ingenious air-conditioning system. I learnt more of his religious philosophy as he rehearsed the theme for a forthcoming sermon, on *zakat*, the Islamic obligation to give to charity. 'If God has given you money, you must share it with poor people. When you see poor people in the market, they have eyes and arms and legs like you. When you see a rich man, has he been given four eyes, four arms and legs? He is lucky and should be thankful to the Almighty.' He then gave a short economics lecture. 'When you give *zakat* at two point five per cent, you give buying power; when buying power comes into the market it becomes demand; to fulfil demand you have to generate supply; and to generate supply you have to have factories and other places where people work, so through *zakat* money comes into greater circulation and all society becomes richer.' It was a fine exposition of Keynesian economics, derived from the Holy Qu'ran, a source nearly 13 centuries older than Keynes. By his account, all modern knowledge and science is anticipated somewhere in the Holy Qu'ran. At some length, he gave me two examples: space travel and heart surgery. He took me through several episodes of Islamic history to refute the common perception of Islam as an intolerant faith, notably the Prophet's return to Mecca and his refusal to take vengeance on its people. As I have often heard from other defenders of Islam, he told me that the Muslim warriors had behaved much better than the Christians during the Crusades.

But then we came to the case of Salman Taseer.

For over four years, this has divided Pakistan and clouded relations with her friends. Salman Taseer was governor of the Punjab. He was assassinated by a member of his bodyguard, Mumtaz Qadri, after intervening on behalf of Aasia Bibi, a poor Christian woman condemned to death for blasphemy, a case that had already divided opinion and shocked much of the outside world. Mumtaz Qadri gave himself up – and was promptly adopted as a national hero by a large body of opinion in Pakistan. Lawyers strewed him with rose petals and queued up to defend him for nothing. Conversely, it was hard to find a prosecutor or a trial judge. At the time of writing, he was a privileged prisoner while Aasia Bibi was in solitary confinement in harsh conditions: although her death sentence was recently rescinded her health has been broken and her release remains uncertain.

The modern world is full of strange heroes. Mumtaz Qadri's case reminded me of Lieutenant William Calley, who received strong support throughout the United States after his conviction for the massacre at My Lai during the Vietnam War. Several state governors campaigned for him strongly, led by Jimmy Carter of Georgia, the future president, who initiated American Fighting Man's Day in his honour. It was no surprise that lawyers and religious politicians and agitators should make Mumtaz Qadri their poster boy, but I was still shocked that SF Rahman had joined them, a gentle, affable, non-political scholar with a genuine respect for other faiths. He wrote a long pamphlet in defence of Mumtaz Qadri, which was submitted on Qadri's behalf to two of the judges who handed down his initial sentence.[3]

We had a polite but animated discussion.

Maulana Rahman's defence of Qadri rested on a Manichean view that the world is now the subject of a terminal struggle between 'the liberal people' and all people of faith. The 'liberal people' will not rest until they have destroyed all faiths, not only Islam. His pamphlet identified Taseer with the liberal enemy, and enumerated all his transgressions against faith in his championship of Aasia Bibi. The governor had himself committed blasphemy, within the terms of Article 295-C of Pakistan's blasphemy laws. This highly contentious Article was added to the Criminal Code at the height of General Zia-ul-Haq's drive for Islamicisation. Unlike most other provisions of the blasphemy laws, it refers only to Islam and requires no proof of intent. It prescribes a mandatory death sentence for anyone who 'by words, either spoken or written, or by visible representation or by any imputation, innuendo or insinuation, directly or indirectly, defiles the sacred name of the Holy Prophet Mohammad (PBUH).'

---

3 Qadri's case has engendered protracted court proceedings, on separate charges of common murder and terrorism. Failing outright acquittal, or referral of his case to the sharia court, his lawyers have tried to annul his conviction for a terrorist crime, leaving only a conviction for murder. If that happened, his death sentence would no longer be automatic and could be rescinded if his victim's family accepted an offer of restitution. This would have given Qadri's supporters an opportunity to pressure and intimidate the late Salman Taseer's family. However, in October 2015 Pakistan's Supreme Court upheld the conviction for terrorism. Maulana Rahman predicted accurately that this would produce mass protests. Mumtaz Qadri was finally executed in February 2016.

Even if one accepts that view of Taseer, did that give Qadri, or any other outraged Muslim, the right to kill Taseer without any legal process? Yes, he answered, because Taseer was a governor and would never be brought to trial. There were many precedents for such action, from the early era of Islam. When those in authority transgress against Islam, or simply fail to enforce the laws which defend it in Pakistan, and are beyond the reach of the law, then any Muslim may take whatever action he believes necessary to uphold Islam. No counter-arguments made any headway. We reached no intellectual or moral meeting point.

LAST THOUGHTS ON CRICKET AND LIFE

It was a relief to get back to cricket. He delivered an exordium on coaching. Why did Test cricketers need it at all, let alone a big entourage of specialists, like football players? 'They sent Imtiaz Ahmed to Alf Gover's cricket school after he scored 300 not out in Bombay [for the Prime Minister's XI against the Commonwealth XI, in the follow-on, a unique occurrence]. I went there myself [during the Eaglets tour of 1952]. I put cut and spin on the ball, but Alf Gover wanted more flight. I modified my style and gave the ball more flight – but then it got even more flight from the batsmen!' Like many older players, he advocates diverting funds from coaches and academies to revive school and college and club cricket. 'We had a high standard, but now they cannot afford it. In college we got through six balls each day. Not any more, colleges allocate only three thousand rupees [about £20] to cricket for the whole season. The Islamia college cricket ground is now over-run with pigeons. What influence are all these coaches having? I watched Pakistan against the West Indies in the World Cup. One run for four wickets, inadequate shots and technique. Nawaz Sharif could do better!' For once the prime minister (a keen club cricketer who played a first-class match) might have agreed with him.

He completed the exordium and it was time to take our leave. He enjoined me earnestly to study the Holy Qu'ran. Soon after, he sent me a beautiful edition in translation, with passages suggested in his fine multi-coloured handwriting. Significantly, most of these echoed the Old or New Testament. But he warned me: 'I have spoken the Holy Qu'ran for forty-seven years and still I feel I have read nothing. I think constantly. Even sleeping, my brain works. If I wrote down my dreams they would be short stories of a very high calibre.'

Before we left, he gave a final assessment of his twin life. 'I was a sinner through and through, but then I prayed and surveyed myself. I don't know how much I have succeeded, but when I have sat at the mats of mosques I have tried to do my best, honestly, earnestly. I am not a money man; what I made God has provided for me. What more could I need?'

I had no doubt that he meant this. But clearly he still believed that he had also deserved the wicket of Garry Sobers in his only Test match.

II

WILL THE REAL ABDUL HAFEEZ KARDAR PLEASE STAND UP?

There were many achievements in AH Kardar's life, but the one which made most impact in the United States was his improbable appearance as a contestant on the popular television quiz show *To Tell The Truth*.

It happened on 13 May 1958 when the Pakistan team were playing a series of exhibition matches in the United States and Canada after their inaugural tour of the West Indies. Kardar had lobbied hard to secure the American visit, as he made clear in his book *Green Shadows*. This is confirmed by a guarded despatch after the event from Clifford Manshardt, the US Information Agency's Country Public Affairs Officer for Pakistan, to his superiors in Washington. 'The Embassy and the USIS was [sic] under pressure from the time the Pakistan Cricket team announced its plans to visit the West Indies to provide grants for the members of the team to visit the United States. As it was impossible to arrange such grants, the assistance of the People-to-People Program was requested through the Agency. The day before his departure, Mr Kardar, skipper of the Pakistan Cricket team, phoned the Cultural Office to ask whether the stop had been arranged.'[1]

1 Foreign Service despatch 6 August 1958, cited in www.eisenhower.archives.gov/researchonline.documents/people_to_people/binder/D/pdf.

The Program was a personal initiative of President Eisenhower launched on 11 September 1956 at a White House conference of a hundred luminaries including Walt Disney, Bob Hope and Joyce Hall, the founder of Hallmark greeting cards. In Eisenhower's own words: 'The aim is to build a massive program of communications between Americans and the citizens of other lands – to establish lasting two-way relationships from which international friendship and understanding could grow. The technique is to be direct – through people-to-people – as distinct from official government contacts.' Eisenhower took a keen interest in his creation and in retirement became its first chairman when it was privatised as a non-profit corporation.[2]

In the event, the Program did Kardar and his team proud, not only rustling up cricket teams to play but whistling them round all the tourist attractions of New York, Philadelphia and Washington DC. It produced a delightful souvenir programme, of which we have a copy from the treasure trove of Afzal Ahmed. The Pakistani-themed advertisers included the Karachi Restaurant at 46th Street near Times Square ('Pakistan and India Authentic Dishes Served At Their Finest'). This has since vanished: the address now houses the Manhattan Psychic Studio.

There was also an optimistic puff for 'Britain's brilliant new 1958 Hillman motor car ... It's peppy ... an excellent choice as a small car for the one-car family.' 1958 was a good year for foreign imports – but the Hillman was up against Volkswagen.

Still more optimistic was a message from the Joint Cricket Leagues of New York, based mainly on West Indian expatriates. They hailed the Pakistanis' visit as 'perhaps the best thing that could happen to cricket in these parts'. Local cricketers 'were eager for the opportunity to greet a worthy aggregation of the exponents of the sport of gentle-men'. They added 'the idea is growing that this season will see a revival of interest in cricket because the popular baseball teams of Dodgers and Giants are no longer with us [having migrated to Los Angeles

2 www.eisenhower.archives.gov/researchonline.documents/people_to_people/binder/F/pdf.

and San Francisco] . . . this Pakistan visit as well as the expected West Indies team invasion later in the season will spark plug the return to the grand old game.'

At Philadelphia SF Rahman, an emergency replacement on the West Indies tour, took four practice swings with a baseball bat and struck a homer with each one. The Pakistanis saw a baseball game at Yankee Stadium which Kardar described as 'an exhibition match against Milwaukee', not mentioning that the two teams had met in last year's World Series, won by Milwaukee. There they met Mickey Mantle, misspelt as Micky by Kardar but helpfully described as 'something like Sir Donald Bradman of cricket'.[3] SF Rahman was given an autographed Mickey Mantle bat, but promptly lost it or had it stolen. He narrated this calmly, clearly unaware of the tragedy this would represent to any American of that time.

The Pakistanis' New York visit included Radio City music hall and 'the numerous first-class [night]clubs such as Stork Club and the Copacabana'.[4] In Washington, the team had a private tour of the White House. President Eisenhower was unable to greet them, but they left him a signed cricket bat with his aide, Earle D Chesney, who played 'a few light-hearted baseball strokes' with it in front of the cameras on the White House lawn.[5]

Kardar's quiz appearance was taped before the Washington visit, but broadcast afterwards. *To Tell The Truth* was a CBS quiz show, devised by Bob Stewart who also gave the world *The Price Is Right*. Sponsored by Geritol, 'the high-potency tonic that makes you feel stronger' and hosted by the genial, bow-tied Bud Collyer, it aired in the prime slot of

---

3 AH Kardar, *Green Shadows* (Karachi: 1959), p.154. For the record, the Milwaukee Braves won 4-3, but the Yankees would edge them 4-3 in the World Series that year, coming back from 3-1 down.
4 Kardar, ibid, p.147.
5 Kardar, ibid, p.151. Eisenhower was pre-occupied on the day of Pakistan's visit with a Middle Eastern crisis and riots in Latin America against Vice-President Nixon. However, he did make time later to greet representatives of the World Amateur Golf Team Championship Conference. Eisenhower was a devoted but not very competent golfer, who liked to practise putting in the White House in his golf shoes. His successors, the Kennedys, complained that several wooden parquet floors were badly damaged by his spikes.

9pm on Tuesdays. Kardar was competing against ABC's Western series *Broken Arrow* (featuring an unusually sympathetic native American protagonist, Cochise, the Apache chieftain) and NBC's hard-hitting detective series *Meet McGraw*.

The quiz formula was simple and engaging and versions have aired until the present day. It came to the UK as *Tell The Truth*, first hosted by McDonald Hobley. Three people stood before a celebrity panel and declared their names and their unusual occupation. One was the real person, the other two impostors. As numbers 1, 2 and 3 they answered questions from each member of the panel. The real person was obliged 'to tell the truth' while the impostors lied as convincingly as they could. The four celebrities then made their choice between 1, 2 and 3 and the quizmaster would invite the home audience to do the same. He would then intone the show's catchphrase: 'Would the real X- Y- please stand up?' Cue astonishment or self-congratulations from the celebrities, who would give their reasons for their vote.

Kardar was number 2 in his panel, each dressed in cricket whites and carrying a bat in an identical casual pose. They each declared his full name, Abdul Hafeez Kardar, and Bud Collyer read out a long affidavit: 'I, Abdul Hafeez Kardar, am Assistant Adviser in the Ministry of Education in the Government of Pakistan. I am also a cricket player. Before Partition I was a member of the India match cricket team and also played at Oxford University when I was a student there. The Pakistan team is now playing in the United States under the sponsorship of President Eisenhower's People-to-People Sports Committee. Since 1951, I have the honour of being the captain of the team.' Pakistanis were then in short supply in New York, and the quiz show used a Syrian, Maan Medina, and an Iranian, Abdullah Mansoor, to impersonate Kardar. After the West Indies tour, he was noticeably more tanned than the other two and make-up had to adjust them. More importantly, neither knew anything about cricket or Oxford or indeed Pakistan, and Kardar helped the quiz show to give them a crash course in all three.[6]

6 Kardar, op. cit., p.156.

The celebrity panellists that day included Polly Bergen (a durable actress and all-round entertainer) and the A-listed Joan Fontaine (misspelt by the star-struck Kardar as Fontain). Another was the character actor Jim Backus, best known as the voice of the cartoon character, Mr Magoo, and the fourth was the syndicated entertainment columnist, Hy Gardner.

A mannered Polly Bergen opened the batting, asking number 2 to spell his full name, a task Kardar managed confidently. She turned to number 1 (Medina) and asked him how long a cricket match lasted. He answered six days, starting in the afternoon with a pause for tea. Naturally, said Bergen and the panel agreed. Jim Backus asked number 3 (Mansoor) which position he played in, and was told 'square leg'. This drew predictable laughs from the panel and the studio audience, which Backus unnecessarily followed by asking number 1 if he played 'round leg'. Maan Medina then had his best moment by correcting him: 'No, short leg.' More hilarity. Backus then flummoxed number 3 by asking the meaning of a 'sticky wicket'. He threw the question at number 2, and Kardar replied metaphorically: 'Anything which is difficult in life.'

Joan Fontaine had her turn. Again number 3 stumbled when she asked for the name given to a superior athlete at Oxford. Even Kardar had to ask for the question to be re-phrased before giving the correct reply of a Blue. Number 3 fared better when she asked the name of Pakistan's UN ambassador, Prince Aly Khan, who had hosted a large reception for the Pakistan team. Fontaine followed up by asking how many children he had – a daring question since she had had an affair with Aly Khan which led to his divorce from Rita Hayworth. Number 3 got the biggest laugh of the night by answering, 'Around sixteen.' Hy Gardner cut in 'Is that cricket?' and moved onto his questioning. Number 1 coped successfully with the name of Pakistan's head of government, volunteering both Iskander Mirza and the prime minister, Feroz Khan Noon, both to be overthrown in Ayub Khan's coup five months later. He turned to number 2 with a question which echoed Bertie Wooster's advice to Miss Tomlinson's girls' school:[7] from which

7 See PG Wodehouse, 'Bertie Changes His Mind.'

London hotel could one see Waterloo Bridge and Big Ben? Kardar then had *his* best moment: 'Normally, I didn't stay in a hotel.'

The bell ended question time, and the celebrities voted. The programme is still available online so it would a cruel spoiler to give the result. Suffice it to say that the panellists were more successful with Kardar than with the next contestants, Faye Snider, a professional circus artiste, and Texas Joe Foster, a former undercover anti-narcotics agent whose story was about to be filmed by MGM.[8]

Kardar was not alone in his television appearance: the manager, Saeed Ahmed Khan, was interviewed on the *Tonight* show by Jack Paar and the whole team appeared on the top-rated *Ed Sullivan Show*, with an estimated audience of ten million.[9] Together they made Pakistan better known as a nation to both American and Canadian audiences than at any time since it came into being. Mr Manshardt was well satisfied with the results of the visit, when the whole team came to thank the US Information Center in Karachi on 9 July 1958 after their return to Pakistan. 'Mr Kardar and other members of his team paid glowing tribute to the American people and spoke warmly of their reception in the United States.' He assessed that 'the Agency and the People-to-People Sports Committee by this means reached a large and influential segment of Pakistani people that is not always touched by other efforts.'[10]

8 *High School Confidential* (1958) in which he was played by Russ Tamblyn. The real Texas Joe Foster appeared in the film himself as 'Henchman'.
9 Kardar, op. cit., p.156.
10 See his despatch, previously cited.

12

IKE TAKES THE STRIKE IN KARACHI

Although President Eisenhower was unable to meet Pakistan's cricketers when they visited the White House in 1958, he made amends on 8 December the following year in Karachi, when he became the first and so far only American president to watch a Test match.

This formed part of a whirlwind visit to Karachi, then Pakistan's capital, which included an elaborate ceremonial welcome, a horse-drawn carriage ride to the home of its new military ruler, Ayub Khan, laying a wreath at Jinnah's tomb, visiting a housing development part-financed by American aid and watching a display of tent-pegging. The Karachi visit was part of a tour of 11 countries in 19 days, described as a 'goodwill tour'.[1] Most of those countries were Asian, and Eisenhower's real purpose was to bolster their governments' resistance to Soviet communism. This was especially true of Pakistan, who had joined the American-sponsored Central Treaty Organisation (then the Baghdad Pact) in 1955. It began to attract substantial military aid from the United States, and American influence had greatly increased in the

---

1 See 'Ike Will See Cricket Match in Pakistan,' *AP*, 1 December 1959. Eisenhower was not accompanied by his First Lady, Mamie. His hostess was his daughter-in-law, the former Barbara Thompson. Mamie found travel and public appearances an ordeal because she suffered from Meniere's Disease, an inner-ear infection which affected her balance and created unfounded rumours of alcoholism. See the review of her biography *His Significant Other: Mrs Ike* by her granddaughter Susan Eisenhower, in the *Los Angeles Times*, 1 December 1996.

officer corps, at the expense of the British. The CIA had supported Ayub Khan's recent coup, and Eisenhower was happy to boost his standing with a presidential visit.[2]

Eisenhower watched about 30 minutes of the third and last Test in Pakistan's series against Richie Benaud's Australians. They had already won the first two, and Pakistan were fighting to avoid a whitewash. It was one of the dullest days in Test history: only 104 runs were scored, 5 watched by Eisenhower as two wickets fell. The presidential visit was a merciful deliverance for the 40,000 spectators.

According to *Dawn,* they gave the president a standing ovation when he entered the National Stadium at 11.40am accompanied by Ayub Khan. Play was delayed as the Pakistan Air Force band played both national anthems, after which both teams were presented to the two presidents. Before entering the National Stadium, Eisenhower had been presented with a green Pakistan blazer and a cricket tie, and he changed into them. To his delight the blazer fitted perfectly: the Pakistanis had asked the White House for his measurements in advance.[3] The Australian manager, Sam Loxton, made a pointed joke when he saw it: 'Good morning, Mr President, I see you have joined the opposition.' Eisenhower laughed heartily and said: 'I think you are all cricketers.'[4] Richie Benaud hastily offered Eisenhower his cap, which he accepted in the interests of neutrality.[5]

According to *Dawn,* Ayub later expressed surprise that Eisenhower knew so little about cricket. However, Eisenhower made two pertinent observations which belied this. During the presentation of the teams, he had recognised Pakistan's Duncan Sharpe as 'the man who did so well in Dacca'.[6] Sharpe had scored 56 and 35 in his debut Test, but there was no reason for Eisenhower to note this for a whistlestop visit in a tour of 11 countries. Either the president was genuinely

---

2 Four American presidents have visited Pakistan – never under a civilian ruler. See P Oborne, op. cit., pp.163-64.
3 See Fazal Mahmood, *From Dusk To Dawn* (Karachi: OUP, 2003), pp.172-73.
4 'Ike watches Test match,' *Dawn,* 9 December 1959.
5 Mike Coward, *Cricket Beyond The Bazaar* (Allen & Unwin, 1990), p.85.
6 Duncan Sharpe: personal interview.

interested in the two teams, or he had received and memorised a thorough briefing.

Much more importantly, to the delight of the Australians, Eisenhower commented to Ayub Khan that he had thought that cricket was meant to be played on grass rather than matting. The Australians had already lobbied Ayub Khan on this point. After the unexpected intervention by the leader of the Free World (and a major donor to his regime), Ayub decreed on the spot that all future Tests in Pakistan would indeed be played on turf pitches.[7]

Eisenhower's visit to the Test was a challenge to the visiting American press corps, whose reports were syndicated to local American media in places where cricket was unknown.

The *Appleton Wisconsin Post-Crescent* ran a story entitled: 'Ike does diplomatic fielding at Pakistan–Aussie cricket tilt.' It put the crowd numbers at 50,000, higher than in *Dawn,* and added a few more details. 'Eisenhower asked to inspect a cricket ball and bat, which were brought to him from the field. He looked at them carefully and then autographed the bat. The two presidents remained at the stadium for about half an hour. Eisenhower asked many questions about the game, a mystery to most Americans. Ayub Khan smilingly tried to explain, sometimes waving his arms in demonstration of what went on. Eisenhower grinned, but there was no indication that he really caught on.'[8]

Another report was entitled: 'Ike disturbing factor in Pakistan cricket match' and blamed the Eisenhower effect for the loss of Saeed Ahmed (caught Harvey bowled Davidson) and the run-out of Ijaz Butt (future chairman of the PCB). 'The Pakistanis were so rattled they promptly lost two wickets and now stand to lose their third straight Test.'[9]

Two reporters thought that American readers needed a little more explanation. As part of a long despatch for the *Chicago Daily News*, Peter Lisagor reported that 'The Mickey Mantle of the Pakistan club

7 Coward, op. cit., But Najum Latif and many Pakistan sources attribute the change to Benaud alone.
8 The *Appleton Wisconsin Post-Crescent* managed to run this story on the very day of the match, 8 December 1959. Wisconsin was then 11 hours behind Karachi time.
9 UPI, 9 December 1959, in www.newspapers.com.

[Hanif] goofed his first time at bat and many in the partisan crowd blamed it on nervousness induced by Ike's presence.'[10]

The much-followed reporter and commentator Bob Considine made the same equation of Hanif Mohammad with Mickey Mantle, in his syndicated report deadlined 15 December 1959. Significantly, he was the author of a major biography of the baseball legend, Babe Ruth. Considine contrasted the dull play in the Test with the earlier display of tent-pegging which had made Eisenhower exclaim, 'By golly!' He continued: 'Ike also saw some cricket in Karachi. Pakistan against Australia. Pakistan president Field-Marshal Ayub Khan, a real hep fellow, was astounded at our president's ignorance of the game. So were fifty thousand fans when Ike left the cricket grounds right in the middle of a 307 to 277 pitchers' battle.

'Another Eisenhower boob came when he was introduced to one of the Pakistani team. Making small talk, Ike said to him: "I guess it's the same in cricket as in baseball: pitchers aren't supposed to be good hitters." Everyone blanched to hear a bowler called a pitcher and a batsman a hitter.'

Considine pointed out that most of his American colleagues were baseball experts and followers of the Washington Senators.[11] 'They have become sensitive to dumb-bell plays. As a man they were enraged when one of the world's foremost batsmen, Haneef [sic] Mohammad, attempted to "score" his batting partner and himself with a bunt and got his partner banished for the day.

'"Imagine trying a squeeze play when you're thirty runs ahead," one of our fellows said. He'll never cheer for Haneef Mohammad.'[12] The president and the reporters did not stay long enough to see Hanif complete a match-saving century.

10 'Ike gets a look at Asia's "vest-pocket" Cold Wars,' *Chicago Daily News,* 10 December 1959.
11 After years of mediocrity in the American League their owner removed them the following year to Minnesota where they became the Twins. A replacement Washington Senators team lasted from 1961 to 1971, and then became the Texas Rangers, years later owned by George W Bush.
12 Bob Considine's UPI despatch 'Anyone for tent-pegging?' was carried in the *Greensburg (Indiana) Daily News* on 15 December 1959.

In spite of the dull play, Eisenhower enjoyed his cricket experience and wrote a civil letter of thanks the same day to 'SM Hussain, secretary of the Board of Cricket Control'. He called it 'a unique opportunity to see two of the world's finest teams matched up against each other.'[13]

13 Cited by Valoise Armstrong, Archivist, Dwight D Eisenhower Presidential Library, Abilene, Kansas. Ms Armstrong was unable to trace what happened to the Pakistan cricket blazer, which mysteriously was not included in the list of gifts he received in Pakistan.

13

FROM MULTAN TO MELBOURNE: THE DOUBLE LIFE OF DUNCAN SHARPE

As of November 2015, 220 people had played Test cricket for Pakistan. One name leaps out of the list: Duncan Albert Sharpe. He had a brief, blazing Test career of three matches against Richie Benaud's visiting Australians in 1959, but then became disenchanted with Pakistan cricket. With the help of Barry Jarman, the Australian wicketkeeper, and the backing of Sir Don Bradman, he made a second life in Australia, where he is still living.

Duncan was the second of four Christians to play for Pakistan. In his debut Test match, he used a bat and boots borrowed from the first, Wallis Mathias. He was the first Anglo-Indian to join the Pakistan team. He will almost certainly be the last.[1]

He came from a community that had been hugely important in pre-Partition India but faced social and pressures after independence in both India and Pakistan. The pre-independence term Anglo-Indian covered British families who had worked and settled in India (such as Rudyard Kipling's) and a much larger population descended from mixed-race relationships, almost invariably between British men, soldiers, civil servants, planters and merchants, and

---

1 Few other Anglo-Indians played first-class domestic cricket in Pakistan after independence.

Indian women. In pre-Partition India, Anglo-Indians became especially important in the railway industry and in post and telegraph offices.[2] Their political leader was Frank Anthony, who estimated their population, at independence, at 800,000.[3] He secured them special status and voting rights under the Indian constitution. There was no matching provision in Pakistan, although the 1973 constitution introduced by ZA Bhutto reserved nine National Assembly seats for Christians.[4]

There is a striking image of Duncan Sharpe in his playing days in Pakistan. He could have been a matinée idol from the 1950s. He was once, quite genuinely, mistaken for Cary Grant.

Duncan Sharpe is a relation of the great English novelist, William Makepeace Thackeray[5] and he wrote occasionally for the Lahore *Civil and Military Gazette* (Kipling's newspaper). At 78, he was a vivid letter-writer and colourful conversationalist as he gave us his own account of his double life.[6]

He was born in Rawalpindi in 1937, into the third generation of a family that had migrated to British India in the mid-19th century.[7] His grandfather served in the Indian army but was killed in the Quetta earthquake of 1935. Until the Kashmir earthquake of 2005, it was the deadliest to strike the current land of Pakistan, causing at least 20,000 deaths.

2 See in particular M Deefholts, *Haunting India* (CTR Books, 2003), p.191, L Bear, *Lines of the Nation* (Columbia University Press, 2012), p.244, Zasha O'Brien, 'The Anglo–Indian Community and their Role during the Raj,' in www.academia.edu/5839877.

3 F Anthony, *Britain's Betrayal in India: The Story of the Anglo-Indian Community* (Simon Wallenberg Press, 2007), pp.92, 144-46. We have not found a reliable estimate of the number in Pakistan after the population transfers at Partition.

4 See R Braibanti, *Chief Justice Cornelius Of Pakistan* (OUP, 1999), p.6. Cornelius is sometimes erroneously described as Anglo-Indian. In fact, he had no English blood. He came from an Indian Hindu family who had changed their name on conversion to Christianity. Ibid., pp.21-22.

5 This also makes him a relation of David Cameron and the comedian, Al Murray, creator of the Pub Landlord.

6 Unless otherwise stated, all quotations from Duncan Sharpe are from telephone interviews or letters from him: in the latter case, we have retained his style.

7 Their roots were in Yorkshire. Might he also be related to Phil Sharpe, the Yorkshire and England batsman of the 1960s? He was not aware of any connexion.

He was the second of three brothers: Robin was the oldest, Marcus the youngest. His parents broke up early in his life and he lived initially with his father, a very reserved man, and his step-mother whom he disliked. He and his brothers were packed off to St Anthony's High School, a prestigious Roman Catholic boarding school in Lahore.[8] Their mother then took over their upbringing. She was a nurse, strong-minded but warm-hearted in character, whose maiden name was Maisie Margaret Marvel Thackeray. 'She was part of Thackeray's family. We used to laugh about it, but I read some of his books later.'[9]

By his own account, Duncan Sharpe took to cricket as a bored teen-ager. He had transferred in Lahore to the Cathedral School, where he became a lifelong friend of one of its best cricketers, Zafar Altaf, later a senior administrator of Pakistan cricket. 'He studied a lot,' said Duncan Sharpe, suggesting that this might have been unusual.[10]

'I hardly played at all in school, but I took it up in a small town called Multan where there was nothing to do, the year being 1953. My two brothers and I were fond of the game, but we were too backward to go forward. However, we ventured down one Saturday to a nearby park and saw a cricket match being played. After the match, some of the officials who attended were from the Multan Cricket Club. They saw us and asked us if we would like to join the Multan CC where practice was on Tuesdays and Thursdays. That's where it all began.'

Duncan Sharpe's cricket idol was Denis Compton. 'I wanted to play for England, like him, and face Ray Lindwall, but here I was living in Pakistan. That killed me. I never imagined I would face him, but in the Pakistan side.

---

8 Source: Marcus Sharpe. The present prime minister of Pakistan, Nawaz Sharif, is an alumnus.

9 She and Duncan are probably not direct descendants, since Thackeray had three daughters who did not carry on his name. The eldest married Leslie Stephen, the father of Virginia Woolf. Thackeray had an extended family, which included a half-sister from his father's Indian mistress. He treated this half-sister very badly, both in life and in his fiction. See Vyvyen Brendon, *Children of the Raj* (Weidenfeld and Nicolson, 2005), pp.1-2, 9, 29, 54-55.

10 Sadly, Zafar Altaf died in December 2015, aged 74.

'After a couple of years, it was advised that playing club cricket in Multan would not give me the recognition to go further in my cricket pursuits, so my club associates said that Lahore was the place to go, as they had higher quality cricketers who would improve my game. I was fortunate enough at the time that my mother, who was a nursing sister, transferred back to Lahore and we all went with her.'

His mother's selfless decision transformed his prospects. 'There were no computers in those days to put me and my eldest bro in the right direction as to which club we would choose, but certain scribes said go to a club called the Crescent CC, that is where a lot of first-class and Test cricketers were bred – including none other than AH KARDAR. [Duncan Sharpe's own upper-case letters, here and below.]

'My brother and I were invited to partake in practice sessions. The good news was that they selected both my brother and me to play in the first eleven and that was a thrill. From memory, I got a seventy and my bro got fifty or so. That was the turning point of where I was to go. I accumulated five consecutive half-centuries in a row. The elusive hundred was missing, however I topped the averages.'

Not surprisingly, he was recommended to Kardar, who came to watch him in the nets. Kardar brought along Zulfiqar Ahmed, Pakistan's Test off-spinner and his brother-in-law. 'Now I've always called off-spinners "fruit for the sideboard". As proceedings went, I played him quite comfortably and a few other bowlers. Word got to me that Kardar was very impressed with the session and said that he would like to see me bat in the middle. And he did – in the first Test against Australia.'

Another important net encounter came by chance. 'My brother and I took a walk from where we lived to the Bagh-e-Jinnah ground to watch the club practice session, and lo and behold we noticed IMTIAZ AHMED batting in the nets. We were very happy when he came up to us and said, "Would you like to bowl a few balls?" That was not a bad session. Little did I know that three years later I would play Test cricket with him. THE FINEST STROKE PLAYER I HAVE SEEN. He compares with Sehwag and Tendulkar. I watched him open against the West Indies [in 1958-59]. He hooked Wes Hall for four fours in a row.'

More important still was working with Fazal Mahmood at a new club, the Universal. Fazal became a lifelong idol and mentor, and he stayed in touch with him every year after he emigrated.

At 17, Duncan Sharpe took a job in the railways, as a clerk. He was winning more notice as an aggressive middle-order batsman, who favoured the front foot, and as a wicketkeeper. He made his first-class debut in March 1956 as a specialist batsman for a combined Railways–Baluchistan side against the touring MCC A team. It was inauspicious: 1 in the first innings and a first-ball duck in the second, caught in the leg trap, in which he was the middle victim of a hat-trick by Tony Lock. Happily, he took some revenge on Lock years later, on another continent, when both were playing in the Sheffield Shield.

His fortunes improved in the next domestic season, when he also kept wicket. In 1958-59, he had two side matches against the touring West Indians. They were unproductive but he was on the selectors' radar, and they made him 12 man for the Test series. At a festival match in Karachi, he shared a hotel room with SF Rahman[11]and tried on his Pakistan blazer for size.

Although his mother had done so much to launch him into cricket, she did not think that it would earn him enough to support a family. He was still working on the railways but also contributing occasionally to the *Civil and Military Gazette,* following the lead of his elder brother Robin.

In 1959, Duncan went on the Pakistan Eaglets tour of England. It was a fine summer and it gave him some of his happiest memories. He outscored his captain, Saeed Ahmed, who had already begun his Test career with a brilliant series in the West Indies. By the end of the tour, he had been made vice-captain.

There were two standout performances. Against Nottingham Second XI at Trent Bridge, he opened and top-scored in both innings: 58 out of 149 and an undefeated 176 out of 268, including 135 before lunch. No one else could cope with the pace bowler Cleveland Lindo, who

11 For whom see chapter 10.

took 13 wickets in the match for 163.[12] He captained the side against a Kent XI led by Peter Richardson. Opening the batting again, in front of the former Kent and England wicketkeeper batsman Les Ames, he scored 50 out of 51 in a few overs. 'I asked for a glass of water, but Peter Richardson said, "No, you've only been here fifteen minutes." When I was out [for 76] Les Ames shook my hand, and said he had never seen a batsman slaughter an opening attack like me. And this was real cricket – not one-day.'[13]

Best of all, his mentor, Fazal, then playing for East Lancashire in the Lancashire League, drove from Blackburn to Stroud to watch him in the two-day match against Gloucestershire.[14] 'He drew up in his sports car ninety minutes from the start but he saw that I was already out, sitting in the pavilion. He was disappointed and said I could not have scored very many. I told him I made sixty-five. His eyes lit up. He took me aside and said, "The Australians are coming. How do you feel about taking on Meckiff and Lindwall and Benaud?" I said I could face anybody, and just to give me a chance. Fazal said, "That's all I wanted to hear."'

He strengthened his case with his performance in a trial match on his return to Pakistan. There were two visiting guest players. Lala Amarnath and the off-spinner, Jesu Patel, who would later ravage the Australians on their visit to India. He scored a century, again as opener. 'Lala Amarnath told Fazal that Pakistan should pick me with their eyes shut.'

Duncan Sharpe had worried about the response to his selection for the first Test in Dacca. But this proved needless. 'There was some possible hostility to me, as Fazal's protégé from the Punjab, but the weight of my runs on the Eaglets tour stopped all that.' He was picked as a specialist batsman at number 5; Imtiaz was still wicketkeeper, at number 7.

---

12 On his day, Lindo was a terrifying fast bowler on the county circuit. See S Chalke, *Caught In The Memory* (Fairfield Books, 1999), pp.38-39.
13 Sadly, he never played in a major one-day match, for which his methods would have been ideal.
14 Stroud was then infamous as a low-scoring spinners' wicket. See Chalke, op. cit., pp.89-90.

Benaud won the toss and sent Pakistan in to bat. DA Sharpe came in at 82 for three when Wallis Mathias was flummoxed by Benaud's googly. Wallis had kindly lent his young rival a bat and some boots. Sharpe faced Benaud confidently and immediately cover-drove him for three. Against a high-quality attack (Benaud, Davidson, Meckiff, Mackay, and his one-time fantasy opponent, Ray Lindwall) he scored most of a partnership of 63 with Hanif Mohammad. At the end of a funereal first day, he was not out 35 as Pakistan reached only 146 for four wickets. The next day he lost two more partners, Wazir Mohammad and Imtiaz Ahmed, but he completed his fifty with a hook for four off Davidson.

He was in full flow when disaster struck. 'That Israr Ali . . . He tried to take a short single to Norman O'Neill of all people at cover-point.' O'Neill, who had also been a professional baseball player, was one of the game's finest fielders. The borrowed spikes failed to save Duncan Sharpe, the non-striker, from being run out by a direct hit.[15]

Pakistan limped to 200 off 105.5 overs. Australia gained only a narrow lead, thanks to Harvey and Grout, but Pakistan's second innings was even limper than the first: 134 all out in 100.3 overs. Duncan Sharpe was top scorer with 35, and alone in trying to counter-attack Benaud and Mackay, who took all the wickets between them. Australia scored 112 for victory for the loss of only two wickets.

The performance was enough to make him an idol, regularly mobbed by autograph-seekers. When they grew too irksome, his amiable brother Robin met them as a substitute and forged his signature.

He did not achieve much in the Lahore Test (his mentor Fazal was absent and Imtiaz captained) but kept his place at Karachi, in the famous Test watched by US president Eisenhower. 'I shook hands with him. He said, "You were the one who did so well in Dacca." I replied, "Yes, sir, thank you very much for remembering it."' In the second innings he made 26, second top score, before falling to Lindwall, the subject of his boyhood fantasies. He shared the highest partnership of

---

15 For Israr Ali, see chapter 5. Duncan Sharpe remembered him as 'pretty nifty and a good bloke'.

the innings, 53, with Hanif, who scored a six-hour century, and helped him to save Pakistan from a whitewash in the three-Test series.

Sharpe's final series average was 22.33, but it was enough for third place among Pakistan's batsmen. He also developed a friendship with Barry Jarman, the Australians' reserve wicketkeeper, which proved more significant for his future.

He followed up with some impressive achievements in domestic cricket, including a century against a strong Indian Starlets team, and 20 victims in seven matches behind the stumps.

Then came a crushing disappointment. It came at the hands of Ijaz Butt – the Widmerpool of Pakistan cricket. Like Anthony Powell's anti-hero, he reappears constantly in the narrative, regularly disparaged but possessed of a mysterious power which wrecks other more compelling characters.

Recently married to the daughter of the selector Chaudhry Mohammad Hussain (a union which also launched him on a business career in Servis Industries), Ijaz was picked ahead of Duncan Sharpe as a batsman and reserve wicketkeeper on Pakistan's tour of India in 1960-61. Sharpe's friend Zafar Altaf, who was selected, told him afterwards that the Indians were relieved. That was no consolation. 'The trip to India destroyed me. It really tore me apart. I deserved that tour. Players now usually get about seven or eight Tests to prove themselves: I got three.'

Although there had been no criticism of Sharpe's selection against Australia, some newspapers turned against him at this point – to rationalise his non-selection. 'That's when all the furore came up. People said that I would not bat well against India, and some said I was not a real Pakistani.' However, some of Duncan Sharpe's contemporaries (including the Test players SF Rahman and Shafqat Rana) have defended his non-selection. They suggested that his head was turned by his Test appearances and that he made unreasonable demands on the selectors as both a batsman and a wicketkeeper.[16] Whatever the truth of this, Duncan Sharpe's disappointment was real and intense when his mentor

16 Source: Najum Latif.

Fazal broke the news of his non-selection. 'I didn't know where to look. Two months ago I was the star of Pakistan. Richie Benaud had said that three players were Pakistan's hope for the future: Saeed Ahmed, Wallis Mathias – and Duncan Sharpe. Now I didn't even make the sixteen for India. That inflamed me into saying, "I've had enough of this."'

In this mood, he took up the offer from his friend Barry Jarman to sponsor him as an emigrant to Australia. It was a huge step at the time, because Australia then took very few immigrants from Asian countries. Fortunately, he had a British passport, as did his partner, Gillian Keelan, daughter of a successful engineer in Lahore. According to Zafar Altaf, 'she put Elizabeth Taylor in the shade.' The then Australian High Commissioner, Sir Roden Cutler VC, was helpful but suggested that Duncan Sharpe might find it hard to adjust to Australian life without domestic servants. This over-estimated Duncan Sharpe's Pakistani lifestyle by some distance.

He and Gillian left for Australia in such a hurry that he missed saying goodbye to his brothers. Both had begun their careers with a drilling company and they were away on a project in the Sind desert. He fixed a farewell meeting at the railway station at Kotri on the way to Karachi – but they missed the train. Duncan Sharpe also missed seeing his infant son, Kevin, the product of a very short-lived marriage. He was raised by his mother, Thelma, in Multan, without knowing his father. However, 45 years later Kevin's teenage daughter Angela discovered her unknown grandfather, Duncan Sharpe, through an internet search. They have yet to meet, but have built a warm long-distance relationship by letter and telephone.

By that time, Duncan Sharpe, Pakistan Test cricketer, had put down deep roots in Australia. He and Gillian settled in Barry Jarman's home state of South Australia, where he had a second first-class career, principally as a specialist batsman. He had many happy memories to share, especially a century partnership with Garry Sobers against Western Australia and scoring 76 against Victoria while a young Ian Chappell was almost strokeless at the other end. 'I hooked Alan Connolly for four. Ian came up to me and said, "Shot, Sharpie!" I quite promptly told him to stay there and watch me bat. Cheeky – that was how I was.'

But there was a more significant meeting after his dismissal. 'Sir Don Bradman had been watching. He took me into the corner like little Tom Thumb and told me I had one hundred, one-fifty, two hundred for the taking, I had Victoria on their knees, but I had given it away. I was stunned. I could only say, "But I'm not Don Bradman."'

After arriving in Australia with very few qualifications outside cricket, he was especially grateful to Bradman for securing him an outdoor job assisting the curator at the Adelaide Oval. It launched a new career, in which he acquired multiple qualifications and became a foreman of parks and gardens, with a staff of 25, after moving to Melbourne.

He and Gillian married and raised six children, first in Adelaide and then in Melbourne where they still live. Although remaining in contact with Fazal Mahmood, Duncan's outlook (and his accent) became completely Australian. He has never returned to Pakistan since emigrating.

His new loyalties were displayed in 1964-65, when Pakistan visited Australia. Rather insultingly, they were given only one Test match, at Melbourne, which was saved for them by Hanif Mohammad. After a century in the first innings, he was given out stumped for 93 in the second. The wicketkeeper tried and failed to persuade the square-leg umpire to rescind the decision, telling him that he had dropped the ball and failed to achieve the stumping. This display of sportsmanship came from Sharpe's friend, Barry Jarman.

Duncan Sharpe saw little of his former colleagues until he played *against* them for South Australia – after helping to prepare the pitch. Told to hurry by his captain, he scored a rapid 43. 'Hanif Mohammad was asked what he thought of me. He said my footwork had improved a lot.'[17] The Pakistanis did not socialise very much on that tour, even with him. 'They kept to themselves. They did not understand Western living.'

Spoken like an Australian.

---

17 On this tour, Hanif was able to compare notes with Don Bradman about breaking his world record score with his 499. He asked Bradman about his 452 not out and Bradman replied that he was just warming up when the declaration arrived.

14

A CLOSE RUN THING:
RAILWAYS VERSUS DERA ISMAIL KHAN

December 1964. Re-elected president Lyndon Johnson plans to escalate the bombing of Vietnam. Students stage a massive sit-in at Berkeley, California. The Beatles release an album with the self-mocking title 'Beatles For Sale'. Dera Ismail Khan is then a sleepy market town in Pakistan's North West Frontier Province: official population around 47,000, celebrated (if at all) for its dates and mangoes and for finely made lacquerwood products and cloth sarongs.

This unremarkable place was the starting point of an epic journey by a group of eager teenagers. The first leg was a ride in a lurching rural bus or a lift on a lorry, on a poor road, crossing the Indus river on a pontoon bridge. This took three hours or more in the heat and dust to reach the nearest rail station at Dera Dariya Khan, just 15 miles away. From there, they took the branch line to Kundian, around 50 miles to the north. Then they waited four or five hours for the mainline train from Rawalpindi to Lahore. After a sleepless overnight journey, they arrived in the great city for the first time and headed for the cheapest hostel they could find.

But these hardships meant little to the young travellers. They were about to make history as the first representatives of Dera Ismail Khan in a first-class cricket match. They knew that they faced tough opposition in the preliminary round of the Ayub trophy, a relatively new competition named after Pakistan's military dictator, Field-Marshal Ayub Khan. The Railways had a high-quality team, with at least seven players in the frame for international selection.

The young men might have done better to miss their trains. The Railways beat them by an innings and 851 runs. It was the biggest victory in cricket history. It seems certain to stay in the record books for ever.

This performance was cited by Norman Preston, editor of *Wisden Cricketers' Almanack* for 1978, in a sniffy note. 'Even ardent followers of cricket in Pakistan are beginning to criticise the proliferation of national and world records standing to their country's name. They say the blame must be placed on the shoulders of their Board of Control, which, it has been said, has repeatedly allowed teams with no first-class status to compete in first-class tournaments.'[1]

It is hard to disagree. Pakistan's cricket authorities have regularly handed out first-class status to weak teams, partly to give more opportunities to cricketers, especially those outside the major centres of Karachi and Lahore, but partly also through political patronage. Before the 1964-65 season, the Board of Control decided to extend the Ayub trophy with a preliminary knockout tournament in three zones. This gave a sudden opening to first-class cricket to many new teams which were not ready for it. There were many heavy defeats in the trophy that year, but none as hopeless as Dera Ismail Khan's.

Yet the match was much more than a freak from Pakistan's cricket politics. We found and interviewed two of the survivors of the Dera Ismail Khan team. They tell a different story – of a group of teenaged friends who played cricket for fun and at their own expense, pitched into battle against mighty opponents who gave them no quarter.

Brigadier MTK Dotani appears as Taimur Hasan on the published scorecard: he opened the batting in both innings, scoring 0 and 0, and bowled two overs. He lives today in a housing complex for retired officers in Rawalpindi, full of mementoes of a distinguished military career. There are few cricket souvenirs apart from the team photograph

1 See Norman Preston's *Notes from the Editor* 'Dubious Records.'

taken on the eve of the match. He identified himself, sitting second from the left. There is no need for him to point out the distinctive profile of his friend Mr Shahid Javaid Khan, sitting second from right. He was the number 3 batsman, on the scorecard as Javed Khan.

Both men are eager to share their cricketing memories. They both laugh readily, but also offer strong views about the past and present state of Pakistan cricket. Brigadier Dotani was a student at Government College, Dera Ismail Khan, one of a group of friends since childhood who loved cricket. When lessons finished they would dash home and then cycle, in the blazing summer heat, to play pick-up matches or hold practice nets at the big former parade ground which the army let them use. They had to do almost everything themselves, collecting kit, preparing the pitches, and finding older people ready to umpire.

Eventually, a government official, Syed Ali, set up a local divisional cricket association, which supported them with some gloves and balls, a kitbag and a man to put up the nets. Even so, they had very little competitive cricket. The nearest local team was at Bannu, about 90 miles away, or even further at Kohat or Peshawar University, which had a fine ground with a lush green wicket.

Shahid Javaid Khan was an engineering student at the University, a keen cricketer looking forward to the University's participation as a new entrant invited into the Ayub trophy. He was devastated to learn that their sports director had withdrawn them, for lack of funds. He discovered that Dera Ismail Khan would be eligible to replace them, and hurried over to the town to sign up their team. Then he had to secure their approval as replacements from the divisional cricket authorities. For this, he enlisted the help of his uncle, an influential lawyer, who did not believe that the DIK team could meet first-class standards. 'But when he saw my eagerness and desperation, he asked me to come over to his place in Bannu.'

Shahid Javaid Khan convinced his uncle who helped him complete the registration formalities. Under great time pressure, he put together a team of college players from Dera Ismail Khan and Bannu, and three or four Peshawar University players, including himself. At the last minute, the University decided to field a team after all. Although Shahid decided to stick by Dera Ismail Khan, they had lost three of their best players. They were hurriedly replaced by enthusiasts from the pick-up matches on the parade ground.

Dera Ismail Khan nearly lost Taimur as well, and the Government College captain, Mohammad Hanif. They had exams looming and their parents did not want them to play. 'We stayed behind with a heavy heart,' said Brigadier Dotani, 'but then the team discovered in Lahore that they were playing Railways and sent us an urgent message to join them.' They prevailed on their parents, and completed the day/night journey to reach the others at their 'pathetic hotel'.

The team had a day of sightseeing and movie-going before they were due to play at the fine Moghalpura Institute Ground, used by the Railways. It was opulent by their standards, lusher than the Peshawar University ground and with abundant spectator space limited only by the railway line at one end, where trains passed every ten minutes or so. This distraction would be another home advantage for the Railways team, not that they needed it.

For the first time, the Dera Ismail Khan players – the oldest was 20 – sensed what they were up against. They were relieved to lose the toss and bowl first. Their bowlers were their main strength and they hoped to make their opponents work for runs. They opened with their youngest player, the left-arm medium-pacer Inayatullah, aged 15. At the other end was the quicker, right-arm Anwar Khan. He made an early breakthrough, dismissing the Railway opener Saeed Butt for just 20. But then 'they totally dominated us, taking boundaries at will,' said Brigadier Dotani. At the end of the first day, Railways had made 419 for two. 'That was a huge score for us,' said Shahid Javaid Khan. 'We expected them to declare. We practised batting in our hotel.'

No such relief. The Railway captain, Bashir Haider, batted right through the second day to allow his batsmen to fill their boots. At the close they were 825 for six. Ijaz Hussain, the wicketkeeper and opening batsman, had made a century, Javed Babar a double century, and Pervez Akthar was not out 301. Tellingly, this was his only first-class hundred. Still no declaration: Bashir Haider batted on into the third day to allow the number 8, Mohammad Sharif, to complete his only first-class century.

There were inevitable fielding lapses, but Shahid Javaid Khan took a fine catch at long-on in front of the railway line, which had the Railways wobbling on 548 for five. At last the declaration arrived on 910 for six – the first time any Pakistani side had passed 900.

The young Dera Ismail Khan side had stuck to their task, bowling 172 overs. The scoring rate of 5.29 an over was high by the standards of the time, but far from contemptible. The young Inayatullah bowled the most overs, 59, which produced one wicket for 279; Anwar Khan had three for 295 off 46 overs, Qaiser Khan, another right-arm seam bowler, had one for 175 off 43 overs and the slow-medium Fazal Matin one for 110 off 22 overs. (The remaining two fill-in overs were bowled by Taimur Hasan, a spinner.) The four main bowlers achieved eight maidens amid the carnage.

Had Bashir Haider declared too late? He opened the bowling himself and Taimur Hasan went out to face him. Bashir was one of the fastest bowlers in Pakistan. During Pakistan's disastrous tour of England in 1962 the captain, Javed Burki, had begged the selectors to send out Bashir to reinforce his depleted attack – but they thought him too wild. The teenaged opener was facing him without a helmet (then unknown), wearing tennis shoes. One spectator was Safdar Ali Shah, a former captain of his college team. He briefed him about Bashir, adding encouragingly, 'If he hits you on the pad it will break your bones.'

Taimur played Bashir's loosener confidently enough. The next one landed, disappeared over him, and was taken by the wicketkeeper nearly 20 yards back with a cartwheel. 'I had never faced a bowler of that pace,' he remembered. 'He took a huge jump and had a very offensive style, like Jeff Thomson. I snicked one and it split second slip's hand. I said to myself "Forget about style, save your life."'

He survived for a while, until Bashir produced a straight ball and bowled him for a duck – 'fortunately'. But the real damage was done by his partner Afaq Khan, another pace bowler of quality, who took seven for 14. Dera Ismail Khan were all out for 32 in 15.3 overs. Six

Dera Ismail Khan batsmen failed to score, and only one, the tailender Anwar Khan, reached double figures. One alone defied the two pace bowlers: Qaiser Khan became the tenth first-class batsman to be given out 'obstructing the field'.

Shahid Javaid Khan was at the other end for this piece of history. 'He was quite a temperamental player. He came over to me and told me that balls were coming to him at the speed of bullets. He was getting frustrated. I don't know what got into his head when he blocked a yorker and then kicked the ball off the pitch. The Railways team complained and the umpire gave him out.' Both of Qaiser's colleagues feel today that the appeal was a little unnecessary.

With a lead of 878, Bashir Haider did not agonise long over enforcing the follow-on. He did not even bother to take a new ball, but simply tossed the old one (fewer than 16 overs old) to his spinners, the slow left-arm Nazir Khan and Ahad Khan, whom many fans rated the best leg-spinner in Pakistan. Nazir was spanked for 18 off six wicketless overs, but his partner caused mayhem at the other end. He bowled Taimur for his second duck of the match. The mercurial Qaiser got himself stumped off him, and Jamil Ahmed, the Dera Ismail Khan wicketkeeper, was run out for 10. Ahad dismissed all the other batsmen without assistance from a fielder, and finished with nine wickets for seven runs.[2] Dera Ismail Khan's second innings closed on 27 – five short of their first, and they had lasted three fewer overs.

The young team made the wearisome journey home, thinking themselves fortunate that they had brought no travelling supporters and that the few scanty match reports had not mentioned their names. Dera Ismail Khan's next scheduled matches – against Rawalpindi teams – were cancelled. They did not reappear in first-class competitions until the 1980s. They then played nine matches, drawing one and losing all the others. Seven were innings defeats, although never on the scale of their predecessors. There is a thriving cricket scene now in Dera Ismail

2 The best nine-wicket haul in cricket history by an overarm bowler. G Elliott of Victoria took nine Tasmanian wickets for two runs in 1857-58 before overarm bowling was legalised.

Khan, at divisional and Under-19 level, with a home ground which it never had before.

None of the young record-breakers ever got another chance at first-class level. Shahid Javaid Khan returned to Peshawar University. He played a few non-first-class matches for them and then many more at club level and for departmental teams in a career as an engineer in public service.

Brigadier Dotani came heartbreakingly close to a second life in cricket. Stationed as an army officer in East Pakistan, he re-invented himself as a pace bowler – perhaps a psychic revenge for his battering by Bashir Haider. He guested regularly for Pakistan International Airlines teams and put fear into their opponents. His best performance – seven wickets for 18 in 14 overs – was watched by Master Aziz, the legendary coach who had tutored the great Test-playing Mohammad brothers (see chapter 3). Master Aziz asked him what he was trying to bowl. 'I told him I didn't know – I just held it like so and let it go.'

The coach told him he was bowling a fast leg-cutter – the stock delivery of Pakistan's greatest bowler, Fazal Mahmood. Master Aziz referred him to Mushtaq and Sadiq Mohammad, leading a national practice session in Karachi, and he arranged to go there on his way to an officers' training course in Quetta. He bowled in front of the Mohammad brothers, who were impressed but wanted to see more the next day.

Cruelly, it rained. As it did for the next two days, by which time he had to report to Quetta. His subsequent career saw him become a personal pilot to General Zia-ul-Haq, as chief of staff and president (fortunately not in the aircraft which crashed and killed Zia) and he retired as a brigadier.

The two friends were therefore marooned: their first-class careers ended in that one match for Dera Ismail Khan, which yielded them both a total of one solitary run. They are still glad to have played, as part of a team that simply loved cricket.

A version of this chapter has appeared previously in The Nightwatchman.

15

A PIANIST BEHIND THE STUMPS

He is understandably vain about his hands. At the start of his career, a colleague in his trade compared them to those of a concert pianist. But the owner has never played the piano. For nearly 20 years, Wasim Bari put his hands at the service of some of the world's fastest bowlers and most bewildering spinners, on all manner of surfaces, whether baked or soaked, manicured or mottled. He claimed 227 Test victims for Pakistan, eight of them English in a memorable display at Leeds in 1971, which equalled the then world record.

Today they are still in beautiful shape, the fingers perfectly aligned, betraying no sign of breaks or even bruises. Wasim Bari displayed them when we met in a somnolent room in Karachi's wonderful Sind club.

His story is one of perseverance. 'My classmates laughed when I said I was going to be a cricketer. I could not even get into the school team.' This happened in the sixth form (aged 12 or 13) in the early 1960s at St Patrick's College, Karachi, a celebrated Roman Catholic college of high sporting and academic achievement. It produced two of Pakistan's four Christian Test cricketers, Wallis Mathias and Antao D'Souza. Wasim Bari had given little cause to impress the school's legendary cricket master, Major Jacob Harris. But he had set his heart on the wicketkeeping spot, in succession to his elder brother.

'Imtiaz Ahmed [Pakistan's wicketkeeper-batsman in their early Test series] was my role model and very popular with my parents too. They often saw his name in the papers or heard it in commentary. "Caught Imtiaz b Fazal" became a cliché. I always thought if I played for Pakistan it would be as a wicketkeeper. I had some natural qualities – good reflexes and eye focus – but above all, I had hard work.'

In every spare moment, he threw catches to himself with a variety of balls, cricket, tennis, golf and squash, bouncing them off every possible surface. 'I recruited boys from the alleys to throw catches and bowl at me on local tennis courts. I asked them to swing the ball either way. In fact, I asked anybody, cricketer or not, to throw things at me, and keep on throwing from different angles. They would plead with me to stop, saying they could not throw any more, their arm had gone.' He played other sports voraciously, including hockey, table tennis and squash. 'I also skipped rope, on the advice of Master Aziz [celebrated coach of Hanif Mohammad, see chapter 3]. He told me that wicketkeepers need strong legs like a boxer.'

However, from an early age, he himself decided that glovework was the key mark of a wicketkeeper. Hence the repeated catching sessions, hundreds a day, alone or with the exhausted helpers. When night at last brought them to an end, like so many other young dreamers he went to bed with his cricket gear.

The hard work was rewarded. The cherished place in the school team was followed by trials for selection at inter-collegiate level. Now 16½ years old, he joined dozens of other hopefuls at open-air nets in Karachi. Each wicketkeeper was given a brief session behind the stumps, keeping to dozens of bowlers he had never seen before. Fortunately, Wasim Bari's session was watched by Wazir Mohammad. The eldest of the five brothers was not only a veteran of 20 Test matches but one of the best judges of cricket talent in Pakistan. 'He saw me and told me to forget college cricket and told the president of the Karachi Cricket Association that he had found the best wicketkeeper in Pakistan.'

That same year he made his first-class debut, for Karachi against Karachi University in the Ayub trophy, under the shrewd and sympathetic captaincy of Waqar Hasan. He scored 11 (run out) and 16 not out and took three catches, two off the occasional bowlers, Alimuddin and Wallis Mathias.

Having broken through to the first-class scene, he resolved to work even harder to stay in it. Pakistan then had few first-class matches, and club cricket was passionately competitive. The City Gymkhana Club was then run by the Test umpire, Shuja-ud-Din, a dedicated man who expected the same commitment from players. He would ride on his scooter to each selected player to warn him to turn up in good time for the start. At another club, the Jang, Wasim Bari was told to wait his turn for selection: they had three senior wicketkeepers ahead of the teenage wonder.

Still only 16, he would round up team-mates and ground staff and ask them to throw cricket balls to rebound at him off a roller. 'The heat would be searing but I would insist on 50 throws to my right, followed by 50 throws to my left. My arms would be bleeding from all the diving on the parched outfields, but I would dust myself down, clean up my elbows and then continue with 50 or more throws each side. This would continue sometimes for hours.'[1] (One cannot help feeling sorry for some of his early collaborators, and hoping that they took satisfaction from his later career.) As narrated elsewhere in this book, he also benefited from long sessions of practice with the left-arm mystery spinner, Prince Aslam.[2] They collaborated to great effect in that year's Ayub trophy final, won by Karachi against the Lahore Education Board, in which Wasim Bari had nine victims. Still only 17, he added another seven victims for Karachi when they won the more important Quaid-e-Azam trophy final against Lahore Greens.

His displays earned him his first representative honours for Pakistan, first against Ceylon (not yet Sri Lanka or a Test-playing nation) and against the visiting MCC Under-25 team led by Mike Brearley, who became his first English victim. He was caught off Majid Khan, then a frontline seam bowler. Alan Knott was the visiting wicketkeeper and they would share a friendly rivalry for over a decade.

1 www.cricketarchive.com/Archive/Articles/12/12934.html.
2 See chapter 1.

The MCC manager, England's former wicketkeeper Les Ames, rated Wasim Bari the best wicketkeeper in the Indian subcontinent[3] and predicted that he would be very successful in England. The Pakistan selectors may have heard this, because they picked him, still only 19, for the short tour of England in 1967.

He impressed in the early county matches in English conditions which were new to him, and was selected to make his Test debut in the first Test at Lord's. Almost immediately, he took a neat catch to dismiss the dangerous opener, Colin Milburn, off Asif Iqbal, then primarily known as a fast-medium swing bowler. Ken Barrington was his other victim off the same bowler, but only after a big hundred, and there were no byes in the England innings of 369. Batting at number 10 in Pakistan's innings, he accompanied Hanif Mohammad for over an hour of his monumental undefeated 187, which saved Pakistan from ruin, before he succumbed to Barrington's occasional leg-spin. In England's second innings, he achieved his first Test stumping, the England captain Brian Close, off the slow left-arm spin of Nasim-ul-Ghani.

There is a fraternity among wicketkeepers, and it was his England rival, John Murray, who first teased him about his 'pianist's hands'. Murray had an unhappy Test match and was replaced by Wasim Bari's new friend Alan Knott. He and Knott compared notes, as they did in future home and away encounters in the 1970s. Knott endorsed his view of the importance of glovework. 'He said it was the sign of a good wicketkeeper. If you are offered four chances, you should accept three, but the most important thing over the whole day is how many balls you gloved.'

His successful debut owed much to the other Pakistan wicketkeeper, Fasiuddin, his senior by nearly ten years. 'My gloves were not very soft, so I asked if I could borrow his gloves. He said, why not? It was very generous of him. His gloves were soft and comfortable. Later Alan Knott helped me. He sent me to Huddersfield, where his gloves were made for him by Slazenger. They were the best available at that time, with soft leather and less padding in the palm so that you could really feel the ball.' Did Fasiuddin ever regret his generosity? He never won

---

3 Ahead of the spectacular Farokh Engineer, who had become India's first choice.

a Test cap and Wasim Bari began a sequence of 28 consecutive Test appearances.

Like Alan Knott, Wasim Bari paid as much attention to the mental aspects of wicketkeeping as to the physical skills. 'In my first representative appearance against Ceylon, I had some excellent advice from Maqsood Ahmed [the free-hitting star of the 1950s]. The danger point is fifteen minutes before each interval – that is when every player relaxes. So that is when to put in two hundred per cent yourself.' He also developed an ingenious mental system for overcoming the disappointment of a dropped catch. 'I would send a message to my brain that it was not a catch at all, so forget about it. Then I would be ready for the next one.' Years after his retirement, he passed this advice to Kamran Akmal, as yet the only other Pakistan wicketkeeper to claim over 200 Test victims.

Wasim Bari was fortunate to play in an era when teams still played specialist wicketkeepers, but he was an obdurate batsman who frequently dug Pakistan out of a hole. In 1976-77 at Bridgetown, he and Wasim Raja shared a tenth-wicket partnership of 133 against a West Indian pace attack of Roberts, Croft, Holder and Garner.

The following year he had two unhappy series as captain, both against England. Pakistan had a weak team, without its Packer players, and he was briefly estranged from them. But in a reunited team he had the chance to show his skills behind a world-class attack led by Imran Khan and Sarfraz Nawaz, and the contrasting spinners, Iqbal Qasim and Abdul Qadir. Against New Zealand in 1978-79 at Auckland, he became the first wicketkeeper to claim seven victims in a Test innings. At a critical moment in his late career, he benefited from a public show of confidence from Imran Khan, and paid him back with 36 catches. He has remained friendly with Imran although he often disagrees with him. 'When that happens I keep a comfortable distance away,' he adds with a laugh. Well, after all, he was used to standing back to Imran. He was able to choose his farewell Test, at the age of 36, at the end of the away series against Australia in 1983-84. It was his 81st, at that time a Pakistan record.

Like many Pakistan cricketers, he had been employed by PIA. Unlike some, he took his airline career seriously, and set out to acquire business skills with the same dedication as he practised his wicketkeeping. After postings in Denmark and France, he was Director of Human Resources for PIA when he retired after 40 years' service. He currently works as a consultant for the oldest logistic company in Pakistan. He has held a variety of posts with the PCB, including selector, chief selector, head of HR, chief operating officer and most recently director of training, in which he gave regular lectures to young players about the dangers of corruption and how to avoid them. He has continued to do specialist assignments for the PCB, including a review of the team's performance in the 2015 World Cup.

He is scathing but diplomatic about some colleagues in the PCB who never mastered the basic skills of the corporate world. 'I had people coming into my office and asking me to write letters for them. They would then expect to become the CEO.' He admires the English and Australian cricket administrations for separating cricket issues from corporate ones.

Sadly, he doubts whether he could fulfil his boyhood dream today of becoming Pakistan's wicketkeeper. The country has lost so much from the decline of school, college and club cricket as a nursery, and academies cannot teach young people how to play competitive cricket. 'We have never developed any systems for spotting talent. It is the same now as in the 1960s. I was very lucky, perhaps even because of God, that my hard work was spotted at the right time.'

He took his leave, and as he and Richard Heller shook hands they compared fingers, his elegant, Richard's generally misaligned after several breakages. He asked Richard gently: 'Did you say you're a pianist?'

16

FACE TO FACE WITH PAKISTAN CRICKET

I f there is one man who understands the face of Pakistan cricket, it must be Jawed Iqbal. Pakistan's popular cartoonist (the street where he lives in his native city is named after him) has drawn all of its leading faces over the last 50 years. There is a fine collection in one of his eight books, *How Is That?*, published in 1980.

A spry, dapper man, looking much younger than his 68 years, he would be an easy subject for his own pencil. He is famous for working quickly. On television, as a party piece he can complete a sketch in under 90 seconds (the time needed by the West Indian spinner Alf Valentine to complete a maiden over). He can work in unfamiliar media: on a visit to England in 1974 he did a sketch on a lady's T-shirt, while the lady was still wearing it.

He discovered early in life his gift for caricature. 'It began in school,' he told me. 'Normally the first people you draw in school are your teacher and any people you don't like, and maybe family members too, and you try to make fun of them. Then people laugh and it gives you encouragement.'

He completed formal training, earning a degree from Pakistan's National College of Arts, and made an instant impression with the first drawings he submitted, while still a teenager, to a prestigious daily newspaper.

He has been a political cartoonist throughout his career, but frequently uses cricket to make his point. His cartoons became especially popular during the time of Zia-ul-Haq, when dissent was strongly discouraged, particularly in the media. 'President Zia was a very difficult man. My best cartoons were in his time. I used to fight with his press information people over certain cartoons and I would tell them they had nothing against the country or against any individual. In fact, President Zia used my cartoons when people asked him to comment on issues. He would say, "See today's cartoon." He never mentioned my name but he knew who I was.' Friends were surprised that he was never a victim of Zia's crackdown, but Zia knew that he had a following.

Although willing to tangle with politicians, he has always kept clear of two subjects: religion and sex. 'The great majority of people here are embarrassed if you touch on these subjects, and I want to amuse people, not hurt them.'

Cricketers have always been his favourite subject, and among them, Imran Khan. 'He is a legend and I think his team of '92 started the love affair of our young people with cricket. He got the whole nation involved, even grown ladies who didn't know anything about cricket.' He and Imran found themselves travelling together frequently within Pakistan and struck up a friendship, particularly when their flight was delayed. They fell out briefly when Imran threatened to sue him for reproducing his image without permission in a special souvenir autograph book, but nothing came of this and he has happily continued to draw Imran as both a cricketer and politician as he sees fit.

Apart from Imran Khan, he enjoyed drawing English cricketers, especially David Gower and Geoff Boycott. He drew them from photographs, using two or three if necessary to get all their features. He dislikes watching cricket on television, or working from television images. 'On TV there is no depth of field. You can't register distance, everything is flat.'

He is a confirmed Anglophile. He admires David Low as a political cartoonist and Tom Webster (creator of Tishy, the horse which crossed its legs) as a sporting one. He was an avid follower of *Punch*, the long-established but now defunct magazine which was a treasure house of British humour. In its time, being published there was a summit for any cartoonist and he submitted work to them on a long European visit in 1974. This opened up new possibilities for him and led him to remodel his style. 'I used to think cartoons were best with minimum lines. Then in Europe, every cartoon was like a painting. Beautiful. Background, foreground, colours, technique ... I could get involved for hours in a cartoon.'

He admires the English for their good manners, their public transport, their reverence for their history – and their tailoring. He is relieved to hear that many noted names still survive from his first visit, including Burberry, Liberty's, Austin Reed and Church's shoes.

The conversation turns to Pakistan's great early cricketer, Fazal Mahmood. In 1954, on Pakistan's inaugural tour of England, Fazal spent the then astonishing sum of £20 on a Daks blazer from Simpson's.

Fazal inevitably figures in his collection *How Is That?* Each caricature of a player is accompanied by a brief ironic pen-portrait. It also has some of his pocket cartoons about cricket, and some samples of advertising featuring cricket, which are historically interesting because the commercialisation of Pakistan cricket was in its infancy in 1980 when the book was published. One is especially striking: he drew a spray can of insecticide as a fast bowler demolishing the stumps of a hapless giant cockroach.

Notwithstanding his admiration for David Low and Tom Webster, his portraits of contemporary cricketers are very reminiscent of the great American caricaturist, David Levine: huge heads, diminished bodies, prominent, slightly exaggerated features with strong etching. He is especially partial to teeth and handlebar moustaches, which often seem to have a life independent of their owner, like the tail of Felix the Cat.

However, unlike most of Levine's targets, Jawed Iqbal viewed his cricketers with striking affection. Apart from a brooding Majid Khan, then in his late career, they have a smile on their faces. He even gave a smile to the famously stern AH Kardar, of whom he wrote: 'He was responsible for starting the nursery of cricket in the country. Some of the saplings [*sic*] became strong trees under his guidance, while others were scared to death by his discipline.'

Intriguingly, he put the biggest smile on the fast bowler Sarfraz

Nawaz, renowned for his combative character on and off the field. He made Sarfraz stoop, but he was still too tall for the box of the cartoon. Perhaps looking a little deeper than many contemporary fans, he called Sarfraz a 'gentle giant'.

The smile on a long-haired Imran Khan is a little thin and his eyes are narrowed and staring away into the middle distance, as if contemplating the imminent destruction of a batsman outside the page. Jawed Iqbal paid him a striking tribute in his pen-portrait: 'Seeing him makes most men wish they were fast bowlers.' He also noted accurately of Abdul Qadir: 'He spins the ball and himself while bowling,' but added waspishly, 'he bats as if he is posing for a still photographer. His inclusion is dependent upon how the groundsman has prepared the wicket.' However, the drawing negated the sarcasm. The great bowler is making a long stride in his bouncy run-up, the intended delivery hidden in both hands. The face has a thin smile showing complete self-confidence. Again, the distant batsman had no chance.

Thirty-five years on, Jawed Iqbal has an undiminished appetite for caricaturing the current generation of Pakistan cricketers. He told me: 'I have been very lucky to make my hobby my profession, and to be honoured for it.' But there is a downside. It is very unusual to have a street named after a living person. 'When people walk down my street, they say, "Very sorry he's gone, he was a nice man."'

17

AFTAB GUL, KEEPER OF THE FLAME

As a young man Aftab Gul was dangerous company. Fellow students were warned against him by their parents. As a student agitator, he was one of ZA Bhutto's lieutenants in his revolutionary challenge to the tottering dictatorship of Ayub Khan. In that capacity, he made his Test debut for Pakistan in 1969 – while out on bail from criminal charges.

Later on he had SAM missiles discovered in his home. This was a murky episode in 1983 under Zia's dictatorship, when a remarkably well-informed police raid found two missiles and used them as evidence of an alleged plot to shoot down Zia's aircraft.

Aftab Gul had no knowledge of the missiles. But their discovery forced him to make a dramatic escape from arrest, flying to London with his nine-year-old son. Luckily their Philippine Airlines aircraft was out of reach of the authorities. He and his son watched the 1983 World Cup (where he supplied commentary for a documentary film). The boy went home[1] and he stayed on in London for the remainder of Zia's rule. He lived in very straitened circumstances, first in the YMCA near Tottenham Court Road, then in a council flat in Fulham, consoled by visits to casinos with his old friends Keith Miller and Jim Laker.

Today, Aftab Gul is a keeper of the flame for the causes he believed in

---

1 He has since become Additional Advocate General of Punjab.

during the 1960s. He is an Advocate of the Supreme Court (Pakistan's equivalent of a QC). In England he might have become a venerated radical barrister in the mould of Jeremy Hutchinson, but not in Pakistan, where he remains a Marxist, with no reverence for authority.

He chose International Democracy Day in 2015 to announce on television that Pakistan was not a democracy. His conversation is peppered with attacks on Pakistan's ruling class, especially those who went to its elite schools and then to Western universities. He has a long roster of controversial clients, including his former Test colleague Sarfraz Nawaz and Salman Butt, Pakistan's disgraced cricket captain after the match-fixing scandal of 2010.[2]

Aftab Gul's chambers are in his former home (where those missiles were found) near the Lahore High Court. He spends many of his afternoons there playing cards, but there was no game in progress when we called on him.

We wanted to find out more about that Test series he played as a student agitator. But he did not stay there very long. His conversation regularly swerves into books, or history, or philosophy, or sociology, or politics past and present. With a touch of melodrama, he began: 'Approaching seventy, you start to run out of time to finish all the world's great literature.' Besides the usual musty law books, his shelves are crammed with fiction and history titles. Revealingly, he has a complete set of Will and Ariel Durant's *History of Civilization*. It is now a little out of fashion, after attacks by jealous academics, but the critic Luke Upward described it correctly as 'the most successful history in history', attracting multi-million sales with its rich mix of epigram and optimism.

Aftab Gul had a respectable middle-class background (his father was a lawyer in army service) but he was at pains to establish his roots in street cricket, like Wasim Akram or Waqar Younis. 'I studied in a co-ed school where cricket was just coming up. We used to play rounders

---

2 For Sarfraz Nawaz, see P Oborne, *Wounded Tiger* (Simon & Schuster, 2014), p.266. For Salman Butt, see 'One step too far,' *The Express Tribune (Pakistan)*, 29 August 2015: Aftab Gul was too radical for the PCB who wanted him off the case.

and some sort of softball. I was playing on the streets. But then I went to Government College, a very prestigious place academically and in sport. Cricket was the only major game. I was at a disadvantage because I got admitted some months into the regular year, but I found out that I might be a good player.' He made his mark there and later as a law student at Punjab University, as a fearless opening batsman and an astute captain.

Aged 20, he played against the visiting Sri Lankans and against the powerful MCC Under-25 team led by Mike Brearley. He was made captain of Central Zone against a Commonwealth team led by Richie Benaud. He scored a sparkling 76 in the second innings until Benaud strangled him on the leg side – a problem which bedevilled him throughout his career.

He was also made captain of the full Lahore side which competed in the 1968-69 Quaid-e-Azam trophy. He faced down a revolt by more senior players and led his unfancied team to the trophy against their arch-rivals from Karachi.

There was a fierce controversy when the last day of the final was abandoned with Karachi poised to win. The ground was ruled unfit for play, officially because of rain but the Karachi players accused the Lahoris of watering it. 'We won that final fairly and squarely,' he declared, 'Well, maybe fairly but not squarely.'

By then he had become a founder member of ZA Bhutto's new Pakistan People's Party and its leading organiser in Punjab University. 'For me, it was all about Bhutto then. My study of socialism and Marx came later. My infatuation was with Bhutto as an individual and that carried me for two or three years. He had a remarkable capacity to raise expectations.'

No one like Bhutto had ever been seen in the young state of Pakistan. After an electrifying speech to the UN Security Council during the 1965 war over Kashmir, Bhutto had dramatically broken with Ayub Khan over his settlement with India at Tashkent, resigning as foreign secretary to set up the Pakistan People's Party. His new party was the first to develop an appeal to the masses. Mimicking Lenin's three-word slogan (Peace, Land, Bread), Bhutto offered Food, Clothes, Housing.

Aftab Gul placed Bhutto in a wave of contemporary leaders who had reshaped political expectations. 'I grew up when there were great charismatic leaders, whom we don't have today. They began with Kennedy. He was a big influence over people like me, although we do not like to admit it since he was a Cold Warrior. Then the Non-Aligned movement was flowering, and we had Nasser and Lumumba and Nkrumah and Sukarno. In China, we had Mao and Chou En-Lai. Then came the 1968 revolutions and people like Rudi Dutschke, Daniel Cohn-Bendit and Tariq Ali. Bhutto had the same charisma, but such vision as well. He was brilliant. He grasped every issue instantly.'

By 1969, Bhutto was on the rise and the political situation in Pakistan was highly volatile. Ayub was ailing and would soon hand over to the hard-drinking Yahya Khan. There were regular strikes, demonstrations and other protests against the enduring dictatorship.

Sheikh Mujib's Awami League party dominated East Pakistan with a programme of six demands for its Bengali population, fiercely resisted by Bhutto, by then the biggest political force in West Pakistan.

MCC flew into this volatile situation for a three-Test tour hastily arranged to replace the tour of South Africa, cancelled in the wake of the so-called 'D'Oliveira affair', which should really be called the 'Vorster affair'. Aftab Gul won his first Test cap against England at Lahore.

The legend is that he was chosen for political reasons, to appease potential student protesters in the Test match crowds. But in reality, he was Pakistan's best available opening batsman, then averaging over 40. In a side match against MCC, he outperformed both of his potential rivals and scored a 50 in each innings. Did he really tell the selectors, 'If I don't play, there's no bloody Test match'? Perhaps – but as a warning, not as a threat. He told the selectors he deserved the place and there would be protests if he did not get it.

He was picked for the Lahore Test. Was he really out on bail? Yes, for charges under the martial law regulations about his activities as a student organiser. 'But there has been too much emphasis on this. The Army came to my house and took away letters and photographs. They found a book – a history of terrorism. They registered charges but I went to the judge at the Criminal Sessions Court and was given bail straightaway on all of them.'

In the match, he helped Pakistan gain a draw with a painstaking 29 in the second innings. He was frequently asked to go into the stands to talk to protesting students. He asked them to stop – for his sake and Bhutto's. They obeyed. It was reminiscent of the United States the previous year, when students were asked to be 'clean for Gene' and present a good image for the anti-war candidate, Eugene McCarthy.

He did not play in the Dacca Test (when the selectors tried to placate protestors by including a token East Pakistani, Niaz Ahmed[3]). However, Aftab Gul returned for the third Test in Karachi. Again he was asked to appeal to demonstrators, but he had less influence there and the match was abandoned after a riot. 'I think that the protests there were not part of the youth movement but really about the way cricket was run in Karachi.'

On the 1971 tour of England, he wore a polo-necked sweater in preference to a tie. He slipped away to betting shops and casinos. He had arguments in Bengali restaurants. Most seriously, he led a group of players who refused to be bounced into signing a cricket bat in aid of victims of the civil war in East Pakistan. Like Bhutto he was fiercely opposed to the Bengali separatists. To avoid embarrassment, the Pakistan government ordered all the tourists to sign. He alone held out, even when they threatened to send him home.

He had little success in the three Tests. The first saw him retire hurt on the third ball, hit by England's fastest bowler, Alan Ward. That brought in the unlikely looking number 3, bespectacled, shambling Zaheer Abbas, to score his epic 274. Aftab Gul bravely returned in the middle order and scored 28.

The second Test was wrecked by rain. He scored 33 in a sound opening partnership with Sadiq Mohammad, and then Pakistan collapsed. In the third Test they shared another sound start in the first innings. In the second, he and Sadiq left Pakistan well placed overnight as they

3 In fact, Niaz was not a Bengali. He was born in Benares (Viranasi) and his family migrated at Partition.

pursued a modest winning total. But he played a horrible shot on the final morning and was widely blamed for opening the path to England's victory.

However, he was highly successful in side matches, scoring well over 1,000 runs on the short tour. After his century at Warwickshire, he was approached by the county as a possible overseas player. His friend Rohan Kanhai took him out for the evening and warned him that he would not enjoy county cricket – the travel, the gruelling routines. Later he discovered that Kanhai was hoping to secure the place for a young relative. 'Still, I think they did better with Alvin Kallicharan.'

There were a few more big domestic seasons. In 1973-74 he scored over 1,000 runs and earned another tour of England, but played only six matches and was never in contention to regain a Test place.

By now, Bhutto was firmly in power but it brought him no preferment. Bhutto warned him not to expect anything: he was too independent and too left-wing. (Years later, in exile, Bhutto's daughter Benazir delivered a similar message.) He retired from cricket, and started a law practice.

He was soon depressed by Bhutto's political opportunism, his relationships with established politicians, and his slide into authoritarianism. But he rallied behind Bhutto after he was ousted by Zia-ul-Haq and put on trial. He bravely volunteered to join Bhutto's legal team. He took down some of Bhutto's scathing political testament *If I Am Assassinated*, dictated in his death cell.

He is slowly writing his own autobiography – working title *No Apologies*. It will be primarily a political memoir rather than a cricket one, and it seems likely to be dominated by Bhutto – as he might have been, rather than what he became. If finished, this book will provoke huge controversy. He is looking forward to this, but he was also proud of a much less contentious effort to preserve the past.

For years, Minto Park was one of the great centres of Lahore cricket – a vast space where dozens of teams could play all at once. Much of it has been lost to thoughtless redevelopment, and what was left was threatened by further development plans. However, he had just won a stay order against these in court, which will delay them and open the possibility of outright rejection. 'I asked the court if it knew it was dealing with our living history.'

Aftab Gul is himself part of Pakistan's living history. He embodies ZA Bhutto's original dream of a democratic, socialist Pakistan which, while predominantly Muslim, would tolerate all creeds and encourage free thinking. It is a dream which Bhutto betrayed – but then died for. Aftab Gul, fiery and irascible though he is, has remained faithful to the dream all his life. More than any other Pakistan cricketer, Aftab Gul answers CLR James's famous question: what do they know of cricket who only cricket know?

18

AN EVENING IN THE LIFE OF
THE PRESIDENT

By Richard Heller

In the summer of 1971, Pakistan was far from popular with Britain's student population. Most sympathised with the Bengalis fighting for secession and there were regular protests against the Pakistan Army's methods in the civil war. They had made the High Commission nervous enough to recommend cancelling the tour to England.

Around a dozen students were slumped in front of the junior common room television set at my Oxford college for the start of the first Test match. Pakistan batted first. Our response was at best comatose, at worst, hostile.

Pakistan's opener (and former radical student leader) Aftab Gul retired hurt on the third ball of the day, which hit him in the face. Few of us believed that the shambling, bespectacled replacement was a Test number 3. We checked his name: Zaheer Abbas. A few armchair pundits from the college third XI fretted about his high backlift. There were early uncertainties, but as his innings developed we realised that we were watching something exceptional. With exquisite anticipation and timing, he turned a well-regarded England attack (Ward, Lever, Shuttleworth, D'Oliveira, Underwood, Illingworth) into a procession of waiters serving his choices from the menu of the day.

Somehow the word went out: you have to see this. The room gradually filled. We stayed with him on radio when BBC television coverage inexplicably disappeared. We willed him past all his milestones, 50, 100, mentally supporting him through his long stutter on 77. The next day, we saw him in his pomp complete 200 and 250. At 261, he became the first batsman of a damp English summer to reach 1,000 runs. A triple century beckoned, even the Test record, still in the hands of Garry Sobers with 365. We were almost as distraught as Zaheer himself when a poorly executed sweep off Ray Illingworth cut him down on 274.

There was much else for us to enjoy in that Pakistan performance – centuries by Mushtaq Mohammad and Asif Iqbal and nine wickets for Asif Masood with his engaging run-up, compared by John Arlott to Groucho Marx chasing a pretty waitress. But it was Zaheer who changed our view of Pakistan as a cricket nation, and left us disappointed that bad light and rain robbed them of the chance to clinch victory. His strokeplay was beyond our reach, at times even beyond our imagination as good deliveries were magically conveyed to the leg-side boundary. But we could identify with his appearance – like a swotty student, the sort who would let you borrow his notes when you missed a lecture.

Nearly 45 years later, I am meeting him for the first time. His friend Qamar Ahmed has procured me an invitation to dinner at his home in the well-to-do Defence district of Karachi.

Zaheer no longer looks like a student, more like a successful businessman. Casually but expensively dressed, he is a little more portly than he would wish, after a serious injury in a road accident on his way to playing golf. (When fit, he plays off 7.)

Qamar and I have arrived on an auspicious day: Zaheer has just been nominated as president of the International Cricket Council. He is coping with an uninterrupted flow of congratulations from well-wishers. It is part of a new ICC settlement in which the president will become a non-executive figurehead. Appointees will be admired cricketers of all nations who carry no political or factional baggage. Zaheer answers the job description. Unlike most of his great contemporaries, he

has stayed out of recent politics and controversies. His spell as manager
of the Pakistan team ended as an unhappy passenger in the dispute over
alleged ball-tampering on Pakistan's England tour of 2006. Since then
he has concentrated on a successful construction business and become
a respected analyst for various media.

We add our congratulations but cannot resist teasing him. We
address him constantly as 'Mr President': when his wife Samina
joins us, she becomes the First Lady. She is Indian-born, formerly
Rita Luthra, who became Samina when she converted to Islam.
She is a sought-after interior designer, with many opulent Middle
Eastern clients. The elegant house shows her influence, but least of
all in the study and trophy room where we sit before dinner. We
immediately dub this the West Wing. We tell Mr President to insist
on a personal jet – ICC One – to take them both to the forthcoming
annual council meeting in Barbados. He takes all this in good part
but is genuinely anxious to hear our views on how he should use his
new status.

Zaheer Abbas is almost exactly as old as Pakistan, born in July 1947,
three weeks before independence in the provincial city of Sialkot.
He was the first-born child of his parents Syed Ghulam Shabbir and
Kaneez Fatima. Five more were to follow him, including two brothers
who played first-class cricket in Pakistan. Wisely, his father had told
his pregnant wife to remain in the safety of Sialkot, while he remained
in his official post in the Rajasthan desert on the Indian side of the
Partition line. He did not see his new-born son for several months, after
a perilous escape from the violence and massacres which accompanied
Partition.

Zaheer's early childhood was spent in a remote desert outpost, where
his father was an officer of the Locust Control Agency. If Zaheer's
powers of application were inherited from his father, one almost feels
sorry for the locusts.

From an early age, he was captivated by cricket. It was a mystery
and something of a worry to his academic-minded parents. Their families had no cricket background and they had hopes of their first-born
becoming a doctor. Dutifully, he kept up with school work but still

played in any kind of cricket match within reach. From age seven, he was playing village matches, travelling long distances by bicycle and several times crossing a deep river (the non-swimming boy had to be carried over by his team-mates). From childhood, Zaheer set himself to make a big score in every innings, as if to prove to his parents that cricket was not a waste of his time.

A move to Karachi brought him the chance to watch his idol, Hanif Mohammad, and to be further inspired by the visiting West Indians, Garry Sobers and Rohan Kanhai. It also allowed him to practise regularly with Intikhab Alam, already a Test player, his future captain, friend and mentor. In spite of regular centuries in school and club matches, Zaheer pleased his parents by virtually abandoning cricket to concentrate on academic study at Islamia College; however, he did become a successful volleyball player, which may later have helped his wristwork as a batsman. Rightly he decided that history would be an easier course than science and medicine. There would be no Doctor Zaheer, nor Field-Marshal Zaheer after he abandoned a half-hearted attempt to join the army.

Cricket kept calling him back, and his best friends were all playing club cricket. One of them, a talented off-spinner, Nazeer Baig, would become better known as the movie superstar, Nadeem.

Zaheer joyously relates the story of his road back into cricket. 'Some of my friends shifted to Nazimabad, and started playing there for one of the city's best clubs, Pak Crescent.' One day they took him to a net session. 'My friend Ali had his bat and kit and proper shoes and white clothes and all that. I had none of that and was wearing sandals, because I wasn't expecting to play. But I asked Ali if I could use his bat if they asked me.' He watched for some time. 'It was getting dark, when someone asked if I would like to bat.' Still in sandals, he padded up and borrowed Ali's bat. As darkness fell, he batted for half an hour. 'They kept changing the bowlers. Why? Because I wasn't getting out and so many other things were happening. I had a stroke for every ball. I could see a top-class off-spinner bowling at me, then the whole of the first team. They could not get me out.'

I am struck how often that phrase recurs as he reminisces. Most admirers think of him as an artist. Indeed, the cricketing scholar KH Baloch, in his indispensible *Encyclopedia of Pakistan Cricket*, compares him to two great artists in as many lines: 'Often a completed innings could be compared to the work of a Van Gogh on canvas. He was truly the Michelangelo of cricket . . .'[1] Zaheer seems to prefer thinking of himself as an accumulator, as if Michelangelo was prouder of having covered the ceiling of the Sistine Chapel than of the brush strokes he used to achieve this.

After that net session, he was invited instantly to play for the Pak CC first team. He declined: he was not in practice, but he did agree to play for the B team. The captain put him down at number 3. 'I thought he was joking, making fun of me. I said number five.' In the event, he had to come in at 23 for three with around 200 needed to win. He contributed an unbeaten 90-odd and his team duly won. 'I tell you what, from that day on my luck stayed good. I was doing so well, people talked about me all over Karachi. They said, this guy does not get out.' Other clubs tried to recruit him. When his team travelled to Hyderabad by train, 'people would offer me good food, cream, bangles and jewellery for my sisters and mother. I told them all it was too little,' he adds with a laugh, surveying his well-furnished room.

Zaheer made his first-class debut aged 18 for Karachi Whites against Punjab University in the Ayub trophy competition, flatteringly named after Pakistan's military ruler. Batting at number 8 in the first innings, he was run out for 4. Promoted to number 3 in the second, he was not out 19 as the match meandered to a draw. His captain that day, Faqir Aizazuddin, has a prodigious memory for Pakistan cricket matches, especially those he himself played in, but he could give me no account of Zaheer's performance, even though they shared a stand of 44 in the second innings.

There were some scattered first-class matches in the next few

1 Dr KH Baloch (with Mohammad Salim Parvez), *Encyclopedia of Pakistan Cricket (1947-48 to 2004)*, published 2005, p.377.

years, particularly for the Public Works Department, a traditional employer of cricketers which rarely expected them to do much public work. On his seventh first-class appearance, for Karachi against East Pakistan, he made the first of 108 centuries. Characteristically, it was a giant one: 197 (batting at number 7) in a partnership of 348 with the Test batsman Salahuddin. Throughout his career, Zaheer never thought his work was done when he completed a century. In 35 of his 108 first-class centuries he passed 150, and 14 of the remainder were not out.

At his zenith, contemporaries noted his attention to personal milestones. Like Geoff Boycott he contrived to score his hundredth hundred in a Test match, at Lahore in 1982-83, the second of his mighty domestic series against India. He set it up by scoring century number 99 for the Patron's XI in the previous match against the Indians. Both sides used this for batting practice and the Indians rested their star bowler, Kapil Dev. Zaheer greeted century number 100 with a quiet celebration, remembering in time to acknowledge the toil of India's slow left-arm bowler Dilip Doshi, a friend from county cricket. Thanks to Imran Khan's delayed declaration, he was able to out-do Boycott and continue to a double century. The one disappointment was the small crowd at the ground. Two more huge centuries followed in the Test series. His last century came in domestic competition in his generally lean final season in 1986-87. It was another not out.

Zaheer believes that the big break in his early career was being asked to join the powerful Pakistan International Airlines team, especially an invitation from Hanif Mohammad to be part of its tour of Ireland in summer 1969. 'I said, "Sir, why not? I would love to." I scored the most runs on the tour. Hanif told a group of eight or nine people, "this guy will break all my records."' The memory reminds him of an important task. 'I must call Hanif now, and say "Your student has become the ICC president."'

His first Test appearance came two months later, in Karachi against New Zealand. The match was overshadowed by the sacking of Hanif Mohammad. In a low-scoring draw, Zaheer did nothing much in the middle order: 12 and 27. He disappeared for the rest of the series, the first which Pakistan lost on home soil. He might easily have become one of Pakistan's one-cap wonders, but a spate of centuries for PIA in domestic cricket forced him back into the selectors' reckoning for the England tour of 1971.

Even then he enjoyed a slice of luck. In the opening first-class match at Worcestershire, the veteran Saeed Ahmed was due to bat at number 3. Once a fearless attacking batsman, Saeed by then was reluctant to face fast bowlers on green wickets. Mushtaq Mohammad says that when this seemed likely, Saeed used to swaddle himself in sweaters and blankets to run a temperature. At any rate, Saeed declined a duel with Worcestershire's Vanburn Holder and his slot went to Zaheer. He scored 110 in 171 minutes out of a completed innings of just 241. He was impervious to a Worcestershire attack with three Test bowlers, being run out in both innings (a malady which affected him frequently in his early career). Zaheer thinks that this is when he was first called 'the Asian Bradman'.

He thereafter occupied the number 3 spot as of right. With the help of the 274 (which remained his highest first-class score in a long career) he completed the short tour with 1,461 runs at an average of over 58: he made 386 runs in four innings in the three-Test series, marred only by a golden duck at Headingley in a match Pakistan should have won.

This series earned Zaheer an invitation to join the mighty World team touring Australia that winter in place of the banned South Africans. He found it hard to believe that he was batting with two boyhood idols, the captain Garry Sobers and Rohan Kanhai. Intikhab Alam and Asif Masood were the other Pakistanis in the party, which also included three Indians, Sunil Gavaskar, Bishan Bedi and Farokh Engineer, who made some heavy-handed jokes about the ongoing war between Pakistan and India. Zaheer announced himself to Australians on the fast wicket at Perth with 112 (run out again) and 52. He played with mixed fortunes in all the representative matches but scored 86 at the third one at Melbourne, which was transformed by Garry Sobers's majestic 254. In the final representative match at Adelaide, Zaheer scored 73 in his only innings – and met the real Don Bradman who came to greet both teams.

'He admired my hands, which were very strong. He told me that he had watched me in the World XI and had never seen any other batsman who had looked as though he would never lose his wicket.'

The Asian Bradman became an easy cliché to apply to Zaheer. Certainly, they had traits in common. They both had an appetite for big hundreds. Even more than Bradman, Zaheer liked not only to dominate attacks but to extort the maximum from those to his liking. Zaheer holds the record for scoring two centuries in a first-class match (eight times). In four of those matches, he scored a double century and a century (another record) – and was not dismissed in any of these eight innings. He scored five consecutive centuries against the Indian attack in Pakistan in 1982-83.

At first-class level, Zaheer is the highest-scoring Asian batsman of all time, with 34,485 runs. The next is Mushtaq Mohammad, with 31,091, then comes Javed Miandad with 28,663. All three tallies were boosted by long English county careers. The highest-ranked Indian is Sunil Gavaskar, with 25,834 first-class runs and 81 centuries, closely followed by Sachin Tendulkar: 25,396 runs and also 81 centuries. For Sri Lanka, Mahela Jawardene's tally was 17,843 and 51 centuries, Kumar Sangakkara's at time of writing was 18,381 and 55 centuries. The constant contraction of English first-class cricket almost guarantees that Zaheer will stay ahead of the pack and remain the only Asian batsman to complete a century of first-class centuries.

But for all his imposing statistics, Zaheer never had Bradman's remorseless consistency. His Test career had surprising troughs between the dizzying peaks. After his brilliant 1971 series against England, his subsequent 20 innings yielded just 410 runs with two fifties, until he redeemed himself with his 240 at The Oval in 1974. Two series against unremarkable New Zealand teams then produced just 95 runs in 10 completed innings. Some of these early problems were put down to the wrong optical prescription, but even when this was corrected there were blips in his career. He did not manage a fifty in Pakistan until he murdered the Indian attack in 1978-79 and ended the Test careers of their four great spinners, Prasanna, Bedi, Chandrasekhar and Venkataraghavan. But after posting a record 583 runs in that three-Test series, he assembled only 157 in five Tests in the return series.

In total, Zaheer played 17 series of three Tests or more. In seven, he had an average of 50 or more (in one he averaged 130 and another 194). In seven, he averaged less than 30. His Test career ended even more anti-climactically than Bradman's: after ten innings totalling 121 runs, he left the scene without a proper farewell. By contrast, in Bradman's worst series (Bodyline in 1932-33) he averaged over 56.

Zaheer was especially vulnerable to the ultra-fast Australian and West Indian fast bowlers of the 1970s, and to the lesser pace of Richard Hadlee and (in India) Kapil Dev. He achieved only three fifties in his two-year excursion with Kerry Packer, in matches where fast bowlers were unleashed on improvised pitches. A prototype batting helmet made his glasses steam up. But like most of Packer's players he strongly defends Packer and praises his lasting innovations, especially night cricket. 'He gave people the chance of entertainment after work. You can't see cricket matches in your office.'

Dramatically, his failures make the Asian Bradman a more engaging hero than the real one. When watching a movie, we need to think that the hero *might* be gunned down by the villains, *might* fall off the cliff, *might* even give way to anxiety or despair.

Like Bradman, Zaheer often battled health problems which may have been nervous in origin: in his case, mouth ulcers, stomach problems and weight loss. Like Bradman, he had less than perfect vision. (With Bradman, this was discovered to the cricket world's astonishment when he volunteered for war service.) Zaheer tells us simply, 'I never took to contact lenses,' despite several experiments, and confirms that he stuck to the same cherished pair of glasses for most of his career, even when they were broken by a (literally) spectacular diving catch in the Sydney Test against Australia in 1976-77.

Like Bradman, he had rifts with other senior players, especially Javed Miandad on the acrimonious Australian tour of 1981-82, which flared into open revolt in the subsequent home series against Sri Lanka.

Unlike Bradman, he never established a grip on the captaincy. He was bitterly disappointed to be passed over first for Javed and then for Imran Khan, whom he described as a boy (Imran was then 29 to his 34). His record as a stop-gap captain was respectable, including a series win against England, but won him few admirers as a tactician or as a man-manager.

Like Bradman, he was not a clubbable man and preferred quiet evenings at home with his family to social functions and nights out with the boys. On his early tours, Bradman filled much of his social duties at the piano (he was a polished performer and even composed a hit song, 'Every Day's A Rainbow Day For Me'). He trained himself to be an accomplished public speaker. Zaheer had no such resources outside cricket. Especially at the start of his English career, he relied heavily on the support of his first wife, Najma, mother of his three daughters, and a small circle of trusted friends.

Zaheer's long county career of course sets him apart from Bradman, as does his role in one-day cricket. Both of them demanded new mental and technical disciplines, particularly county cricket. 'Many counties came after me in 1971,' he tells us. Majid Khan was a big influence on his choice of Gloucestershire. 'He told me Graham Parker [the secretary/manager] was a very nice man.' Moreover, his friend Sadiq Mohammad was already enjoying life there while qualifying.

One-day cricket suited him well, in its more sedate opening era before fielding restrictions, power-plays and improvised shots with massive bats. His ability to manœuvre the ball round the field generated 2,572 runs in one-day internationals at an average of nearly 48. In the 1979 World Cup semi-final, he made a peerless 93 against four West Indian pace bowlers who had previously subdued him. His partnership of 166 with Majid Khan set up a Pakistan victory which later batsmen threw away. During his full international career, he scored at 5.09 an over in an era when four an over was a brisk scoring rate. He helped Gloucestershire take two one-day titles during the 1970s – their first successes since WG Grace at his peak a hundred years earlier.

County cricket was tougher initially. The circuit was physically demanding, the weather was cold and damp, he was often lonely and homesick and even hungry. He found that workaday seamers could get him out too easily on green wickets. His first English season produced only 353 runs at an average of 25. The second began with a big undefeated century, but the next one did not arrive until August and his final county average was 30. He resented the delay in the award of a county cap, but accepted the need to prove himself in new conditions. His tightened his technique without sacrificing any artistry. He developed his offside repertoire and the cover drives which made older spectators remember an earlier champion. Already the new Bradman, Zaheer became the new Hammond. He is the only batsman to hold both titles simultaneously.

The first of two hot summers, 1975, saw a big improvement. The second, 1976, passed him into legend: over 2,500 runs at an average of 75. No one had scored that many runs since the English first-class programme was reduced in the previous decade. As an established star, with the affectionate nickname of 'Z', he gave the county a regular thousand runs at a high average in each of the next five seasons. In 1981, he made up for a washed-out May by scoring 1,000 first-class runs in June, needing only 27 days.

Apart from the sheer weight of runs for the county, Zaheer had an aura at the crease. His team-mate Alastair Hignell wrote a beautiful essay on batting with him. 'When he got to the crease, Z entered a world of his own, where all that mattered was the bat in his hand and the possibilities it offered.' Hignell soon learnt not to ask him for advice on the wicket or the bowlers (he would only get worried, said Zaheer, with the clear implication that they made no difference to *him*). 'I also learnt to count to six, as Z regarded it as entirely natural that he should farm the strike and only right and proper that if anyone should be running to the danger end, it would not be him.'[2]

Even as an established star, he had some negative experiences with the county. He had clashes with management over small issues: wearing a sunhat instead of a county cap, not turning up at sponsors'

2 Alastair Hignell, 'The art of Z,' in www.cricinfo.com 29 November 2010.

events. He was disappointed over the captaincy. His later years with Gloucestershire were troubled by his mystery illness, uncertainty over his future as their overseas player and some stress in organising his benefit. The final version of his appeal, in 1983, simply asked people to contribute to 'the best batsman in the world.'[3]

Despite these occasional problems, Gloucestershire made him a firm Anglophile. 'I respect British guys,' he tells us. 'I learnt a lot from them. Whatever you say, they are nice and have some class in them.' For a second, he gives us a challenging look, as if daring us to defy him.

The congratulatory telephone calls subside and the president takes us in to dinner. The outside temperature is still 35 degrees C so we enjoy it in his garden, scented with roses and jasmine, under the moon and stars reflected in a discreet pool. All the dishes are excellent, spicy but subtle. One can understand his longing for curries in the early homesick days at Gloucestershire.

The conversation reverts to his new role at the ICC. Will he have any power? How much will he be allowed to say? 'I want to use my experience to help world cricket through the ICC.' For his own country, he wants to bring back international visitors (he was encouraged by the recent short stay by the Zimbabweans, although this had to be confined to Lahore) and, above all, 'to secure the resumption of Test cricket with India'. Like many others, he deplores the decline of school, college and club cricket in Pakistan ('the standard was very high in my time') and the loss of school and local authority maintained grounds. He has a big personal agenda for international and domestic cricket, but 'I know I must listen carefully before making statements, and find out what the ICC wants from me and how they want me to do the job.' He will be cautious in his opening overs. 'If there is one thing I learnt as a batsman, it is not to give my wicket away.' (The same self-image recurs.) 'Don't leave the crease, and don't give a bad call.'

His friend Qamar Ahmed assures him that he will be able to make a big contribution in private, because of the respect he enjoys in world cricket, especially in India. I suggest that he will be the constitutional

3 Hignell, ibid.

monarch of cricket, like Queen Elizabeth. He will be a public symbol of the best qualities in the sport, and in private he will enjoy her prerogatives, to be consulted, to advise and to warn. He seems taken by the idea.

On the way home, I glimpse some young men playing an improvised cricket match under street lights. The batsman has a high backlift and brings off a beautiful flick to the imaginary midwicket boundary. Just like his neighbour, Mr President.

19

A GLIMPSE BEHIND THE CAMERAS

Thanks to President Ayub Khan, television reached Pakistan in 1964 through the Television Promoters Company, a public–private partnership between the state and the Japanese company, Nippon Electric. Its first transmission in November 1964, from a makeshift studio in Lahore, featured a speech by Ayub Khan followed by a table tennis match. This output (in black and white) was enough to fascinate viewers at a public demonstration. Their response, followed by a 90-day trial, persuaded the government to give the go-ahead. Initially limited to Lahore, transmissions began in Dacca, Rawalpindi/Islamabad, and Karachi over the next two years; Quetta and Peshawar had to wait until 1974. Colour arrived in 1976. It was nationalised in two stages in 1967 and 1971, but unlike the BBC, PTV has carried commercial advertising since its beginnings.[1]

Official PTV figures in the following table show the initial growth and reach of television in Pakistan, although they naturally omit the number of television sets acquired and viewed illegally.[2] The high ratios

1 See S Logan, 'Television in Pakistan,' in ed I Banerjee, *Asian Communication Handbook* (UNESCO, 2008), 'Pakistan Television,' in A O Thomas, *Imaginations and Borderless Television: Media, Culture and Politics Across Asia* (Sage, 2005), O Samiuddin, *The Unquiet Ones* (HarperCollins, 2015), pp.230 et seq.
2 Source: PTV Facts and Figures 1981 and PTV Basics 1989. Cited in 'History of PTV' on www.scribd.com/doc/29742078.

of viewers per set illustrate the extent to which television viewing was
a shared experience, in which people gathered around sets in cafés and
public places or friends' houses.

Year	TV set count	Est viewers	Pop covered %
1964	NA	NA	9.3
1970	123,000	985,600	32.0
1975	405,000	3,240,000	54.9
1980	937,000	7,500,000	77.5
1985	1,436,610	11,492,800	81.8
1990	1,504,200	12,033,600	86.4

PTV's initial cricket broadcasting was limited and cautious,[3] but
this was transformed in the 1970s when two brothers, Akhtar and
Athar Viqar Azeem, gave fans innovative and informed coverage of an
increasingly successful team.

Athar, the younger brother, spent over 30 years at PTV but is now
senior vice-president of a private network, HUM TV. Lunch in its
canteen is an excellent experience, testing recipes for its 24-hour food
channel. He was virtually press-ganged into PTV in 1972 after a chance
encounter with its head of news and current affairs, Muslehuddin. 'He
took me by the hand, led me to a room and said, "This is your room,
and you have joined PTV."'[4] Although a total tyro, he quickly made
a reputation as a producer of live current affairs programmes. The
network then turned to him and his brother for cricket coverage. They
knew the game better than anyone else, especially Athar, a talented
college and club performer, but had no experience of transmitting it or
indeed any other sport.

They taught themselves. Athar, still producing current affairs programmes, put in six-hour shifts in an outside broadcast van. Staffing
was much smaller than today and he had to do dozens of tasks on his

3 For which see O Samiuddin, op. cit., pp.232-33.
4 See 'Flashback: Going Live,' *Dawn*, 1 October 2011.

own. The staff he was given were not always much help. 'The cameramen did not know the fielding positions. When I said, "Show Asif Iqbal at gully," they would say, "Where's gully?" I had to teach them all the positions.'

Another problem was to train commentators to follow the monitor after learning on radio to describe everything they saw. He developed a new pairing, the emotional Iftikhar Ahmed and the analytical Chishty Mujahid. Partly under the influence of General Zia-ul-Haq, whose English was less fluent than earlier rulers, he gave 20 per cent of the time to Urdu commentary from Munir Hussain, and later Bashir Khan, who became a power in advertising.[5]

Like the commentators on BBC radio's *Test Match Special*, Iftikhar Ahmed and Chishty Mujahid became celebrated for banter. Occasionally, this got them into trouble, as in the Karachi Test against Australia in 1980. In the midst of a joke they were startled by a roar in the stadium. They had missed the dismissal of Kim Hughes, Australia's top scorer, caught at slip by Majid Khan off the new, hitherto unknown, off-spinner Tauseef Ahmed.[6] Out, they declared, and then asked the expert summariser, Hanif Mohammad, to explain. 'They passed the mike immediately to Hanif for his reaction. But Hanif had not seen the dismissal either. He normally used to arrive late, with an omelette, which he was eating when it happened. So he described the dismissal as he imagined it: Tauseef's delivery, Hughes's edge, the chance accepted by Majid. In the action replay, it was exactly as Hanif described.'

Athar Viqar Azeem's favourite television coverage was of Majid's century before lunch in Karachi against New Zealand in 1976. This innings, in the first series telecast from all PTV's centres, gave a big boost to the following of Pakistan cricket, and Majid also provided another great moment, the six off Dennis Lillee which sealed Pakistan's win in Sydney, in 1977. It was Pakistan's first victory in Australia, and as at The Oval in 1954, it was gained through a charismatic bowler

5 O Noman, *Pride And Passion* (Karachi: OUP, 1998), pp.173-74.
6 See chapter 23.

taking 12 wickets. The last hour was televised and presented Pakistan to viewers as a brilliant winning team. This image was dented slightly by the struggling Packerless team in England in 1978. 'We used to take an hour or so after tea from the BBC. When I cut to live coverage of the first Test at Edgbaston, four wickets went down in no time [this was Chris Old's spell of four in five balls]. My controller said, "we asked for live coverage, not the highlights."'

However, with the Packer players restored, Pakistan reconquered viewers in the exciting home series against India in 1978-79. By then, General Zia-ul-Haq had taken power. His military regime instituted a fierce crackdown on the media and interfered regularly in the content of PTV programmes.[7]

Athar did not recall any special pressure from Zia's regime, but he was careful to give full coverage of Zia's frequent visits to cricket matches. 'If say, the Australian Premier went to a match he would get shown once or twice. But in Pakistan we had to show the head of government constantly, sitting and appreciating the cricket. If this was not done, someone would ask why we were not showing General Zia doing so and so.'

He also mentioned two cases of self-censorship. In 1980, the commentators avoided describing the West Indian fast bowler, Sylvester Clarke, hurling a brick at a spectator in Multan, for fear of being subpoena'd in criminal proceedings. During India's visit to Pakistan in 1982, a fire broke out in one of the stadiums. 'We went back to the studio and played a song. When my manager asked why we weren't showing the cricket, I told him that I had seen the fire and did not want to show this to India.'

When interviewed by *Dawn*, Athar Viqar Azeem had strong words about present-day coverage of disturbances. 'Today a public riot would be telecast to a ridiculous depth. Not only is there a ratings war among channels but live coverage is done by immature people.'[8]

In less pressured conditions he televised squash: Jonah Barrington

7 See Jaffrelot, op. cit., p.416 and pp 73 and 202 of this book.
8 'Flashback: Going Live,' *Dawn*, 1 October 2011.

thought his coverage superior to the BBC's. He also answered a request to organise the transmission of the cricket matches in Sharjah developed by Abdul Rahman Bukhatir and Asif Iqbal. 'I covered Sharjah for fourteen years. I advised them on the creation of the stadium and then on camera coverage. We turned Sharjah cricket into a social get-together, with Indian artists and Bollywood stars and television personalities from Pakistan. We showed celebrities watching the cricket but we covered every single moment of cricket.' He brought over English and West Indian commentators, including Tony Lewis and Tony Greig. Deprived of his usual buses, Henry Blofeld liked to fill time by describing well-dressed Asian female spectators.

All the while, Athar Viqar Azeem was improving the technical coverage of Pakistan cricket. He began with three cameras, one at each end and one at square leg, 'but we never missed a thing'. He increased them to five, and independently introduced several innovations normally attributed to Kerry Packer, including pitch reports, copious player interviews, colourful graphics and stump microphones. These were switched on, and broadcast in real time, when Mike Gatting had his famous spat with umpire Shakoor Rana in 1987. Second only to Packer, and ahead of the BBC and the Australian Broadcasting Corporation, he used 12 cameras for the World Cup in 1987, whose staging was shared between India and Pakistan. 'The BBC was happy to take our signal,' he said proudly, 'but they did not do this for India.'

Perhaps his greatest legacy was to capture two of the greatest moments in Pakistan's cricket history: Imran Khan's dismissal of Gundappa Viswanath in Karachi on Christmas Day 1982, and Javed Miandad's last-ball six in Sharjah in 1986. His footage has had more viewers since then than the world's present population.

The standards which he and his brother set for cricket coverage were acknowledged by Asad Azeem Shan, currently a senior director and producer at PTV Sports. He cut his teeth in the 1996 World Cup, the second to be staged in the Indian subcontinent, which PTV covered in partnership with the private company TWI. While Athar Viqar Azeem had used 12 cameras for the 1987 World Cup, Asad was surprised to discover TWI using 36 for a single match. He himself learnt how to deploy 36 cameras, although he cannot always get them. 'There are twelve cameras in Lahore dedicated to sport, and if I want more I have to borrow them from other centres. The twelve in Lahore are not reserved for cricket, and PTV has a mandate to cover all sports. And we sometimes lose cameras to current affairs, to cover a government minister making a speech.' This seems an ill-judged demand by any politician ('We are leaving our coverage of the Test match to bring you the minister of state opening the new sewage plant') but Majid Khan, former head of sport at PTV, confirmed to us that this has been a regular problem.

Asad Azeem Shan said that by 1996 television coverage had expanded to make the World Cup a universal event for Pakistan. 'Each and every home had access to PTV's terrestrial service, by antenna, even in remote areas. People took television sets out to the roads to share with their neighbours.'

To this day, all of Pakistan's international matches, and its major domestic ones, for both men and women, are available on PTV's terrestrial sports network. The fee, payable through electricity bills, is 35 rupees (equivalent to 23 pence) a month. This situation owes much to a decree of General Pervez Musharraf, who was embarrassed in 2003 when Pakistan television viewers missed a one-day international against New Zealand because of a disputed claim by the private network, GEO TV, to own the rights. Protecting matches for PTV's terrestrial viewers is undoubtedly Musharraf's greatest gift to Pakistan cricket.

Unfortunately, the general's writ did not extend to the English Cricket Board . . .

20

A FORGOTTEN FOUR HUNDRED: THE EFFICIENT BUT UNLUCKY AFTAB BALOCH

The Sind club in Karachi is a world away from the teeming, turbulent city that surrounds it. In its magnificently stuffy public rooms and well-manicured gardens, one may readily subside into a vanished past. On our first visit, we mentally populated the club with the entire cast of PG Wodehouse.

We continued the fantasy when we met Aftab Baloch there, a Pakistan cricket star of the 1970s. Eventually we identified him as a much nicer version of the Efficient Baxter. Compact and athletic at 60, Aftab Baloch did not wear horn-rimmed spectacles and would never have ganged up with Lady Constance to make Lord Emsworth's life a misery. But like Baxter he was remarkably efficient in every job he undertook – batting, bowling, fielding in any position including wicketkeeper, and captaincy. Like many Pakistan cricketers, he endured capricious treatment from selectors and administrators, first as a player and later as a national coach.

Along the way he completed one of the least-watched and least-rewarded quadruple centuries in first-class cricket: 428 in February 1974 as the 20-year-old captain of Sind against Baluchistan.

Birth records are not always reliable in Pakistan, but he is officially the youngest of the eight players to have passed four hundred (Bill Ponsford and Brian Lara did it twice). Don Bradman was 21 when he posted his then record-breaking 452 not out for New South Wales against Queensland in 1930. When Hanif Mohammad broke that record, with 499 for Karachi against Bahawalpur in 1959, he was 24.

Aftab Baloch was the son of MS Baloch, a notable figure of Indian pre-Partition cricket. He told us: 'Everything I learnt at cricket was from my father, he was my guide and my creator,' although he also had some advice from the legendary Master Aziz. Aftab Baloch caught the eye as a schoolboy in Karachi and broke into first-class cricket aged 16. He averaged over 76 in his debut season, to which he added 28 wickets at under 19 apiece. He won a call-up for the third and last Test against New Zealand, in November 1969, still only 16. He scored a painstaking 25 in his only innings, which helped Pakistan earn a decisive lead. The selectors then discarded him.

He had an unhappy two seasons with Pakistan International Airlines, but then came into his own with teams for Karachi or Sind. In 1972-73, he had a fine all-round season, averaging 52 with the bat and taking 19 wickets with his off-spinners. He also demonstrated a flair for captaincy. Appointed over several more senior players, he led Karachi Blues to success in Pakistan's BCCP Patrons' Trophy.

The following season he captained Sind province in a first-class programme expanded by Pakistan's cricket supremo, AH Kardar, their former captain. Sind's first opponents in the Quaid-e-Azam trophy were Baluchistan. The province had never been a power in Pakistan cricket, although, as their name suggests, Aftab Baloch's family had their roots there, as horse breeders and dealers. Baluchistan had only just returned to the competition and played all their matches away, since the province was undergoing a long insurrection which tied down 80,000 Pakistani troops.

Baluchistan won the toss and batted first at the National Stadium, Karachi. They subsided to 93 all out off 360 balls (Pakistan was then conducting an experiment with eight-ball overs. Not surprisingly, given the climate, this was unpopular with fast bowlers).

Aftab Baloch came out to bat for Sind at 116 for two. A sparse crowd watched him put on 302 with Bashir Shana. At the end of the second day, he had scored 326 not out, with Sind 642 for three. 'People started coming to the ground on the third day, thinking I was going to break Hanif's record.' They included Hanif himself, who watched him make 400 and generously urged him past his own 499.

It was not to be. Aftab Baloch was caught at mid-off for 428. 'It was a full-blooded drive and he stuck out his hand.' He had batted for 584 minutes and helped to add 712 runs in three partnerships, the last of them worth 174 with a teenaged Javed Miandad. By contrast, Hanif took 635 minutes over his 499 and was at the wicket for the entire team innings of 772 for seven declared. Bradman needed only 415 minutes for his 452 not out. He added 739 with seven partners before the declaration at 761 for eight.

Although he failed to break Hanif's record, Aftab Baloch set one of his own which is likely to last forever. Only 100 of his runs came in boundaries. To score the other 328, he had to run well over three miles. No one else has run so far in a single first-class innings. Aftab Baloch was unaware of his record and made nothing of it. 'We were all young, myself, Javed Miandad and Nasir Valika [another partner]. Javed was only 17, Valika under 19. We were too quick, and instead of taking fours we chose to take runs in twos or threes.'

Aftab Baloch let the innings continue. The next batsman, another teenager, Mohammad Akram, lost his head in the crisis of 828 for five and was out for 2, but Javed Miandad went on to complete his maiden first-class century.

Javed does not even mention this century in his sparkling, spiky autobiography *Cutting Edge*. Like many other Pakistan cricketers, he underplays his successes in domestic cricket. In truth, Baluchistan were very weak opposition. They used ten bowlers who ended their first-class careers with a combined total of 99 wickets. Statistically, they were the poorest attack ever to bowl at a quadruple centurion, but they still demanded immense stamina, and weak attacks often require more concentration than strong ones.

Aftab Baloch eventually closed the Sind innings on 951 for six (scored off 1,438 balls), the highest first-class score in Pakistan. He was not tempted to push on for the thousand, and although Baluchistan fared much better in their second innings, Sind completed victory

by an innings and 575 runs with more than a day to spare. In a nice
gesture, he put on Mohammad Akram to bowl at the number 11, and
the disappointed teenager took the first of only six first-class wickets.

The 428 brought Aftab Baloch a reward of 500 rupees (then equivalent to around £21) to add to his 30 rupees a day match allowance.
Hanif had received an official gift of 10,000 rupees for his 499, then
equivalent to around £750. Aftab Baloch finished the season with over
1,200 runs at an average over 52 and picked up 19 wickets as a relief
bowler. His reward was inclusion in Pakistan's 1974 touring party
to England – but only as reserve wicketkeeper to the incomparable
Wasim Bari. He played seven matches on the tour, scoring 101 in four
completed innings. 'Established players were in the side and I didn't
get any chance in the Tests, or even in the first-class fixtures against
the counties.' He did not even get batting practice in the touring team's
nets. Management tried to assign him Room 428 in the team's hotels.
Some players might have found this reminder galling when they could
not get a bat on the tour, but Aftab Baloch still finds it amusing.

He returned to Pakistan and put in another big domestic performance: over 1,100 runs at an average over 65, helped by a double
century against his favourite opponents, Baluchistan, and 40 cheap
wickets. At last, he was recalled to the Pakistan team, for the second
Test against the West Indies. In the second innings Pakistan were in
some trouble, five wickets down and only 189 ahead. Against an attack
of Roberts, Julien, Holder, Boyce and Gibbs he made 60 not out, helping to add 156 in two partnerships. This set a target beyond the West
Indies' reach and saved the match and the series.

He was promptly discarded – a victim of cricket politics when an
enemy briefed the all-powerful AH Kardar against him. That was the
end of his Test career. He was kept out of Pakistan's increasingly powerful batting line-up by Javed Miandad, whom he had mentored. He
went to England and had two excellent seasons with Rishton in the
Lancashire League, then returned to domestic cricket and played his
last first-class match aged only 32.

No one has played fewer Test matches after scoring a quadruple
century, with the exception of the Indian, BB Nimbalkar, who never

played any. He was marooned on 443 not out in a Ranji trophy match for Maharashtra in 1948, when the opposing captain, the Takore Sahib of Rajkot, led his Kathiawar team off the pitch. The Maharashtra team begged him to return for a few overs, to allow Nimbalkar the chance to overtake Bradman's then record 452. But His Highness had had enough fielding and forfeited the match.

Nimbalkar aside, Aftab Baloch must be the least rewarded quadruple centurion.[1] He has no regrets, except to recall a missed opportunity to meet Graeme Hick, scorer of 405 not out (in 555 minutes) for Worcestershire against Somerset in 1988. During England's tour of Pakistan in 1999-2000, Aftab Baloch was working for PIA as stationmaster at Karachi airport when he saw Hick and the England party heading for their flight. 'I asked to talk to him but he moved to the plane and we didn't speak. He didn't know me, I was just another spectator, but I would like to have introduced myself as Aftab Baloch who made 428.'

If Graeme Hick reads this, we would be glad to put him in touch with another member of the very exclusive 400 Club.

A version of this chapter appeared in the British magazine Backspin, *issue 9.*

---

1 According to Najum Latif, Mohammed Iqbal 'Bala Natha' scored the first 400 at any level in Pakistan, and had an Eaglets tour of England. Despite the admiration of Sir Donald Bradman, he too was a victim of cricket politics.

21

THE 'WORSTEST EVER DEBUT'
OF A MATCHWINNER

The story of Abdul Qadir, magician and matchwinner, has 'made in Pakistan' stamped right through it. He took all but three of his 960 first-class wickets for Pakistani teams.[1] His four sons have all played first-class cricket in Pakistan and he is teaching a new generation of Pakistani cricketers aged six to 13 at his cricket school in Lahore.

In his office, he tells that story at the pace of an express bowler rather than a spinner. His right hand, which propelled 55,785 leg-breaks, googlies and flippers in first-class and major one-day cricket matches, constantly twists and whirls, as if he wanted to bowl them all over again.

Abdul Qadir was one of four children, raised in a tiny house in Dharampura, a poor and crowded district of Lahore. He is proud of his Pasthun family origins. His father migrated to Lahore and earned a tiny salary reading prayers at a local mosque; he also taught the Holy Qu'ran to local people for nothing. It was barely enough to raise a family, and they sometimes missed meals. His father had no sporting interests, and there were no other older relatives to inspire and teach his second son to

---

1 The others came in a frolic for the Rest of the World v MCC at Lord's during Pakistan's tour of England in 1987.

play cricket. 'But he did pass on my cricket values – excellence, honesty, respect for opponents. In my career, I never had sharp exchanges with opponents' – although later he narrates a famous sledging clash with Ian Botham at Lord's in 1982.

As a boy, he played all kinds of street games, especially marbles, but never played any kind of cricket until he was around 11 or 12, when friends asked him to make up the numbers in a pick-up match. Reluctantly, he agreed. He struggles momentarily for words to express his performance and finally pronounces 'it was the worstest ever debut'. The local rule was for the newcomer to bat first. The friends placed a bat in his hand, told him how to hold it and explained that he had to defend the three sticks behind it. He was clean bowled, first ball, and walked off. The others bid him to return. 'That was only a trial ball.' The bowler delivered again – and clean bowled him. Two golden ducks and he did not bowl. He repeats 'the worstest ever debut'. But his team won the match, and when he returned home in the evening as people set off for prayers, the whole street asked for details of the victory. 'I saw for the first time that cricket could earn me respect from the elders. It inspired me to stay with cricket.'

The boy worked hard and improved. As a teenager, Abdul Qadir became a leading batsman in school teams and organised local matches in the open space near the Fortress Stadium. To support his frail father, he went to work at a local bookstall. The owner paid him 30 rupees a month (about £15 at the then official exchange rate) – 5 rupees more than his father was earning each month. His team-mates secretly paid the stall owner to release him for cricket matches: thus, he became a professional cricketer without even knowing it.

By now he had decided to become a spin bowler, to save energy in the heat. He was entirely self-taught, practising hard in the nets and experimenting continually – even in his dreams. 'I used to go to bed with a cricket ball and as I was falling asleep I used to imagine various grips and what the ball would do.' This method helped him discover three or four different ways to produce the standard deliveries in the leg-spinner's repertoire.

At one game by the Fortress Stadium, he was spotted and recruited

by the best local club, the Dharampura Gymkhana. As often happens
in Pakistan, the newcomer had to watch the seniors and prepare nets
and pitches for them before he even had a chance to practise, let alone
play a match. When they put him into the first team, he obliged them
with a century and five wickets. His all-round performances gained
him a place in Government College, Lahore, a long-established pipeline
for cricket talent, and he hit 145 in the inter-college final against their
rivals, Islamia.

From there, he went to work and play cricket for the Water and
Power Development Association at 230 rupees a week (around £10 at
the current exchange rate), and then an even better offer came from
the Habib Bank – 750 rupees a week (around £32). He was an early
beneficiary of Kardar's system of commercial teams – his father was
surprised that cricketers got paid.

At the Habib Bank, he was at number 7 in a powerful batting line-up
including Mohsin Khan and Javed Miandad. It led him to concentrate
on bowling, a decision reinforced on his first-class debut, aged 20,
against the United Bank in the SA Bhutto Cup (another product of
the Kardar–Bhutto era). He received a shocking lbw decision on the
front foot. 'I went to the toilet and wept and decided never to put my
pads on again.' When Habib Bank took the field, the regular bowlers,
including Test opener Liaquat Ali, were unable to penetrate. When
finally given the ball, as the sixth bowler, Abdul Qadir took six for 67.
His photograph appeared in *Dawn* newspaper over the caption 'Abdul
Qadir Wrecks Opponents.' Not surprisingly, he felt like a champion.

He wrecked 25 other first-class opponents in that first season and 67
in the next, which earned him a Test debut against England. His figures
were modest (the number 11 batsman Bob Willis at a cost of 82) but
he did well enough to keep his place and capture six for 44 in the next
Test. He remembers a match fee of 3,000 rupees (then about £168).

Abdul Qadir finished with 236 Test wickets, most of them gained
with maximum mystery and melodrama. His nine for 56 against
England at Lahore in 1987-88 is the best bowling performance by a
Pakistani in a Test innings. The previous year, in Faisalabad, his six for
16 reduced a powerful West Indies to 53, then their lowest Test score.

He thrived especially under Imran Khan, who suggested that he add a small French beard to help overcome resistant batsmen during matches and resistant ladies after matches. Also for psychological reasons, he decided to modify his natural easy action into the oblique whirling approach which still has thousands of imitators.

More important than any of those 236 victims (and the 132 he added in ODIs) was his hold on the cricket world's imagination. In an era dominated by pace bowlers, with a few finger-spinners as supporting cast, he kept alive the art of wrist-spin bowling. His successors acknowledge their debt to him. He got lucrative offers from overseas (especially apartheid South Africa) – all rejected until he was 43 and his Pakistan career was over. He was tempted by one proposal from AR Lewis, 'a beautiful man with beautiful thoughts', but told him: 'I cannot sell my heart, my heart belongs to Pakistan.'

His cricket academy transmits his values as well as his techniques to the next generation of Pakistan cricketers. On its gates is a giant poster with a tribute to him, as King of Spin, from Shane Warne (who misspells 'sincerely') but there are many more posters with improving precepts and verses from the Holy Qu'ran. The academy is approved by the PCB but independent of them: he devised its training methods. Like its founder, whatever international players it produces will be 'made in Pakistan.'

A version of this profile appeared in the Cricket Society *journal.*

On his first English tour in 1982, Abdul Qadir received this tribute from an unknown poet:

> *The bold English batsman appears at the crease,*
> *And tries not to show any fear,*
> *But the ball's in the air, it'll spin who knows where?*
> *From Abdul the bowling Qadir.*

22

MOHSIN KHAN: FROM CRICKET TO THE MOVIES AND BACK AGAIN

Beginning with the charismatic all-rounder Salim Durani in the 1970s, scores of Indian Test cricketers have tried their hand as movie actors. Some, like Kapil Dev, were wise enough to play themselves, but Sunil Gavaskar,[1] Vinod Kambli, Sandip Patil, Syed Kirmani and Yuvraj Singh all chanced their arm in dramatic roles. Yuvraj's father Yograj was a one-Test wonder for India but notably more successful than his son as an actor.

Few Pakistani cricketers have tried to emulate them. Fazal Mahmood, Pakistan's good-looking master bowler, was sought after by several famous directors in the 1950s. In advance of Pakistan's inaugural tour of India in 1952-53, he got a flattering offer from Mehboob Khan to play the second lead in a big-budget drama, *Aan*: he decided to stick to cricket. A few years later, when George Cukor came to Lahore to make *Bhowani Junction* he met Fazal and said he would have preferred him as the lead to Stewart Granger.[2]

---

1 Gavaskar's first outing was in a Marathi movie *Savil Premachi*, while he was still opening the batting for India. In spite of his following, it made a duck at the box office. He had better luck with a cameo as himself in *Malaamaal*, derived from the American comedy *Brewster's Millions*. He performed 'Ya Duniyemadhye Thambayaala Vel Konala', a song explaining the meaning of life in cricket terms.
2 Fazal was tempted just once in front of the camera, by the pioneering director Anwar Kamal Pasha. The movie was a Moghul costume drama and Fazal was embarrassed by the costume. He walked off the set after a week and the project sank into the dust.

Pervez Sajjad, Pakistan's metronomic slow left-arm bowler of the 1960s, worked extensively on the other side of the camera as an assistant to his brother, the celebrated director Iqbal Shehzad. The brooding fast bowler Sarfraz Nawaz was offered Punjabi film roles, especially after marrying the Pakistani movie superstar Rani, but never appeared on the screen. Abdul Qadir and Imran Khan rejected movie offers. Shahid Afridi managed to play himself successfully in *Main Hoon* – a sentimental offering about a young boy who wants to be the next Shahid Afridi. In 2015, Shoaib Akhtar was set to make his film debut with a singing role in the Pakistani action movie *Sikander*, directed by Moammar Rana.

However, one Pakistani Test cricketer built a solid second career as an actor before returning to cricket. Mohsin Khan was a dashing top-order batsman from 1977 to 1986. His highlight was at Lord's in 1982 when, converted into an opener, he hit a double century in the first innings and a shared run-chase for victory with Javed Miandad in the second. His second career stemmed from his marriage to Reena Roy, an established Indian screen star, who retired and pushed him as an actor instead. Beginning with *Batwara* in 1989, he had dramatic roles in 13 Indian movies, ending with *Mahaanta: The Film* in 1997. He performed in over 40 Pakistani movies, both features and made-for-TV. He then served the PCB in several roles during a turbulent time for Pakistan cricket, most successfully as chief selector and then acting coach in 2012 when Pakistan beat England 3-0 in a dramatic Test series at 'home' in the UAE. He was understandably miffed when they failed to reappoint him and now works as a freelance and forthright cricket analyst on television. On a talk show some years ago, he hit on a motivational slogan which achieved wide currency: 'Don't Play With Pakistan, Play *For* Pakistan.'

When Mohsin Khan talked to us about his two careers, he stressed immediately that he wanted to be thought of as a cricketer, not a movie star. But there is a strong tang of showbiz and celebrity chat shows in his conversation. Many other stars, from both worlds, were name-checked as 'very dear personal friends ... we shared such a lot ... I have deep respect for him ...' He did not have a bad word about anyone, only

oblique references to 'dirty politics' or 'some unpleasant things happened.' At times, he seemed to be playing himself in one of the 'good
guy' roles he was given on screen.

Although his cricket identity is paramount, he takes pride in his
movie career. Statistically, he is the only major Test star with more
movie credits than caps: 45 Test matches against 53 credits. That is
a fair rejoinder to critics of his acting. Unfortunately, we found a fair
number in a random sample of Pakistani movie-goers. They called him
stiff and expressionless and unable to spark with other actors. Hmm.
'Why should they tear the wings from anyone's dream?' We watched
many of his clips. Predictably, he was often out-acted and out-danced
by the more experienced performers, but he stayed in character and had
a good line in sincerity.

Did he have any acting ambitions or experience in early life? 'None
at all. In fact, I was so camera-shy, I could not bear photographers as a
boy or even as a Test cricketer. I would let the press people take a few
shots and then tell them that was enough.' He grew up sports-crazy in
Karachi, where he was born in 1955. His father was an officer in the
Pakistan Navy, while his mother, who had been educated in the United
States, had a long career as a teacher and vice-principal. 'My father
encouraged my love of sport, but my mother was strict about making
me get a good basic education.'

At Kulsoom Bai Valika school, near Karachi airport, he excelled at
tennis and swimming as well as cricket, and in his teens he became
junior badminton champion of Pakistan. He spent a year at DJ Science
College and then was admitted to the National College at Karachi,
largely (he admits) as an all-round sportsman. His college subjects were
Physics, Chemistry and Mathematics. Their schedule was demanding.
He even gave up regular cricket, and played casual pick-up games with
his friends.

His entry into big-time cricket was a typically Pakistani story. Early
one morning, he was summoned to the room of his physics teacher, Mr
Mukarram, who doubled as a sports teacher. 'He told me the college
were playing an important match and had lost its top player through
injury. Would I replace him? Now at that time inter-college cricket

was of a very high standard. I told him I had played no serious cricket for ages.' But his teacher prevailed on him. He went to the match and found he was opening the batting. 'I said I was only there to make up the numbers but the captain insisted.'

Inevitably, he made a century. An international umpire was on duty at the match and asked him where he had been playing. 'I said, "Nowhere, sir, just in the street, and this was my first big game," and he said, "Look, son, you have to pack everything else up and start playing cricket."' He took this advice back to his father, who agreed. Soon after, he was selected for Karachi Under-19s, and scored a triple century, and there was no looking back then, with first-class selection for Karachi and Pakistan Universities.

A decisive step was to join the Habib Bank team, one of many corporate teams called into being to employ cricketers by AH Kardar. 'Next to Almighty God, I owe my cricket career to two people. One was Mr Mukarram, whom we all called Sir Mukarram. The other was Mr Wadiwalla of the Habib Bank. He said, "I don't want Test cricketers in my team. I want upcoming talent so that we can convert them into Test cricketers."' Besides Mohsin, this astute policy benefited Javed Miandad and Abdul Qadir.

Strong performances in domestic cricket earned him his first Test cap in the third Test in Karachi against England in 1977-78. Wasim Bari was his first captain, a cautious leader of a side weakened by the loss of five stars to Kerry Packer. In a dull match, he scored 44 at number 3: it took 137 balls although he permitted himself a six. He went on the return tour of England, with a still Packerless team, in a dismal summer. He was the most consistent batsman, averaging over 38 without ever scoring a fifty. He had already played two English seasons in the Lancashire League as a professional for Todmorden, and would give them four more before playing two for Accrington. 'England became my second home. I loved Todmorden especially, the people were fantastic to me. I bought a house there.' It has since been sold but he revisits Todmorden whenever he can for as long as he can.

The return of Pakistan's Packer players cost him his Test place for two full series against India. He came back in for two troubled series under Javed Miandad's leadership, away to Australia and home to Sri Lanka, which culminated in outright revolt against the captain. Under pressure, he left the uprising along with other Habib Bank employees in the team. The Sri Lanka series gave him a new berth as an opener, in which he scored his first Test fifty and soon after, the first of his seven Test hundreds.

The next was his landmark double century at Lord's, the first by a Pakistani in a Test in England. He made exactly 200 off 386 balls in eight-and-a-quarter hours, against an attack of Botham, Jackman, Pringle, Ian Greig and Hemmings.

He remembers a headline about him (clearly lifted from Handel's 'Messiah'): LORD OF LORD'S. Several English friends asked him why during the 200 he had failed to put his forehead to the ground to thank Allah at each fifty. He replied, 'I thanked my Allah in my heart, but I put it to him that I would put my forehead to the floor only when we won the match.'

Imran declared on 428 and England failed by two runs to escape the follow-on. In their second innings, the home team succumbed to the golden arm of Mudassar Nazar, previously regarded as a part-time medium pacer, but Pakistan were frustrated by a combination of rain, long innings by Tavaré and Botham and a last-wicket stand between Taylor and Jackman. Pakistan had to make 76 to win in short order. Opening with Javed Miandad, Mohsin Khan scored 39 in an unbroken stand of 77. It was achieved at the then scorching rate of 5.85 an over, principally by superb running between the wickets. He then kept his promise to Allah.

As an opener, he enjoyed several productive and happy years in the strong team which developed around the axis of Imran Khan and Javed Miandad. 'We had so much talent and Imran made us accept challenges and fight to the last ball.'

He achieved several further records. In 1982, he became the first Pakistani to score 1,000 Test runs in a calendar year (off nine matches). Within them was a curious record which he will almost certainly keep. At Lahore against India in 1982-83, he scored 101 not out in a second innings total of 135 for one. This is the smallest Test innings to contain a century.

In 1983-84, he became the first Pakistani to score two consecutive Test centuries in Australia. There was one disappointment. Sir Donald Bradman, who had watched the start of his 149 in Adelaide, was taken ill before Mohsin completed his innings, and had to leave his box. 'I never met Sir Don, and I never saw Garry Sobers in Pakistan[3] – the saddest things in my cricket life.' He had to be satisfied with Sir Don's comment, relayed to him by Ian Chappell: 'This boy can bat.'

Meanwhile, he had met Reena Roy, the woman who changed his life. 'It actually happened in London. I was in England to play my Lancashire League season and she was touring with her sister. It was her sister I met first and she then introduced us. I did not know who she was! I was never keen on movies, Pakistani or Indian, and had never seen her on screen, but her sister told me that she was one of the top heroines of India. I was really attracted by her attitude. She was unaffected and seemed to be a very modest, humble person.'

A friendship began and before long they had fallen in love. When their relationship became known, he was worried by how the public would receive it in both countries. 'Amazingly, there was no hostility at all. I made so many friends in India, and she had a huge following in Pakistan. She travelled all over the country on an unrestricted visa and received immense love and affection. I was so proud of the way our government [of President Zia-ul-Haq] and our people reacted to her.'

Their lives had reached a crossroads. 'I was at the peak of my career when we fell in love and so was she. I asked her if she wanted to carry on, and told her I had nothing against it, but she told me she was tired of working and wanted to pack it in and have a family life. I told her that was fine, and continued as a full-time cricketer. In our culture, to be honest, we don't want our wives to work.' He kept up his cricket career and joined Pakistan's tour of India in 1982-83.

There he had a persistent stalker – Reena's friend JP Dutta. 'He even

---

3 Apart from his tour with the West Indies in 1958-59, Sobers made only one visit to Pakistan, as captain of a World XI which played a one-off match in aid of flood victims against Pakistan in December 1970, when Mohsin Khan was 15. Mohsin did not miss much: the great man was out for 0 (bowled Salim Altaf) and 25 (caught Wasim Bari bowled Sarfraz Nawaz).

came to the Test match in Bangalore, where I agreed to meet him before
the start of play. I discovered that he was a top director. He said that
he had a role for me. I told him I was totally involved in cricket and
I wanted to play for my country as long as possible. He asked me to
think about it and I agreed. He actually came back to me at the lunch
interval. I asked him why, and he said, "I am waiting for your answer."
He was showing me so much respect I felt I had to honour him and I
said, "Look, I promise that when I leave cricket I'll do it." He accepted
the promise and I was glad to escape.'

In 1983, he and Reena were married in Bombay and Karachi, both
occasions drenched with stars. 'It was a huge ceremony in Karachi,
huge, huge, huge …' Air Marshal Nur Khan, revered chairman of
Pakistan's cricket board, was one of the attendees, along with his team-
mates and hundreds of other important guests. The security was intense
to keep out gatecrashers.

Their daughter Jannat was born a few years later and would become
the subject of a bitter custody battle: she would eventually live with her
mother and her name would change to Sanam, but she was born into
what was at the time a happy marriage.

However, Mohsin was becoming discontented in his Test career and
had informed Imran privately that he intended to retire. He was planning a permanent move to his beloved Todmorden but he and Reena
went to stay for a fortnight in Bombay, where he received a call from
JP Dutta. He acted out their dialogue, as if from a script.

"'I have come to know that you are planning to quit cricket."

"How the hell did you know that?"

"Don't worry about that. Now, do you remember your promise?"

"Yes, but I was just trying to get out of that thing without using any
bad words to hurt your feelings."

"Well, I will still take that as a promise, and are you ready to keep
it? You are in Bombay and we can meet. I have a film on now and I
need a third hero. I have already cast Dharmendra and Vinod Khanna."

"What am I going to do in that company?"

"Leave that to me. Think about it.'"

Reena worked on him. She was the producer of Dutta's film and saw it as the perfect vehicle. Again, he acted out the dialogue. "'I am going to launch you whatever you decide. This is a great subject and why don't you take this on, and work with top-class actors and a top-class director?"

"'Well, I have always accepted challenges." He telephoned Dutta and accepted. He asked plaintively, "What am I going to be doing in this film? I know nothing about acting." Yet again, Dutta replied, "Leave that to me."'

Looking back, he is convinced that Dutta wanted him simply for his publicity and box-office value as the first Pakistani cricketer to appear in an Indian film. 'But perhaps my personality helped – I was given the role of a really honest police officer.' He was regularly cast thereafter as a police officer, reflecting the Bollywood convention that honest characters are shown either as policemen or poor people. He cited Amitabh Bachchan, who achieved stardom playing poor angry young men. Did he ever work with Bachchan? Unfortunately not, a project fell through, but 'I got to know him very well, he is a very good human being.'

This debut movie was *Batwara*, a big-budget drama, released in 1989. He played one of three brothers from a princely family, coping with their loss of power and status in the early years of Indian independence. Apart from Dharmendra and Vinod Khanna in leading roles, the cast was studded with established character actors. Dutta was intelligent enough to direct Mohsin as a cricketer, not as an actor. This carried him through one complex and intensely dramatic scene (his police character returns to his family home in a palace, runs to greet his father and brothers and then talks to them while concealing that he has just been shot in the back by dacoits). 'Dutta told me to imagine that I had scored a century but my team had still lost. I would rejoice in the century when I saw my father but feel the pain of defeat because I had been badly wounded. After this instruction, I was able to bring off the whole scene in a single take. The whole unit clapped when it was finished. It felt like scoring a century.'

He was fulsome in praising Dutta. 'After Almighty God, all the credit was to that director. He made me so comfortable.' However, his personal favourite performance was in *Saathi*, directed by Mahesh

Bhatt, and released in 1991. He plays a good brother who forsakes a life of crime – and has a dramatic confrontation with his bad brother who does not.

In all, he would make 13 Indian movies, invariably as a good guy, but often inexplicably adorned with a stage moustache. They all had directors and actors of repute, including Saeed Jaffrey,[4] who appeared with him twice, including his last Indian production *Mahaanta: The Film,* directed by Afzal Khan. Mohsin played yet another good guy, Raj Malhotra, who gets murdered at the behest of a wealthy businessman, Mahesh, and his evil father, Kedar, even though their real target is his younger brother Sanjay, but when Sanjay discovers Raj's murdered body it inspires him to revenge . . .

In all his roles, Mohsin Khan drew on his cricket experience. 'Timing the ball helped me in all my film work, especially dialogue. It helped me get a sense of the pace of a scene.'

Footwork was another obvious asset when he had to dance. This happened in most of his roles, because the Bollywood conventions had changed and leading men, once strong and still, had to dance as well as leading ladies. 'I had never done anything except disco dancing. If you want a laugh, watch me in *Gunehgaar Kaun.*' (We watched a clip: he is no Gene Kelly, but the scene works.) 'I think I learnt to cope.' He was intrigued to learn of the success of Darren Gough and Mark Ramprakash in *Strictly Come Dancing.*

After *Mahaanta* he made a string of films in Pakistan. The first was a big-budget suspense thriller, *Raaz,* in which he was the male hero opposite Pakistan's most popular actress, Babra Sharif.[5] Other leading actors were Mustafa Qureshi and Mueen Akhtar; the director was Iqbal Yousuf, son of the celebrated director/producer SM Yousuf.

---

4 Saeed Jaffrey sadly died as this book was being written.
5 Mohsin held out for her. Babra Sharif made several appearances at Pakistan cricket matches to promote her films. She was put out in 1978-79 in Karachi when the crowd paid more attention to the thrilling conclusion of the Test match against India than to her arrival at the ground. However, she herself was a genuine fan and enjoyed talking cricket with Mohsin Khan between takes. She retired over 20 years ago after 143 movie appearances, and pursues many other interests, particularly animals. She receives many offers of comeback scripts. One sounds very promising – a cricketing version of *Sunset Boulevard.*

The story derived from the Audrey Hepburn thriller *Wait Until Dark* – but with a gender reversal. Mohsin's character, also called Mohsin, is driving his Mercedes when he sees Babra's character, Anita, surrounded by gangsters. Anita is a crime reporter whose brother is missing. Mohsin saves her. They fall in love. They are given the customary romantic duet in the song 'Jabtak Jaan Hai', running around a gorgeous and conveniently empty beach. She is noticeably more fluent and expressive, but again their scene works and he shows to better advantage when it shifts to a speedboat and the two of them stand still.

Then Mohsin gets a head injury and loses his sight. He is captured by the gangsters. Anita disguises herself as a beggar, steals into the gangsters' lair and rescues Mohsin. He gets another head injury, which restores his eyesight. He helps Anita find her long-lost brother after a big fight with the gangsters. Anita marries Mohsin as the happy ending.

In spite of the cast and production values, the film did not perform at the box office, although he and Babra worked together again three years later on *Pyasa Saawan*.

Mohsin rejoined Pakistan cricket after Majid Khan became chief executive of the PCB in 1996. ('Apart from being a world-class cricketer, he was the nicest man I have ever met.')

His marriage to Reena Roy was finished. 'Certain things didn't work out.' Bollywood gossip magazines have carried accounts of the break-up, and the subsequent custody battle over their daughter, but he refused to say anything, for his daughter's sake. He did make one oblique comment: 'If you're not comfortable in one place, you have to get out of that place instead of disturbing yourself mentally and disturbing the other person.' His daughter is grown up and still living in Bombay. He is in touch with her almost every day and he is now happily remarried, to a cousin, and living in the Defence section of Karachi.

As an administrator, he did his best work for Pakistan cricket as chief selector at its most troubled time in 2010, above all by recalling the discarded Misbah-ul-Haq as captain. This single decision transformed Pakistan's fortunes. He and Misbah had a close relationship ('he is a great player and a fine gentleman'), which deepened when he assumed a temporary role as team coach in 2011. The PCB chairman, Ijaz Butt, wanted Mohsin to continue as chief selector, but he refused to combine the roles. His first assignment as coach was a visit to Sri Lanka, with Mahela Jayawardene and Kumar Sangakkara in their prime. Pakistan won the series in all three formats, Tests, one-day internationals, T20. Not surprisingly, the new PCB chairman, Zaka Ashraf, asked him to continue, and Pakistan comfortably won their next series, away to Bangladesh.

Then Pakistan played England, 'at home' in the UAE. England were then ranked number 1 in the ICC Test rankings, Pakistan number 5. Pakistani media were gloomy about the team's prospects as they departed for the UAE. He was asked if he expected to draw a single Test match. 'I said that the boys were playing very hard. I could not make any promises, but I asked the media to wait and see.'

As coach he concentrated less on technical advice and more on giving the players strategic awareness. 'With Misbah, I always had two or three game plans, and if one didn't work we switched to another.' Above all, he inculcated national pride and mental toughness. 'I warned them that anyone who made less than one hundred per cent effort would be dropped, no matter how senior.' He was backed strongly by Misbah-ul-Haq and Younus Khan (also a 'great cricketer and fine gentleman').

Remembering Imran, he told his players never to give up on victory. In the second Test, England needed only 144 to win: he held a team meeting and told them not to focus on England's small target but to substitute one of their own and bowl England out for less than 100. They responded by dismissing England for 72.

Pakistan won all three of the Test matches. It was the high point of his career with the PCB. In retrospect, he is glad that England insisted on DRS: 'No one could say that we won through umpiring mistakes.' He is also proud of asking for lively pitches to be prepared at Abu Dhabi and Dubai, rather than the zombie pitches of the 2015 series.

After three winning series, he might have expected to keep the job. Instead, he departed in acrimony. Officially, the PCB wanted a permanent coach from overseas with formal qualifications (he had none). He referred darkly but obliquely to 'conspiracies ... dirty stuff ... and some kind of nepotism,' and finished with a fine exit line. 'I said this will happen over my dead body. This is not my team but my country's team. I don't want any disgrace to the players or the team.' Like the honest policemen he so often played on screen, he handed in his badge and walked away into the sunset.

Summing up his two lives, he told us: 'Cricket was my identity. Anything I am was because of cricket and playing for Pakistan.' The critical movie-goers we spoke to would agree. Certainly, he found it easier to carry his bat than carry a motion picture. As an actor, he might not belong at number 3, but he was a reliable middle-order performer who built many important partnerships.

23

TAUSEEF AHMED, THE HERO
OF EVERY NET BOWLER

He does not look like Lionel Richie any more. Tauseef Ahmed
sported the singer's trademark Afro in February 1980 when he
came from nowhere straight into Pakistan's Test team against Australia.

Aged 21, Tauseef was drafted into Pakistan's net practice for the first
Test in Karachi against the visiting Australians led by Greg Chappell.
He was a useful off-spinner at the Pakistan Gymkhana Club near the
airport, and was recommended to Pakistan's captain, Javed Miandad,
and his predecessor, Mushtaq Mohammad, now the team coach. 'Javed
Sadiq gave them my name. He was a cricket enthusiast from England
and knew me from the club.' Mushtaq and Javed Miandad accepted
the recommendation even though the Test squad already had an
experienced off-spinner, Ilyas Khan. He was yet to play a Test but had
completed four first-class seasons in which he had taken 81 wickets.

Tauseef Ahmed bowled at the Pakistan team for a day in the nets.
'They liked me and asked me to come back the following day.' So he
gave them another day's practice, after which Javed Miandad told
him to go to the team's hotel, the InterContinental (now the Pearl
Continental) and stay there overnight. 'I thought they were playing a
joke on me, but Javed Sadiq came with me, on the captain's instructions. He told reception that I was a new member of the squad and
they should give me a room.' Not surprisingly, the man at the desk

decided to check these instructions. He was put through to Javed Miandad, who told him to put Tauseef in Zaheer Abbas's room, which would not be used because Zaheer was allowed to stay at his home near the hotel. 'When Zaheer rang the room at night, to pick up his messages, he was surprised when I picked up. He asked, "Who are you, what are you doing in my room?" I explained and he said, "OK, stay there."'

The following day, Tauseef took part in a practice match with the team. The one after was supposed to be a rest day before the Test match, but he had a club game for the Pakistan Gymkhana, and there was no reason for him to miss it. At 12:30, another friend, Riaz Malik, called him out of the game. He was another enthusiast from England, owner of a cinema in Bradford. 'He told me I was in the Test team. I didn't believe him, but he told me to go home and check. I found a crowd there and thought maybe there was something in it.' He had been announced in the squad of 12. The final choice was between him and a batsman, Mohsin Khan.

Ilyas Khan had been discarded. Tauseef had impressed three key players in the practice nets, Zaheer Abbas, Majid Khan and the left-handed Wasim Raja. They believed that Australians were traditionally vulnerable to off-spin and that Tauseef would give their present team more trouble than his rival.

Naturally, Ilyas Khan was bitterly disappointed. He may even have believed a wild newspaper report that the unknown Tauseef's father was a millionaire who had bribed Mushtaq and Javed to pick his son. Tauseef scorned this canard. 'That was a cock-and-bull story. My father was a compounder, a druggist who made up medical prescriptions as a doctor's assistant. He showed the reporter his clothes and asked, "Am I a millionaire?"'

Tauseef did not sleep. He discovered that he, not Mohsin Khan, would be playing, but he had none of the right kit. Asif Iqbal (newly retired) kindly gave him his Pakistan cap. Riaz Malik provided him with two pairs of trousers and two shirts. Another friend borrowed some boots for him from his nephew (he had never needed them before). 'They were one size too small and I had to play a five-day Test in them. They were very painful. I discovered that I had wounded my heel when the match was over.'

Australia batted first. Bruce Laird was out early, lbw to Imran Khan, but Graham Yallop and Kim Hughes slowly built a partnership. Javed Miandad brought Tauseef on against the left-handed Yallop, whose last Test innings had been a century against England. Tauseef had no idea who he was. 'My mind was a blank.' He quickly settled into line and length and Yallop played cautiously for 15 balls against the unknown mystery bowler. 'Then I turned one away from him and beat his defence and he was caught behind.' It was also the first victim for a new wicketkeeper, Taslim Arif. Shakoor Rana, later to become notorious, was the umpire who raised his finger. 'He told me that evening that he did not give him out because of my appeal but because he heard a noise and Majid Khan appealed from slip.'

Tauseef got through 30 overs and two balls in his borrowed boots and ended up with four wickets for 64, virtually identical figures to those of his left-arm spin bowling partner, Iqbal Qasim. His other victims, all caught, were the top scorer, Kim Hughes, Rodney Marsh and tail-ender Geoff Dymock. He could not name them when interviewed on radio.

When Pakistan batted he was at number 11 – and out first ball, bowled by the left-arm spinner, Ray Bright. But the dream continued in Australia's second innings, when he claimed Hughes and Dymock for a second time – and the prize wicket of Greg Chappell. Seven cheap wickets for the unknown bowler on his Test debut, and a comfortable win for Pakistan. 'Javed said, "Don't surround him and congratulate him, he'll faint."'

Of course he was retained for the next Test at Faisalabad. This was tougher going as Australia amassed 617, but he was the most successful bowler, dismissing Hughes (again), Marsh and Beard for 77 runs off 33 overs.

There was a little anxiety for him when Ilyas Khan was selected for the Punjab Governor's XI in the subsequent side match against the tourists at Multan. His rival took four for 62 in the first innings, but they were not enough to displace Tauseef in the team for the third Test at Lahore. He picked up two more hard-earned wickets in another high-scoring draw: Allan Border twice passed 150.

His final tally of 12 Test wickets in the series secured him a job. 'Haroon Rashid recommended me to United Bank and I played in their team for the next fourteen years.'

After the fairytale beginning, his international career was a stop-start affair of 34 Tests over 13 years and 70 one-day internationals. He had to fight for the off-spinner's place – not against the luckless Ilyas Khan but against a different rival, Nazir Junior. He was not chosen for an overseas tour until Sri Lanka in 1986, but eventually visited all the current Test-playing countries except Zimbabwe (South Africa were still banned).

He and Iqbal Qasim took nine wickets apiece in the pulsating Test match at Bangalore in March 1987, so nearly won for India by Gavaskar's brilliant innings of 96. 'It was a terrible wicket. My off-spinners kept rearing and hit batsmen in the stomach and chest. Our pace bowler, Salim Jaffer, never bowled a ball. On the rest day, Iqbal Qasim and I met Bishan Singh Bedi in the West End Hotel. We asked him how to bowl on a pitch like that. He told us, "Just keep a good line, the ball is turning." The next day our line was too good for all the Indians except Gavaskar. Bedi was called a traitor for giving us advice. He said, "I have been giving this advice for years to Indian bowlers without success, but these two picked it up in ten minutes."'

In that low-scoring game, Tauseef's two innings of 15 not out and 10 were vital contributions. In the second innings, he shared with Salim Yousuf the only fifty partnership of the match. He was also proud of staying with Imran Khan for 90 minutes to save the Karachi Test against the West Indies in November 1986, and of batting for a total of four hours in his two not-out innings in the drawn Test at Melbourne in January 1990. 'I faced Merv Hughes with Ijaz Ahmed. He was an unpleasant man who sledged us. When I left a ball alone success-fully, Ijaz would say "shabbash, shabbash." Hughes got frustrated. He charged down the pitch at me shouting "shabbash, shabbash". He didn't know he was saying congratulations.'

But his biggest batting moment was a scrambled single at Sharjah in 1986, which enabled Javed Miandad to strike the most famous individual shot in cricket history – his winning six off Chetan Sharma in the one-day international against India. 'I remember rushing to the pavilion with Javed as the crowd invaded the pitch. They were mostly Indians, Pakistanis and Sri Lankans. The Arab police knew nothing about cricket and just hit out randomly to try to control the crowd. I got hit by a baton. Then people showered Javed with money but I got nothing. Someone wrote a song: "Javed got a hundred thousand and Tauseef got eight dirhan."'

He retired with 93 Test victims. They cost him nearly 32 runs apiece, but he went for only 2.27 runs an over. He now coaches the best Under-16s and Under-19s in Karachi, preaching his values of control combined with sharp spin. Like so many coaches, he deplores the influence of the doosra on young players' bowling actions.

Tauseef is now bald and avuncular. Did he still admire Lionel Richie? 'I'd never heard of him. I was given that name by Sunil Gavaskar.' He is a contented man, always willing to re-tell his story as the Cinderella who was given the ball in a Test match by a fairy godmother.

But what of Ilyas Khan, forced through no fault of his own into the role of an Ugly Sister? He carried on in domestic cricket, retiring nine years after his rejection with 282 first-class victims. He continues to serve Pakistan cricket as a match referee. We happened to meet him in that capacity shortly after interviewing Tauseef. We asked if he resented the way he was discarded and never got a second chance. He shot back, 'I think about it every single day.' But his son Junaid recently began his first-class career, also as an off-spinner.

With a fitting touch of fairytale melodrama, Ilyas Khan declared: 'My son will avenge me.'

24

SHOAIB AKHTAR: INSULTS AND INJURIES

S hoaib Akhtar was the fastest bowler to play for Pakistan and one of the very few in cricket history known to have broken the 100 mph barrier. He attracted controversies at the same speed. To make it easier to follow his dizzying career, this list of major incidents or allegations involving him is drawn from his appropriately named autobiography *Controversially Yours* (Harper Sport India). With the help of Indian author and journalist Anshu Dogra, it offered pungent but often perceptive judgements on latter-day Pakistan cricket and its leaders.

Circa 1980: age 5-7, steals and eats other children's school lunches.

Circa 1991: age 16, runs away from home after regular physical punishments.

Circa 1992: age 17-18, assorted college pranks including motorbike riding, playing cricket outside girls' section, impersonating one lecturer, terrorising another with firecrackers.

1994-95: age 19, survives violent streetfighting in Karachi between armed political/ethnic gangs and army, argues with employers, PIA, over unfair treatment and walks out on them.

Bowling against PIA team, injures five of their players in revenge, screams and swears outside their dressing room, dragged away by team-mates.

1997: age 22, on Pakistan A tour of England, plays practical joke on unpopular coach, Agha Akbar,[1] who fines him and delays next international appearance.

1997: age 22, home Test debut v West Indies, rows with captain Wasim Akram and other senior team members who attempt to exclude him, refuses to make them drinks, condemned in dressing room for 'bad attitude'.

1998: age 22, on Test tour of South Africa, distracted by almost-nude female spectators but takes five for 43 in spell of electric pace. Knees swell, sent home after ODI in Zimbabwe. On return to team, rents car although does not know how to drive. Loses control, drives car over high curb, cannot afford repair.

1999: age 23, Kolkata Test v India, bowls Rahul Dravid and then Sachin Tendulkar first ball. Second innings, in collision with Tendulkar who is run out, crowd riots and arson interrupt match.

1999: age 23, bowls Pakistan to World Cup final, but after defeat is accused by Nawaz Sharif 'accountability bureau' of partying with girls. Demands proof of charges, is told that he looked tired on morning of match. Accuses captain Wasim Akram of planting this rumour, which WA denies. SA then walks out on bureau.

1999: age 24, on Australian tour, accused of throwing, ICC ban, overturned after PCB intervention. Banned for violation of curfew.

---

1 Shoaib seems to have added to the injury by misnaming him. The coach on that tour was former Test player Agha Zahid.

2000: age 24, ignores Imran Khan advice not to tour West Indies. Tours in pain but is allowed to enjoy beach life and dancing. No guidance from management. Plays in Trinidad Test when unfit, breaks rib.

2001: age 25, comeback in New Zealand, spell of five wickets for 2 in ODI. But followed by hamstring injury in New Zealand and then called for throwing by NZ umpire. Assessed by human movement specialists, University of Western Australia, which reveals naturally double-jointed elbow. ICC ban overturned.

2001: age 25, depression causes early withdrawal from England tour.

2002: age 26, breaks 100 mph barrier during demolition of touring New Zealanders, but recording technology not recognised by ICC. Begins speed duel with Brett Lee. Fears ICC bias against him and has renewed anxieties about knees.

2002: age 27, throws water bottle at abusive spectator in Zimbabwe, one-match ban.

2003: age 27, breaks 100 mph in World Cup, this time recognised by ICC. Sledging row with Matthew Hayden. Dressing-room squabbles and row with captain Waqar Younis. Sacked after Pakistan failure in tournament.

2003: age 27, tampers with ball in ODI in Sri Lanka, banned and fined.

2003: age 27, fears death in heat of Peshawar Test v Bangladesh, bowls in ice jacket.

2003: age 28, pulls out of Test on New Zealand tour, with groin strain, but is photographed jet skiing.

2004: age 28, retires hurt with rib injury in home Test v India, accused in leaked PCB report of faking despite evidence from bone scan.

2005: age 29, sent home with injury in ODI series in Australia, coincides with unjustified rape accusation, leaked to media, complains of no support from PCB.

2005: age 29, plays for Worcestershire CC, accused by chairman of being selfish superstar. Returns and has best home series, versus England.

2006: age 30, threatens to sue Greg Chappell, Indian coach, over throwing allegation. Acute knee pain prompts second operation.

2006: age 31, returns to team for ODI series v England after Darrell Hair ball-tampering accusation aborts Oval Test. Rows with captain Inzamam-ul-Haq.

2006: age 31, banned substance, nandrolene, detected in drug test. Banned for two years but succeeds with appeal. Later meets retired judge who imposed ban in restaurant and shouts at him.

2006: age 31, confrontation in South Africa with Bob Woolmer, who refuses to believe he is injured.

2007: age 31, dressing-room fight with Shahid Afridi and Mohammad Asif in World Cup. Five-year ban, which prevents him joining IPL, later withdrawn after political intervention.

2008: age 32, attacks PCB chairman Nasim Ashraf for unfairness towards him, including deliberate preparation of dead pitches. Ashraf sues him for defamation. Action withdrawn after SA reluctant apology.

2008: age 32, on television, claims to have rejected approaches from match-fixers to underperform. Risks penalty for not reporting to ICC.

2009: age 33, dropped from T20 World Cup squad, treated for skin condition which PCB leaks falsely as genital warts.

2012: age 36, in retirement, says match-fixing commonplace in Pakistan cricket because players are underpaid.

Pakistan captains, officials, fellow players, coaches, politicians condemned by SA or in clashes with him:

Shahid Afridi
'Agha Akbar' (Agha Zahid, coach)
Nasim Ashraf
Mohammad Asif
Ijaz Butt
Intikhab Alam
Inzamam-ul-Haq
Shaharyar Khan
Zakir Khan (long-serving official)
Geoff Lawson
Javed Miandad
Ramiz Raja
Wasim Raja
Nawaz Sharif
Waqar Younis
Wasim Akram
Yawar Saeed

List of PCB personnel admired by SA:

Lt Gen Tauqir Zia, chairman
Subhan Ahmed (long-serving official).

25

THE PARALLEL CAREERS
OF MOIN KHAN AND RASHID LATIF

Both came from Karachi. Both competed for the roles of wicketkeeper-batsman and later captain of the Pakistan cricket team.

But Moin Khan and Rashid Latif had contrasting personalities and playing styles. Moin Khan was a noisy wicketkeeper, constantly cheering or chivvying his bowlers and fielders and winding up opposing batsmen. Rashid Latif, Pakistan's best wicketkeeper since his early idol Wasim Bari, was athletic and spectacular but much quieter, staying in his personal zone. Both were strokemaking batsmen who frequently contributed important runs down the order, but Moin was more rumbustious and unorthodox.

Rashid Latif was an independent man who waged a long personal campaign against corruption in cricket, both in Pakistan and across the world. He clashed repeatedly with fellow players and with authority. He was politically active with the MQM, the party established to represent emigrants from India, which became the dominant force in Karachi, after fierce and often brutally violent struggles with other factions including the national government. Moin Khan was equally honest but less confrontational and not political.

After retiring as a player, Rashid Latif had coaching assignments with the PCB and then with the Afghan national team: he left both of them on issues of principle. Moin Khan served successively as coach, manager and chief selector of the Pakistan team, his tenure ruffled only by a synthetic media storm during the 2015 World Cup when he went out for a meal in a casino.[1]

Even as rivals, the two men remained friends. Their easy relationship was visible when they appeared together in October 2015 on a television programme for the Geo TV network. They bantered and joked and then fed each other slices from a large gooey cake.

They have become rivals again in that they both run cricket academies in Karachi, which meet in regular tournaments.

Both of them are turning out hard-working and proficient young cricketers, but a visit to each one reveals some significant contrasts, both social and personal.

Moin Khan's is located in the well-to-do Defence Housing Authority of Karachi and forms part of a fee-paying residents' sports and recreational club, which also offers tennis, badminton, a swimming pool and a gym. Rashid Latif's is in the less affluent area of Nazimabad-Federal B. It has no fees and is used only for cricket.

When we went to visit, Moin Khan was supervising preparations for a televised university T20 tournament that very evening and, soon afterwards, a T20 tournament for corporate teams during the month of Ramadan. 'I pioneered this type of tournament five years ago.'

His academy was initiated in 2009 and became functional in 2011. It had not been going long enough to feed players into the national side, but some boys had progressed to regional teams at Under-16, Under-17 and Under-19 level and another was playing for the Pakistan Navy at grade 2, just below first-class. 'There is a tradition in Pakistan of players breaking through at a very early age, and we need to maintain this. We have at least three outstanding talents here who could make it, with luck and hard work.'

Moin Khan's younger son Azam began as a wicketkeeper-batsman at the academy. The young man was selected for Karachi Under-16s but

1 See 'PCB asks Moin Khan to return home,' www.espncricinfo.com 24 February 2015 and Qamar Ahmed, 'Moin Khan deserved a better deal,' *Dawn*, 27 February 2015.

faced cruel personal attacks over his weight. He answered them with a century off 60 balls. 'He plays all his matches as if they were T20. I was a fast scorer myself, but mostly before T20. I had just one season of it, but I scored the first T20 century in Pakistan.'

As of October 2015, there were 300 boys at the academy, divided by age and talent. 'They normally start at seven but there are about twenty, with exceptional early talent, who have been allowed to start at ages five and six.'

No girls? 'Not yet. I have been asked to provide facilities by many local girls' schools. This is something we're planning for the recent future.' (A rare entertaining stumble in his polished English.)

There are 13 coaches, led by his elder brother, Nadeem, who holds an English Level 3 qualification. Moin Khan does not coach himself: 'I monitor everyone and I sometimes lecture on different cricket topics.

'Most of our boys live locally, but we have some from surrounding areas. Anyone can come who wants to learn cricket. But we have to charge fees to make it sustainable.' There is a range of charges to be a member of the Sports Club itself, ranging from a basic 14,000 rupees a month (around £92) to a lifetime family membership of 350,000 rupees (around £2,300). Then there is a top-up fee for a boy to receive three days' coaching each week at the academy: 1,000 rupees a month for members, 3,000 rupees a month for non-members. A few of the most talented boys get six days' coaching a week and there are some scholarships available. ('I approach people for these.')

To put these fees in perspective, in November 2015 a local website was advertising school principal jobs in Karachi at salaries of 35,000 to 50,000 rupees a month.[2] Like many others, Moin Khan is concerned that high-quality cricket is becoming too expensive for more and more families, those of professional people.

He himself came from a middle-class family: his father was an administrator at two major construction companies. He showed early promise as an opening batsman for Zaifia Memorial School, Karachi,

2 See www.jobs4u.pk/school-principal-jobs-in-Karachi.html.

but had no ambitions as a wicketkeeper. In a typical story for many Pakistan cricketers, his destiny was shaped by answering an emergency summons. 'Our wicketkeeper got injured and the teacher asked me to take over. On that day I got two catches and a stumping and made a few runs so that started me as a wicketkeeper.'

He was then 13, and he progressed so rapidly that he made his first-class debut as a specialist wicketkeeper aged only 15 years 10 months, for Karachi against PIA in the Quaid-e-Azam trophy.[3]

His most enjoyable experience was keeping to Saqlain Mushtaq. 'I got loads of stumpings, especially from his doosra.' He enjoyed re-telling the story of how he had invented the name in Australia, with some help from the journalist Qamar Ahmed. 'I used to shout "shab-bash, shabbash, doosra". It was easy to use this as a code, because none of the Australians would recognise it. I said this when I kept for him in Hobart in 1999 and he took six for forty-one.' When Saqlain was interviewed by Australian journalists afterwards and asked what the delivery was called, he did not speak English very well and he simply repeated the word 'doosra'. Qamar Ahmed obligingly translated it for them. Literally it meant 'the second one' but he added that in Pakistan cricket it signified 'the other one'. They all followed this invention, and the next day they solemnly cited the 'doosra' as the standard name for the new magic ball.

Moin continued, 'Saqlain had the cleanest action of any bowler, including the doosra, but other bowlers were more controversial. It is very difficult to deliver. There were doubts about Muralitharan, Harbhajan Singh and Saeed Ajmal when they starting imitating Saqlain.' Like so many others, Moin Khan was deeply worried about the doosra's influence on young bowlers. 'Last season there were 43 bowlers in domestic first-class cricket who were called for suspect actions. At the academy we have to correct so many boys who are chucking after imitating Murali and Saeed Ajmal. It's the fault of umpires and referees for allowing them. The authorities should make videos of Saqlain as a model for them.'

3 December-January, 1986-87. He scored 10 and 5 and had two catches and a stumping.

He had to leave for a meeting. He gestured towards the nets, all full of young players working intently. His free-flowing speech became a little slower and more solemn, as if he was coming to terms with his academy's responsibilities. 'This is the only game which our whole nation plays and it is the unifying factor of the country.'

We met Rashid Latif twice at his academy. The first time, in 2013, he spoke primarily about his dramatic and hugely courageous decision to walk out of the team, with his friend Basit Ali, during the tour of South Africa and Zimbabwe in 1994-95, in protest over match-fixing. He was vice-captain but had lost all faith in his captain, Salim Malik, over a series of apparently irrational decisions on team selection and fielding first after winning the toss. He received credible death threats on his return to Karachi and told us that MQM helped to 'swallow me up' during the following months to protect him from potential assassins. During the next few years, he became the principal source of allegations against players accused of match-fixing – although intermittently he was asked to captain them in the national side. He presented his charges in media interviews, through a much-followed blog and ultimately in sensational testimony to the Qayyum Commission, in October 1998. The latter was supported by secret audio recordings, although their evidential value was reduced when it emerged that passages had been excised – he said, because of bad language.

Few modern cricketers have sustained such stress over such a long period. Not surprisingly, he spoke about this tersely and reluctantly. Two years later at his academy, he was slightly mellower but still independent and serious-minded. As a tour guide, he spoke more sparingly and reflectively than Moin Khan.

As already mentioned, the academy is located in Nazimabad-Federal B, a socially mixed area of Karachi and most of the intake is local. 'Our boys mostly have a middle-class or lower-middle class background, with just one per cent from the upper class.' It occupies a larger space than Moin Khan's academy, with three grounds and 16 turf wickets. At the time of writing there were 125 trainees, ranging from 11 to 19, although it took some boys of nine and ten during its summer camps. It was boys only, but he was studying proposals to add programmes for girls. 'It will take some time. We have too many things at hand at the moment.'

There are no fees – thanks to a socialistic business model. 'We hire out our three grounds at large fees to multinational companies, at night or at weekends. The rental income of five hundred thousand rupees allows us to give the free training.' In effect, the multinationals are subsidising the boys. The academy also receives private donations and receives some indirect but valuable support from the city government of Karachi in the form of electricity and free land for car parking. He has put some of his own money into the academy, and posed proudly on the English roller which cost £8,000. He paid for it from his earnings at the celebrity-studded Lashings Cricket Club.

Even with these sources of income, the academy is sometimes severely stretched by its support for its poorer trainees. 'Cricket equipment is expensive for middle-income and lower-middle-income families. We try to get cast-off bats from players to give away to them, and we ask our business renters to give us their used bats and balls. When Mohammad Sami first came to the academy he had no boots, nor did many other boys. We got the local sports association to donate them last year's stock from Adidas and Nike. After Ramadan, we sometimes have a financial crisis because we have given away so much equipment and clothing to players. We have no cash and we have to wait for the cheque from the multinationals.'

As Mohammad Sami's name might suggest, Rashid Latif's academy has been going longer than Moin Khan's. Other Test-playing graduates included Younus Khan, the batsman Asim Kamal[4] and the brilliant leg-spinner, Danish Kaneria, currently under an indefinite ban from international and domestic cricket after alleged involvement in match-fixing.

Rashid Latif has campaigned continuously against corruption for over 20 years. Nonetheless, he has been a persistent champion of

4 The third batsman to be dismissed for 99 on Test debut (in 2003 at Lahore against South Africa).

Kaneria: friendship for a pupil he once mentored was more important to him than maintaining a public stand.

As mentioned, for many years he exposed alleged domestic and international wrongdoing in a regular blog. It has been silent lately: was there any sinister explanation? No. 'I don't write as much as before, but if I notice anything I try to write and I still speak occasionally on these issues.'

He has told the ICC incessantly that power-plays and fielding restrictions have made it easier to fix one-day matches. He continues to campaign for a delay of at least 30 seconds in the transmission of all cricket events, as a check on the huge volume of illegal betting on individual deliveries.

Not surprisingly, an institution offering superb coaching for nothing is hugely oversubscribed. There are trials every two years for Under-13s, Under-15s and Under-19s. They usually attract up to 600 boys but only 25 are selected from each age group. 'The British Council and a major NGO wanted to sponsor more boys, up to a thousand, but I refused. We did not have the time or the resources for that number.' However, the academy has offshoots in Burewallah (home of Waqar Younus) and Abbotabad – both free, like their parent.

His full-time coaching staff is four, supplemented by some part-timers. They make their charges work hard as we learnt from a young wicketkeeper-batsman, Wasi-ud-Din. We had met him before, when he was loaned to our Wounded Tiger touring cricket team, along with his academy colleague, a genuinely quick bowler, Saifullah.

Wasi-ud-Din had been coming for six years, since he was 12. He was now studying computer science at college, but showed up at the academy every afternoon, six days a week in the heat of June, for at least three hours of batting and wicketkeeping practice. Then he went home to study and complete college assignments. But the hard work had paid off. He had earned selection for the Karachi Under-19 team while Saifullah had appeared in first-class cricket for the Sui Southern Gas Corporation.[5]

---

5 According to *CricketArchive*, he played for them as a wicketkeeper-batsman rather than as a fast bowler, which suggests that Rashid Latif's academy fosters versatility.

Like all of Rashid Latif's pupils, Wasi-ud-Din has received lectures on the evils of corruption and training in basic life skills, including time management, punctuality and keeping track of their personal finances. Rashid told us, 'The academy is meant to educate them in every phase of life to be a good citizen of the country.'

Rashid Latif came from a lower-middle-class background. His father worked for a foreign oil company in Karachi but was not well paid. 'When I grew up in the 1980s, he was earning four thousand rupees a month [around £200] but he managed to educate all of his children, four boys and two girls.' Rashid is married with four children – none of them cricketers, he said, matter-of-factly.

Unlike Moin Khan, he always wanted to be a wicketkeeper. His first-class debut, aged 18, was inauspicious: his team, Karachi Whites, were dismissed for 57 by Pakistan National Shipping Corporation. But he was not out, with 7, and managed 21 at number 9 in the second innings, besides taking a catch and a stumping. He was chosen as second wicketkeeper on Pakistan's successful tour of England in 1992, and replaced Moin Khan in the final Test at The Oval. Geoff Boycott bet five pounds that he would not make 35. He produced a sparkling 50 and Boycott generously handed over ten pounds.

In 37 Tests, Rashid Latif claimed 130 dismissals. His rate of 3.51 victims per Test is better than any other Pakistan wicketkeeper, except, curiously, his much-criticised successor, Kamran Akmal. Characteristically, he gave Kamran advice and moral support during his roughest patch. He had many challenging bowlers – notably Mushtaq Ahmed, Saqlain Mushtaq and Danish Kaneria on worn pitches – but surprisingly he says the most challenging of all was Aamir Sohail, an occasional left-arm spinner. 'I never knew what the ball would do.' Mohammad Sami was the fastest bowler he ever kept to. 'Wasim and Waqar never hurt my hand, but Mohammad Sami did, when I took a catch off him in a side match in Kent in 2001.' Like Wasim Bari, he is proud of the state of his hands, with no fingers broken.

The sun began to set and the ground cooled very slightly. As the practice sessions wound down, he greeted some of his pupils and gave them a few encouraging words. He completed a few telephone calls and then considerately offered a lift back to the Sind club, sparing us another long awkward journey by tuk-tuk.

Rashid Latif has often been a controversial figure, but he has many admirers who would like to see him back in the mainstream of Pakistan cricket. 'Oh, no. I have too much television work to join the PCB. I would find it very difficult to work with them, and really prefer to work in my own way on television and in the academy.'

If his pupils bring the same technical and moral strength to Pakistan cricket as he did, that would be a much bigger legacy than anything he could achieve as an administrator.

26

A TALE OF TWO UMPIRES

I n 1987, after his on-field confrontation with England captain Mike Gatting, Shakoor Rana became a demonic figure in the British media. Perceived as incompetent, officious and biased, he served as the archetypal Pakistan umpire. The *Sun* newspaper even promoted a dartboard with his face on it: readers who threw a double-top would zap him right between the eyes.[1]

By 2015, Pakistan's Aleem Dar was recognised as one of the world's finest umpires. In his elegant fedora, he had established a new image for his country's officials: calm, scrupulous, authoritative. At the time of writing (January 2016) he has just completed 100 Test matches as umpire – the third to achieve this (after Steve Bucknor and Rudi Koertzen) and at 47, the youngest. He has also umpired 178 one-day internationals.

He was one of many players who took up umpiring after giving up hope of a top-flight career as a player. Having made that decision, he pursued his new goal with great dedication, as he narrated to us below.

However, behind Aleem Dar is a less familiar story, of how Pakistan has set out to improve the status and standard of all its officials. This emerged from the 27-year career of Aleem Dar's domestic colleague, Javed Ashraf.

---

1 See *Sun*, 10, 16 and 21 December. Readers had better taste than the paper realised: only ten were ever sold. According to the website www.the-saleroom.com.

Aleem Dar was born in the provincial town of Jhang, in the Punjab in 1968. 'I belong to a middle-class family. My father was an attorney in the police service. I was always very fond of cricket, but he was posted frequently to different cities and most of them had no proper cricketing facilities, so I never got any coaching or training. I actually started proper cricket only when my parents shifted to Gujranwala City when I was in my teens. Then I got admitted to Islamia College, Civil Lines, Lahore [a famous cricket nursery], on the basis of cricket and did my BA in Humanities. I had two colleagues in college who went on to play Test cricket – Aaqib Javed and Wasim Akram. I also played a lot of cricket against Saqlain Mushtaq and Saeed Ajmal. Meanwhile, I joined the P&T Gymkhana Club, which produced two other Test umpires apart from me: Athur Zaidi and Asad Rauf.'

As an off-spinning all-rounder,[2] he had a first-class career of 17 matches spread over 11 years. His top first-class score was 39 but there were several centuries at grade II level, including two in the same match against the Services XI. 'After realising that I might not join Pakistan's squad of Test cricket [a fine example of meiosis] I started umpiring as I wanted to stay connected with cricket. My early days of umpiring were quite tough and rough. I did my umpiring course and conducted grade two and then grade one matches. I was very lucky to officiate in nineteen first-class games in the first year of my umpiring career.'

The first was in March 1999: Sargodha versus Lahore City, in the company of the experienced Siddiq Khan. He was 30 years old – four years younger than the Sargodha captain, Akram Raza. The score-sheet shows no lbws but seven caught-behinds: it is impossible to tell how many he gave. 'Within fifteen months I got selected to the panel of International Umpires by the PCB because of my excellent performance in domestic cricket.' In a short period, he became an International Elite umpire and won three awards in succession as ICC Umpire of the Year.

Disclaiming any special gifts, he said: 'I just try to put in my best

2 Several reference sources refer to him wrongly as a leg-spinner.

during the performance of my duty.' He is convinced that the general standard of international umpiring has risen markedly. 'The contributing factors are a better and tough assessment system and rankings, clearer rules and regulations, better pay packages and a sense of competition.' He has become a firm believer in DRS, to reduce the risk of one bad decision changing the course of a match. 'It definitely helps an umpire to be more judgemental. It is not easy for an umpire to change his decision, but you need to have a brave heart and mind to accept the reversal of the decision you gave first.'

Aleem Dar received what he called 'a meagre amount' for his early umpiring from the PCB. He remembered his fee for that first-class debut match as the equivalent of US$50. He became an early 'shop steward' for his colleagues and to this day he has continued to lobby the PCB to make umpiring an attractive profession for Test cricketers on retirement. He is worried that Pakistan's cricketing exile has cut off its umpires from their international colleagues. 'Due to my ICC commitments, I conduct very few local games, but I try to give more chances to other Pakistani umpires to conduct international ones. A few upcoming umpires are in touch with me and I share my experience with them when I do get free of the ICC. I also contribute to local workshops within Pakistan.'

Throughout his international success, he has sought to give something back to his homeland. He made an immediate personal donation of 1 million rupees (around £6,600) to help victims of the earthquake which struck northern Pakistan in October 2015. He has been involved for some years in the Pakistan Veterans, who raise funds for many grassroots initiatives. In 2013, he opened the Aleem Dar Cricket Academy in Lahore, with almost a hundred boys and girls. They include 25 boys with impaired hearing, who receive free coaching and equipment. It supports 16 talented boys from poor families, who would be unable to afford the fees and charges. It offers special financial aid to a number of hearing-impaired boys who have been selected for the Pakistan Deaf People's team, and to another academy boy selected for Pakistan's Under-16 tour of Australia.

He would like to do more. 'My obsession is to open a school offering speech therapy and language classes for hearing-impaired boys and girls, and to build a sports complex for them.'

Praise be, there is another umpire Dar on the horizon. His elder sons are playing good club cricket in Lahore, but the youngest, Hassan, who is 15, has become fond of umpiring. 'He regularly holds friendly games to assess his skills.'

Like Aleem Dar, Javed Ashraf went into umpiring because it was the best way to express his love of the game. He had no first-class career but played for 17 years as a wicketkeeper and opening batsman just below that level, and made a lone one-day appearance for Faisalabad against the Habib Bank.

Unlike Aleem, his debut as an umpire was accidental rather than deliberate: he answered an emergency summons from the Lahore Gymkhana club because he had a pair of black trousers. He found that he enjoyed the job and a few years later, in 1994, he was persuaded to go on a local course at the Gaddafi Stadium supervised by the Test umpire, Khizer Hayat. This was part of a sustained effort by the PCB to improve umpiring standards, an effort which survived many convulsions within the PCB and, indeed, in Pakistan cricket generally.

From 2000 onwards, the former Test umpire Khalid Aziz produced a programme for the PCB of arranged courses and examinations for umpires. Many good umpires came through this, including Aleem Dar, Asad Rauf and Ahsan Raza (a major casualty of the attack on the Sri Lankan cricketers in 2009[3]). In 2004, the PCB introduced a new progressive structure with three panels, grade II, grade I and elite. All new umpires begin in grade II and have their performance evaluated at the end of each season. If there are good reports on their work, they are promoted to grade I. There is a similar exercise from promotion from grade I to elite.

However, Javed Ashraf believes that the PCB needs to do more for umpires, particularly on pay. 'Bangladesh may not be much of a cricket power, but they pay their umpires handsomely and they give them central contracts. Aleem Dar once lobbied PCB chairman Ijaz Butt to

3 See chapter 32.

improve umpires' wages and establish central contracts, but there are still only three Pakistani umpires on central contracts. They get paid sixty-five to seventy thousand rupees a month [around £430 to £470] but all the others, including me, are paid only match fees. For a first-class four-day match in Lahore, my fee would be twenty thousand rupees [around £135] and there would be another twenty thousand rupees added for a match out of the city. In India, they pay umpires eighty thousand rupees for a first-class match.'

He makes a caustic contrast between the pay and status of umpires with those of coaches. 'There are coaches in the regions and at the National Cricket Academy taking home over one hundred thousand rupees a month and getting paid right through the year – but they do not correct boys with illegal bowling actions. We call these boys for throwing but they still get into the National Academy. I once supervised a camp at the National Academy and there was a young off-spinner with a really bad action. I had to call his first delivery. He had been in the academy for a month, and I asked the coaches what he had been doing there. They said they were working on his action.'

Like many others in Pakistan, he is rightly alarmed at the decline of school and club cricket. Recently, he helped to organise the most prestigious club tournament in Lahore. It needed 16 good teams from the 135 registered clubs in Lahore. The organisers found eight. Nearly all the others were ghosts, clubs which existed on paper to cast votes or benefit from patronage.

Although far less well known than Aleem Dar, Javed Ashraf is further proof that Pakistan currently has a dedicated corps of proficient umpires. They are a greatly under-used resource, and a mark of giant change from the days when Pakistan umpires were demonised by the outside world.

27

PAKISTAN'S CRICKETING SUFFRAGETTES

In the early drama of Pakistan cricket, women appear only as mothers or extras. The greatness of women such as Amir Bee and Shaukat Khanum appears by reflection, through the testimonies of their famous sons, the five Mohammad brothers and Imran Khan. Sisters and girl cousins appear in photographs of family cricket matches, but usually as spare fielders or spectators.

For the first 30 years of Pakistan, only a small percentage of girls managed to play any organised cricket. These were nearly all from the wealthier classes, attending the elite schools and colleges which offered cricket to them, and with parents who could drive them to the rare local tournaments. However, they had no opportunity to progress further. The Board of Control for Cricket in Pakistan did nothing for women's cricket and local clubs and associations had no women's teams. Moreover, young women cricketers generally faced strong family pressures to give up the game and prepare for marriage or, just possibly, a career. Not even the mighty Burki cricket dynasty produced a woman cricketer. The former Pakistan captain Javed Burki was surprised when we raised this point with him, explaining that Burki girls pursued sport 'as runners and things, not in ball games'.[1]

In 1977 (four years behind India) a Pakistan Women Cricket

1 P Oborne, op. cit., pp.423-24.

Association (PWCA) came into being at the Lahore College for Women, and its secretary, Azraa Parveen, a former wicketkeeper, tried to establish a network of Universal Women's Cricket Clubs.[2] These early initiatives were strangled almost at birth, partly by factional fighting,[3] but more importantly because of the rise to power of General Zia-ul-Haq. His regime took Pakistan's women cricketers from the shadows to the darkness.

Partly from personal conviction and partly from political expediency, Zia allied himself with ultra-conservative Islamic forces in Pakistan. Under their influence he subjected women to some of the most oppressive laws ever devised by a modern state.

In the 1973 constitution adopted under ZA Bhutto, women had been guaranteed fundamental rights including equality before the law, equal rights to enter any lawful trade or profession and equal rights to enter public service. Zia began by removing these protections. He began by withdrawing all the guarantees of women's rights under the 1973 constitution, which prepared the ground for legislation in which the value of a woman's evidence in any investigation or court proceedings was given half the value of a man's.[4] This provision combined with Zia's infamous Hudood Ordinances which imposed fierce controls on women's sexuality and subjected female rape victims to a particularly cruel form of Catch-22. The Ordinances criminalised all consensual sex between women and anyone other than their husbands, and introduced punishments which included amputations, public whippings and stoning to death.[5] Such an offence was defined as *zina,* meaning for a married woman, adultery and for an unmarried one, fornication.[6] Because of the evidential ordinance, a man could accuse a woman of a

2 See www.espncricinfo.com/db/National/PAK/Associations/PAK.

3 For which see the Report on Scrutiny of Women's Cricket Associations submitted to the PCB in January 2003.

4 This legislation also discriminated against all non-Muslims, so that a Muslim woman's testimony retained the same value as a non-Muslim man's.

5 These punishments were also applied to a range of theft and property offences.

6 See eds Rutherford, Capdevila, Undurti, Palmary, *Handbook of International Feminisms* (Springer, 2011), p.136; ed Tomalin, *The Routledge Handbook of Religions and Global Development* (Routledge, 2015), pp.222 et seq.

zina offence with no need for any corroboration but the woman would
need at least one independent witness to defend herself. Worse still, a
female rape victim required four independent witnesses to sustain a
charge against her rapist – and without them she would face a charge
of *zina*. The Hudood Ordinanaces resulted in a dramatic increase in
Pakistan's female prison population. In 1979 this was only 70, but by
the end of Zia's rule, in 1988, this had risen to 6,000. The great majority
of the new intake were women accused of *zina* offences after failing to
prove charges of rape.[7]

Zia had to back down to a limited degree in the application of the
Hudood Ordinances under protests from a newly formed Women's
Action Forum which was well funded and well connected. However,
they remained on the statute book, even after the fall of Zia and during
the premierships of Benazir Bhutto. Finally, they were replaced by a
new Protection of Women (Criminal Laws Amendment) Act in 2006
under President Pervez Musharraf.

The Ordinances were simply the most extreme example of a public
policy of coercing women back into the *chador* and the *chardiwari* (the
veil and the four walls of the home).[8] One important consequence of
this policy was the denial of rights to women at work. The government
was reluctant even to admit that women worked outside their homes,
let alone give them new opportunities to do so or any protection when
they did. Most women workers did remain at home, in cities, making
or selling goods on terms dictated by middlemen.[9]

Given this climate, it was not surprising that Zia also cracked down
on women's participation in the performing arts and sport. Essentially,
they were banned from competing in any public sporting contest,
or even watching one. This was another form of sexual control. As
already noted, Zia's favourite preacher, Dr Israr Ahmed, believed that

7 See M Lau, 'Twenty-Five Years Of Hudood Ordinances – A Review,' in the *Washington
and Lee Law Review (2007)*; Abira Ashfaq, 'Voices from Prison and a Call for Repeal: The
Hudood Laws of Pakistan,' in *New Politics*, Winter 2006; Amnesty International report
'Hudood Ordinance – The Crime and Punishment for Zina' (2003).
8 Tomalin, op. cit.
9 See 'Pakistan: The Status of Women and the Women's Movement,' on www.mus-
limtents.com/aminahs world/Pakistan_women.html.

cricket encouraged erotic fantasies in women and wanted it banned from television.[10] He and his fellow zealots were obsessed by the idea that participating in sports would allow women's bodies to be seen by men, especially by those they were forbidden to marry under Islamic doctrines.[11]

Ironically, this provision gave a very slight encouragement to cricket at the expense of tennis, badminton and athletics, because cricket clothing covers more of the body. However, it still forced girls to play any organised match in *shalwar kameez,* or other voluminous clothing, behind closed doors, without male officials or coaches, and without the support of male members of their families.

The power and cultural influence of religious zealots survived Zia's death. The arrival of Benazir Bhutto, Pakistan's first female head of government, did nothing to silence them. In fact, it may even have encouraged them to bear down harder on Pakistani women seeking a public profile in sports.

It was against this background of oppression and hysteria that the Khan sisters of Karachi decided to form Pakistan's first women's cricket team. Without exaggeration, they could be described as the suffragettes of cricket in Pakistan. Like Britain's suffragettes, they challenged a system previously reserved for men. They may not have broken the law, but they certainly broke the rules.

Like the suffragettes, they faced down fierce hostility not only from men but from other women. Although they never endured prison sentences and hunger strikes, they were confronted regularly by terrifying threats.

Above all, they liberated their sister cricketers, even though other women, including their bitter rivals, would reap the benefits and carry women's cricket forward in Pakistan.

Shaiza Khan and her younger sister, Sharmeen, began their struggle by choice. Their father, Mohammed Syed Khan, was the wealthy

10 See page 73.
11 See H Haqqani, *Pakistan Between Mosque And Military* (Palgrave Macmillan, 2005), p.144; Esposito, Voll, Bakar (eds), *Asian Islam In the 21st Century* (USA: OUP, 2008), p.157.

owner of a successful carpet business with factories throughout
Pakistan and in England. He could afford to have them educated
in England, and they learnt their cricket in the peaceful setting
of Shrewsbury, where they attended Concord College boarding
school.

Encouraged by the advent of Benazir Bhutto, they returned to
Pakistan in 1988 and, still aged only 19 and 16, they made their first
effort to create a representative women's team. They promoted a match
between their XI and a team of Pakistan male legends including Javed
Miandad and Zaheer Abbas. The announcement produced a storm of
hostility from fundamentalists. 'They said what we were doing was
un-Islamic and they would not permit it,' said Shaiza Khan in a radio
interview in 2014. 'We argued that if Benazir Bhutto could become
prime minister and meet ten men round a table, why could we not
meet a men's cricket team?'[12] This point was lost on the fundamentalists. They issued death threats against her and her sister, as reported
in newspapers. Urged by her father, she agreed to replace the male
opponents with another women's team and play a match against them
behind closed doors. Wryly, she said that the cancellation gave her more
publicity than the match itself would have done.

In spite of her concession, the death threats continued. The Karachi
police commissioner urged her to cancel the substitute match, for fear of
fundamentalist riots. 'But we had to go ahead. If we had called it off that
day, the cause would have died forever. We had full police security at our
home and an escort to the stadium. There were no spectators, except for
eight thousand policemen, including the police commissioner. Straight
away after the game, we were flown back to London. Our father said,
"You stay there, and when this country's ready for you, come back."'

They followed his advice, and their cricket prospered at club and
county level in Middlesex. They went to Leeds University, where
Shaiza, a leg-spinning all-rounder, became captain. They were even in
contention for places in the England squad for the Women's World Cup
in 1993, but were discovered to be ineligible.

12 BBC World Service, 'Sporting Witness,' broadcast 7 December 2014.

They could have continued with a comfortable cricket life in the English summers, and perhaps eventually qualified for England. Instead, they watched England's women beat New Zealand at the World Cup final at Lord's and decided there and then that they would play in the next competition in 1997 – for Pakistan.

At that time, the World Cup was run by the International Women's Cricket Council (IWCC). They notified the IWCC of their intention to raise a Pakistan team and in turn were notified of the required conditions. They would have to return to Pakistan at least a year in advance, get themselves registered by the cricket board, raise a team and play at least three international matches before the start of the World Cup.

So Shaiza abandoned her work for a doctorate (in Textile Engineering) at Leeds University, returned to Karachi and, in January 1996, founded the Pakistan Women's Cricket Control Association (PWCCA). It was registered as a company and won the endorsement of the Pakistan Cricket Board, which had recently undergone one of its periodic coups d'état. Its chief executive was the highly experienced Arif Abbasi – from Karachi. He endorsed the PWCCA and it secured recognition from the IWCC. Sharmeen followed her sister back to Karachi after completing her first degree at Leeds.

With these formalities completed, the sisters placed dramatic advertisements inviting girls and women all over the country to come to trials for Pakistan's first women's team. If selected, they would play in a specially arranged tour of New Zealand and Australia to qualify for the World Cup. Hundreds replied. Most had never played cricket before. They were attracted by the prospect of an exciting trip and the chance to do something different in their lives. 'We found around twenty with potential,' said Sharmeen Khan.

One of these was a teenager, Kiran Baloch. Unlike most of the others, she had received encouragement from her family, particularly her father, who had played some first-class matches in the Quaid-e-Azam championship. She recalled: 'He watched me in family matches with my cousins and saw that I was getting better. He taught me off-spin and leg-spin and the basics of forward and back play.'

None of the triallists had played at school. Other than Kiran, the most promising recruits were hockey players. 'They were used to watching the ball and running after it, and they were not afraid of the hard ball,' said Shaiza Khan.

The fundamentalist threat had receded slightly, but some of the triallists needed protection from their own families. It is now time in the story to salute the contribution of Mohammed Syed Khan. He created a secure cricket complex for his daughters, with three turf wickets, in the grounds of his carpet factory in Karachi. He converted a tennis court into a practice net with a bowling machine and built a new hostel where all the triallists could live. Initially, he had hoped that the venture would attract other commercial sponsors, but he ended up by meeting all these costs himself. He would fund the entire operation for almost a decade.

This was forced on him by two new factors. First, Arif Abbasi was replaced as chief executive of the Pakistan Cricket Board by Majid Khan. Majid was notably less sympathetic to the idea of any women's international team and was in any case pre-occupied by the fall-out from allegations of match-fixing in the men's international team.

Secondly, the Khan sisters' organisation ran into a problem which had bedevilled Pakistan cricket from the very beginning. This was the Lahore/Karachi feud. They were based in Karachi. They now faced an intense challenge to its status from the surviving branch of the Pakistan Womens' Cricket Organisation, which was still based in Lahore.

It would have been nice if the Lahore and Karachi arms of Pakistan cricket could have come together at this point as a joint national team. This was not possible. The Lahorites lobbied the International Women's Cricket Council to annul the sisters' team's right to represent Pakistan women on the qualifying tour and the subsequent World Cup.

With the support of England and New Zealand, the Khan sisters crucially managed to retain their organisation's international recognition. But within Pakistan, Lahore was a stronger force.

The Khan sisters were excluded from any PCB stadium or facility and denied the services of any coach or other employee of the PCB. Shaiza and Sharmeen Khan found one of their own, the experienced Australian Judy Davies.

Meanwhile, the Khan sisters set out on their qualifying tour. It cost Mr Khan around US$100,000 and superficially he had nothing to show for it. The team were completely outclassed by their Australasian hosts. They lost the first match by ten wickets after being dismissed for 56. Then things went downhill. They lost by 408 runs (the biggest margin in any one-day game) and then by 374 runs after posting the lowest-ever one-day score: 23 all out.

But they had made history. Astonishingly, they were the first women's team to represent Pakistan overseas *in any sport* outside the Olympic Games. That was after nearly 50 years of independence. Most important of all, they did qualify for the World Cup in India.

They only just made it. The Lahorite PWCA lobbied even harder against them and the Pakistan Cricket Board put their team on an 'exit control' list at ports and airports to try to stop them leaving the country.

At this stage, the Khan sisters pulled off a daring stroke in blatant defiance of the authorities. To reach India, they were forced to slip out of Karachi airport in small separate groups, wearing ordinary clothes, with their kitbags hidden in cartons. Once on the aircraft, and safely out of Pakistan airspace, they each went into the toilet and changed into their Pakistan uniforms.

Kiran Baloch remembered the exhilaration of that moment. 'It was out of this world. Ever since I was a child, I used to see men's cricket on television and wonder when we would have a Pakistan team of our own. That dream came true – and then we wore our Pakistani colours and stood under the flags with our national anthem.'[13] They managed to collect only 11 players and had to wheedle substitute fielders when needed from their Indian hosts.

Results in the World Cup were little better than the qualifying tour (five big defeats) but there were some signs of improvement and the team put Pakistan on the world map of women's cricket. Shaiza Khan was told at the opening ceremony: 'You won by being here.'

On their return, Shaiza and Sharmeen Khan became locked in a

13 BBC World Service, ibid.

seven-year struggle with the PWCA for the title-deeds of women's cricket in Pakistan. This was conducted in the courts (some of the associated litigation and counter-litigation was still not exhausted as of December 2015), through lobbying politicians and adminstrators and through the media.

The mutual bitterness shocked a PCB inquiry chaired by Javed Zaman, a famously robust individual. This reported in January 2003 that the 'war of words between the various associations surpassed all norms of decency. The most deplorable aspect of their controversy was that they consumed most of their time and energy for mud-slinging and raising shabby objections upon each other's private life to establish their legitimacy.'[14]

As always, the feud was more bitter because both sides genuinely thought that they were right. We pass no judgement at this distance on either of them, but we can speculate on the huge stress the feud imposed on Shaiza and Sharmeen Khan, as they continued to maintain the *only* Pakistan women's cricket team in being. Under Shaiza's leadership it played 40 one-day internationals, 14 in Karachi and the others in New Zealand, Australia, India, Sri Lanka, and Ireland, and three scattered Test matches, against Sri Lanka, Ireland and the West Indies. Most were heavy defeats, but there were fine individual performances and victory eventually arrived in Karachi, in 2001, against the Dutch. Pakistan then edged the series with four wins to three. In 2000, Shaiza and Sharmeen Khan were the first Pakistani women to be elected to the MCC. They organised a special one-off match between Pakistan Women and an MCC team – which they won. They showed us the congratulations they received from Sir John Major and from the Queen.

There were more important victories on the home front. The team began to attract favourable media coverage – and a stream of new recruits. Some defied their families, none more dramatically than Sajjida Shah, who went on hunger strike when her parents refused to let her join the team's Irish tour in 2000. They gave in after a week and she

14 Report on Scrutiny of Women's Cricket Associations, submitted to the PCB in January 2003, p.1.

became the youngest-ever international cricketer, aged officially 12½, when she played in the second ODI against Ireland.[15] When still only 15, she set another record, unlikely to be broken, as her off-spinners took seven wickets for four against Japan.

Throughout this period, the Khan sisters' organisation managed to retain its status with the IWCC. Then they suffered a cruel blow. The independent IWCC (their guarantor of international recognition) disappeared and the International Cricket Council took over responsibility for women's cricket across the globe. All national governing bodies were then directed to develop women's cricket in their own countries.

Over time, this shift would bring major benefits to Pakistan's women's cricketers, but it signalled the end for the Khan sisters' role. In 2004, when they played a domestic series against the West Indies in Karachi they knew it would be a last hurrah. They lost the one-day series 5-2, but produced a stupendous effort in the only Test match at the National Stadium, Karachi.

Once again, they had to fight for its recognition. The Pakistan Cricket Board wanted them to play as Sindh. They refused, and Arif Abbasi advised them robustly to break into the stadium at night and paint PAKISTAN over any reference to Sindh on the scoreboards or stands. This turned out to be unnecessary and it went ahead as a recognised Test match.

Shaiza Khan won the toss and batted. Kiran Baloch opened with Sajjida Shah, still only 15. Kiran Baloch later remembered: 'We were very charged up and we knew we needed to have a last good show against West Indies on our home ground and our home city, to show that we could play in a Test match. People kept asking, can girls play for four days?' Shaiza Khan told her: 'You love batting, so just go on, I won't declare.'

Sajjida Shah and Kiran had already set a record for a women's opening partnership, 242, when Sajjida was cruelly dismissed on 98. At the end of the day, Kiran was 138 not out. Shaiza Khan told her to bat on in the same vein, because the individual Test record was in her

15 See 'Grealey plays captain's role,' *Irish Times,* 26 July 2000.

grasp. 'Luckily, Shaiza was on the pitch with me when I scored two hundred, and then she pushed me and really held me together to get the next fifteen runs to get the record.' It duly fell, but Shaiza Khan let her continue, to make it harder for anyone to take it from her. When finally dismissed for 242 Kiran had batted for 584 minutes – still the longest innings ever played by a woman.

When the West Indies batted, it was Shaiza Khan's turn to set records. She claimed seven cheap wickets in the first innings with the help of a hat-trick, only the second by a woman in international cricket. Then in the follow-on, she claimed another six, grabbing another world record. But they had taken a long time. 'I bowled all day, around fifty-five overs. My fingers were bleeding but I had to do it because my other bowlers were getting tired. I knew I had to take the responsibility.' They were both disappointed when the West Indies escaped with a draw, but then, said Shaiza Khan, 'The world records over-ruled the feeling and no one remembers the Test match, only the world records.'

After the West Indies' visit, neither of the record-breakers played for Pakistan again. They refused to join the new 'unified' structure proposed by the PCB and effectively left women's cricket in the hands of the rival Lahore group.

Over the last ten years, women's cricket in Pakistan has advanced far beyond the shadows and darkness inherited by the Khan sisters. The international team has climbed up the world rankings. It won a gold medal at the Asian Games in 2010 and President Zardari found it politically profitable to associate himself with them.

It has a structure of domestic tournaments, is covered regularly on television and attracts commercial sponsorship. The top players have central contracts and do product endorsements. This prospect has helped to break down resistance to women's cricket even in highly conservative households.

Shaiza and Sharmeen Khan now run the family carpet business. They survey the changes in women's cricket from the ground created by their father as a nursery and a sanctuary for their talent. Shaiza Khan reflects: 'I have very memorable feelings not only about being the first captain or playing in Tests or the World Cup but about being the person who introduced cricket to women in Pakistan. When I see girls playing in the street, everybody says that's your doing.'

And so it is, a heroic achievement. Today, there is a statue of the great British suffragette Emmeline Pankhurst outside Parliament in London. Perhaps one day a statue of Shaiza and Sharmeen Khan will be erected at Karachi's National Stadium to mark their heroic struggle not just on behalf of Pakistan's female cricketers but ultimately on behalf of all Pakistani women.

28

CRICKET UNDER THE GENERALS

The Pakistan army has never much liked cricket. The military sport has always been hockey. In 1954, a young army officer, Shuja-ud-Din, was selected for the tour of England. His commander-in-chief, Ayub Khan, called him 'a waster'.[1] By contrast, many of the early Test cricketers served in the air force, which was a keen sponsor of the game.

The army has nevertheless played a crucial role in Pakistan cricket. This influence can be dated back to the coup d'état which established military rule in 1958. The coup leader, Ayub Khan, might not have enjoyed cricket, but he was quick to realise the impact on his regime of a successful team – or an unsuccessful one. When he seized power, the Board of Control of Cricket for Pakistan (BCCP) was based in Karachi, so Ayub arranged for it to be moved to military headquarters in Rawalpindi. In 1960-61, the BCCP introduced a new competition intended specifically to spread first-class cricket beyond the big cities of Karachi and Lahore. They named it the Ayub trophy – so that the new teams and their supporters would associate their status with

---

1 He ignored Ayub and had a remarkably full cricket life. He played 19 Tests, served as a national selector and became a passionate and respected author and broadcaster about the game. He retired from the army as a lieutenant-colonel. Even as a prisoner-of-war in India for three years, he continued to write his regular magazine column about cricket, and received £100 from the MCC for equipment.

Field-Marshal Ayub. This move backfired because the new trophy produced regular mismatches, notably Railways against Dera Ismail Khan.[2]

Ayub was angered by the unbroken dull draws on Pakistan's tour of India in 1960-61. He called the team *goondas* (thugs) and ordered the sacking of Fazal Mahmood as captain. He decided that the next major tour, England in 1962, would be under military management. His choice fell on a towering, bluff brigadier, 'Gussy' Hyder, who had served with distinction in World War Two in Iraq, Libya, Italy and Greece, but was better known as a polo player than as a cricketer. This move also backfired. The team performed calamitously, losing four Tests with one draw. The brigadier was openly mocked by senior players,[3] and could offer little support to an inexperienced and reluctant captain, Javed Burki. Since Burki was the son of a general who was one of Ayub's ministers, the heavily censored media were able to pillory the team as a coded attack on the government.[4]

Ayub's other major intervention came as his regime was crumbling in the face of secessionist agitation in East Pakistan, and worker–student agitation in West Pakistan, exploited by ZA Bhutto and his then new and radical Pakistan People's Party. Pakistan were about to play a hastily arranged series of three Tests against England. To reduce the opportunity for further agitation in the crowds, he had the opening Test in Lahore cut to four days and pressed for the English visitors to meet a demanding programme of side matches – and play a Test in Dacca, where his government had lost control. These moves were of little value to him: ill and depressed, he quit in favour of General Yahya Khan before the series was over.[5]

Yahya had too many problems to interfere much with cricket, which he left in civilian hands. That said, his government made some last-minute attempts to use cricket to win support in East Pakistan.[6]

2 See chapter 14.
3 Unfairly, say his surviving family.
4 P Oborne, op. cit., pp.176-77.
5 See P Oborne, ibid., pp.195-202.
6 See P Oborne, ibid., pp.208-9, especially on the selection of a teenage Bengali, Roquibul Hasan.

The national team only won two Test matches during the 1960s when Ayub Khan's military regime was at its height. Test performances only revived with the election in 1971 of ZA Bhutto and the return of civilian rule.

Bhutto stripped from the army its role in cricket, as in many other areas of national life. He appointed AH Kardar, his childhood acquaintance and Pakistan's magisterial first Test captain, as chairman of the BCCP, with a mandate to re-structure the game. Kardar's reforms meant the sport was in much better shape by the time General Zia seized power in 1977.

Like Ayub Khan, Zia had no real interest in cricket. But he realised more quickly than Ayub that the team's fortunes were important to him and he tried hard to link himself to its successes.

His first cricket challenge was to deal with Pakistan's Packer players. He began by resisting their return to the international team. But then the Packerless team was overwhelmed on the short tour of England in 1978. The next series was against India – after a gap of 17 years. His regime was still shaky and he could not afford Pakistan to lose with a weak team at home to its arch-rivals. So he reversed himself. He sacked the civilian leadership of the BCCP and installed its first military chairman, Lieutenant-General KM Azhar, who had conquered 1,300 square miles of Rajasthan during the 1965 India–Pakistan War. Azhar's first instruction was to get the Packer players back. Thanks to his nephew, Arif Abbasi, he achieved this and Pakistan overpowered India in a thrilling series.[7]

Zia was fortunate in presiding over a Pakistan team which grew steadily more exciting and successful. His main personal impact on it was to order more television coverage from the monopoly state broadcaster PTV,[8] and his choice of Azhar's successor – retired Air Marshal Nur Khan.

Nur Khan has a claim to be the best sports administrator any

7 Arif Abbasi: personal interview. We have also seen the manuscript of his forthcoming memoirs, to be published as *Inside Outside* (Ushaba Books).
8 See chapter 19.

country has ever produced. He took Pakistan hockey and squash to a pinnacle.[9] In four years in charge of cricket, supported by the commercial acumen of Arif Abbasi, he secured a huge increase in income from sponsorship and the sale of broadcasting rights. This funded major investments in new or improved cricketing infrastructure and helped to support a greatly expanded domestic and international programme. After an initial hiccup with a players' revolt against Javed Miandad, the national team became increasingly exciting and successful as Javed and Imran Khan established their relationship. Internationally, Pakistan led the world in appointing match observers and campaigned for third-country umpires. Nur Khan initiated the alliance with India which seized the staging of the 1987 World Cup.

Despite his high rank and achievements, Nur Khan cannot be considered a military chairman of the BCCP. He had left the air force nine years earlier and did nothing to favour his old service in the BCCP – still less the army. He was a superlative decision-maker who always acted in the interest of the organisations he served. Zia was sensible enough not to interfere with Nur Khan's work, although he took care to associate himself with its successes. He watched matches frequently and visibly and gave awards to the players.

Zia appointed General Safdar Butt as Nur Khan's successor. But he also made him chairman of the vastly more important Water and Power Development Authority, which limited his ability to 'militarise' Pakistan cricket even if that had been his intention. Safdar Butt's successor, General Zahid Ali Akbar Khan, also combined the two jobs, although he served most of his term under civilian governments following Zia's death in an air crash.[10]

After the departure of Nur Khan, Zia made one vital personal

9 During the 1960s, he had also turned PIA into a world-class airline.
10 General Zahid Ali Akhbar Khan gave most of his attention to WAPDA, as was revealed years later when the Pakistan authorities tried and failed to have him extradited from Bosnia on charges of unlawfully transferring property valued at 267 million rupees: see 'Wanted WAPDA chief jumps through legal loophole to escape capture,' *Express News* (Pakistan) 8 July 2013. He subsequently returned to Pakistan and the case was settled by a plea bargain, in which he agreed to pay back nearly 200 million rupees. See 'NAB moves against lawmakers, former AGP,' *Dawn*, 18 September 2015.

intervention in Pakistan cricket, when he helped to persuade Imran Khan to cancel his retirement plans in 1987.

However, although Zia was the longest-serving and the most severe of Pakistan's military rulers, his overall personal impact on Pakistan cricket was surprisingly limited.

The most important military influence on Pakistan cricket came from General Pervez Musharraf and his appointee, General Tauqir Zia. Musharraf went further than any of his predecessors in appointing military personnel to administrative posts. In 2003, a journalist from *Dawn* calculated that there were over a thousand of them in jobs formerly occupied by civilians.[11]

Nonetheless, it was surprising that Musharraf and his nominee had such impact on Pakistan cricket. They were both phenomenally busy people. In his memoirs, Musharraf claimed that he worked for 15 hours a day in his first year of office.[12] He had a huge agenda of ongoing crises, including urban violence, organised crime, economic stagnation, rampant corruption and mismanagement in the public sector, and military confrontation with India. His choice for the PCB, Tauqir Zia, retained two vital military responsibilities and Musharraf soon gave him another one.

We spoke to each of them and the starting question was obvious. Where did they find the time for cricket?

TWO GENERALS REMEMBER . . .

After a period of exile in London and Dubai, Pervez Musharraf returned to Karachi ahead of the 2013 elections. As of November 2015, he was compelled to remain in Pakistan where there are several separate legal proceedings against him arising from his days in power. The most serious accusations, which he has vehemently

11 '1027 civilian posts occupied by servicemen,' *Dawn*, 30 October 2003, cited in C Jaffrelot, op. cit., p.340.
12 P Musharraf, *In The Line Of Fire* (Simon & Schuster, 2006), p.334.

denied, relate to the assassination of Benazir Bhutto.[13] He has survived four assassination attempts and still has a host of enemies.
But with an appointment, it did not take long to be admitted to his
home in the Defence district. It is comfortable but not opulent. His
enemies have never accused him of enriching himself from office. He
has been active on social media and has become a relaxed and genial
interviewee.

Musharraf has clearly learnt to pre-empt criticisms that he had little
experience of cricket. He began dramatically by mourning his 'seven
lost years' in Turkey as a child which stopped him becoming a cricketer.
He loved all sports but had to concentrate on soccer and volleyball. On
return to Lahore, he did play in his class team at Forman Christian
College. 'I was a very good fielder, exceptionally good. In one match,
a batsman hit a huge skyer. I ran for the ball and made the catch but
another fielder ran for it as well. He ran straight into my face. I fainted
and dropped the ball. I woke up with people all round me. My eye was
black and swollen for over two weeks.' He clearly felt that this honour-
able wound was proof of his commitment to cricket.

Musharraf in office had a paternalistic view of Pakistan cricketers,
and this was influenced by another school experience. As a runner, he
was motivated by the physical education teacher, Mr Munby. 'When I
went in for the mile, there were always better athletes than me, but he
told me never to think that they were going to beat me. In my mind,
I should go onto the track as a winner.' As ruler of Pakistan, he often
fretted about the team's morale, especially in playing white teams, and
thought that he should give them a winner's mentality, with pep talks
like Mr Munby's. 'I saw our team huddled around itself. I told them
not to do that, and to go out and mix with other teams. I also noticed
that many were not confident being interviewed in English – so I told
them to speak Urdu.'

Unlike earlier teams, largely drawn from the best schools and
colleges, many more recent Pakistani cricketers came from rural vil-
lages and were ill at ease in formal situations. With a touch of Jeeves,

13 See www.nation.com.pk/editors-picks/16-Nov-2015/no-ecl-relief-for-musharraf.

Musharraf commented: 'They even had to be taught to dress properly, how to match trousers with a shirt and coat.' He was reminded
that AH Kardar had taught Pakistan's first England tourists how
to use a knife and fork. 'Quite so. These things should be taught.
I got lessons in them in my army training. And Tauqir Zia started
English lessons.'

To Musharraf, good turnout and discipline were as important to
cricketers as to soldiers. They would then bring credit to their country
as smart soldiers do for their unit. This outlook influenced his choice
of Tauqir Zia.

It followed a period of exceptional turbulence, even by Pakistan
standards, in cricket administration. In 1999, anger over Pakistan's
World Cup defeat led the prime minister, Nawaz Sharif, to secure
the removal of the experienced PCB chairman, Khalid Mahmood.
He was replaced by an ad hoc committee, led by an industrialist,
Mujeeb-ur-Rehman. He had no cricketing history, but was the
brother of the man heading Nawaz Sharif's so-called Accountability
Bureau, which had targeted corruption among his political rivals.
Not surprisingly, Musharraf ousted Nawaz Sharif's appointee when
he took power. His first pick as a replacement was the veteran Dr
Zafar Altaf.

Tauqir Zia took up the narrative, at a meeting a fortnight later at
the Lahore Gymkhana. His manner was more austere than his former
commander's. He spoke as a military man, not a politician. 'I had just
been promoted as a corps commander. Musharraf rang me up ten days
later and asked me who would be the best chairman for the PCB. I said
Imran Khan, but since he had become involved in politics he should
ask if he had the time. I don't know if he did but he appointed Zafar
Altaf, who had been secretary of agriculture in government. But after
forty days, Musharraf rang me up again and said I had better take over
cricket.'

Back to Musharraf. 'I wanted a good administrator and a good leader
of men, because the sportsmen I had seen in life and in the army were
often ill-disciplined. I knew that Tauqir Zia had been a very good leader
of men as a divisional commander. He was a confident leader and men

followed him. He was a pretty good cricketer. Maybe outside the army he might have reached a higher level.'

Tauqir Zia: 'I reminded him that he had just appointed Zafar Altaf, and I had just taken over an important command only a month ago. He said, "No, you can handle it." Then six months later, the Indians massed forces on our border, so Musharraf promoted me to command our forces there, over a quarter of a million troops.' He enjoyed gossiping about cricket over the hot line to his Indian opposite number.[14] 'Then, on top of that Musharraf put me in charge of Pakistan's first nuclear war game. I had four headquarters, in Islamabad, Lahore, Mangla, and Gujranwala. I could give only twenty-five per cent of my time to cricket.'

The first task for both men was to deal with Judge Qayyum's report on match-fixing. By chance, the final version was delivered to the PCB and the Sports Ministry on the very day that Musharraf took power in his 'counter-coup' (his expression) on 12 October 1999. It was not made public until May the following year, when the cricket world was also rocked by match-fixing accusations against Hansie Cronje of South Africa and two former Indian captains, Kapil Dev and Mohammad Azharuddin. There have been repeated suggestions that Musharraf and Tauqir Zia sat on the Qayyum report and applied pressure to reduce the penalties against Pakistan's condemned cricketers.[15]

Both of them denied this emphatically. Musharraf said: 'My policy direction was very clear. Punish the man for match-fixing.' He seemed genuinely puzzled when reminded of suggestions that he had pushed for lighter sentences. 'I would not interfere like that, without knowing the gravity of the thing. Why should I tell Qayyum to give lighter punishments? These are rumours with no base.'

Tauqir Zia was much more familiar with the detail of the Qayyum report. He claimed that he did not see it until May. 'I had already decided to make it public. The Pakistan team were in the West Indies, and I gave a press conference which released the report in the Marriott

14 P Oborne, op. cit., p.453n.
15 See P Oborne, op. cit., p.395, O Samiuddin, op. cit., pp.385-86.

Hotel in Islamabad. Whatever people say is totally wrong. If anyone sat on the report, it was Justice Qayyum himself because he had to examine evidence from about three hundred witnesses.' He went through the Qayyum recommendations, emphasising that only Salim Malik, the former captain, had been condemned for match-fixing. All the other named players were condemned for other reasons: Ata-ur-Rehman for perjury, Wasim Akram, Mushtaq Ahmed, Inzamam-ul-Haq, Saeed Anwar and Akram Raza for failure to give full co-operation to the inquiry. 'We implemented every one of Qayyum's recommendations. People should check the report and what happened afterwards before they speak. We did not pursue one proposal from Qayyum, for the chairman or a senior officer of the PCB to overwatch the team's performance and behaviour on overseas tours. I rejected this, because the ICC had just appointed the Anti-Corruption Unit under Lord Condon to supervise cricketers' behaviour. There was no point in duplicating this.'

He mentioned one other significant personal initiative, not part of the Qayyum report. 'Because no betting is allowed in Pakistan, all bookmakers are criminal. I asked President Tarar and the chief executive Musharraf [his chosen title, to emphasise his constitutional credentials[16]] either to crack down on bookmakers and drive them out or else register them to get some public revenue. I have never had any response to this suggestion since I first made it in 2000.'

As the 25 per cent chairman of the PCB, Tauqir Zia had to respond to many other problems which were not of his own making. In the aftermath of 9/11, Pakistan endured a short period of international exile. This was ended by visits from Sri Lanka and New Zealand, but then a bomb blast in Karachi led the New Zealanders to go home and Pakistan wandered around the world, playing one-day series in Australia, Sri Lanka, Kenya, Canada and even Morocco.

At home, Tauqir Zia had to deal with a land dispute between the PCB and the army. It might have exposed him to a conflict of loyalties, but the issue was resolved by arbitration, in favour of the army. He also had to resolve a challenge to the PCB's five-year television deal with

16 P Musharraf, op. cit., p.144.

Ten Sports/ARY. He pulled rank on one of his challengers. 'Someone from TWI [the losing company] tried to take us to court. He was a retired naval commander. I said on television, if he was so good, why did he retire at the level of a colonel? I asked people to listen to a general instead. There was an investigation under Shaharyar Khan, it found that everything was transparent.'[17]

In spite of these crises, and the demands of his military appointments, Tauqir Zia did more than most PCB chairmen to create and implement a personal agenda. It reflected a military mindset. 'When he takes up a command, a leader must have a vision, for the short term and the long term, otherwise it is impossible to make plans. It was the same with Pakistan cricket. We needed a five-year plan. The first task was to get our record-keeping right. Then I presented a statement with a Vision of every aspect of our cricket: infrastructure, grassroots training, cricketers' welfare, media, marketing, identifying the roles and responsibilities of everyone in administration. It also went into details such as lights in the stadiums.'

Infrastructure was his top priority. 'The Vision was to develop ninety cricket grounds and when I left we already had sixty-seven. Most importantly, we went out to Baluchistan and the interior of Sind.' He put fewer resources into Lahore, where cricket was well established but made a point of reviving Minto Park, which had been a cradle of first-class cricket. He had a genuine sense of Pakistan's cricket history. He subsidised some major historic works[18] and handed out jobs or pensions to former great players, including Fazal Mahmood, Hanif Mohammad and Imtiaz Ahmed.

His greatest pride is the development of the National Academy, in Lahore, and eight others in the provinces. 'They were not intended for the established stars, players of twenty-five or more. We wanted to develop players of twelve to eighteen, by age group. We also provided accommodation for players and officials instead of five-star

17 See S Khan and A Khan, op. cit., pp.42-43.
18 Including the indispensable *Chequered History of Pakistan Cricket* by Shuja-ud-Din Butt and Salim Parvez.

hotels. That saved ten million rupees a year. We also aimed to generate income by giving coaching to private individuals and overseas
teams. We took in players from the UAE and Nepal and earned a lot
of money.'

One feature of the National Academy reflected his military training. 'We added a Research and Analysis Wing, to show players their
strengths and weaknesses and those of their opponents. In other words,
know your enemy. We made videos of our matches and our opponents'.
Ten days before starting a series, the Pakistan players came to the
Academy to watch.'

Musharraf warmly endorsed his appointee's achievements. 'He
did a very good job in spreading cricket in Pakistan. He developed
many cricket grounds, with lighting for night cricket and electronic
scoreboards, then opened the National Academy.' He also received a
tribute from an unexpected source. Alone among modern PCB chairmen, Tauqir Zia was mentioned with approval in Shoaib Akhtar's
autobiography.[19]

All of Tauqir Zia's new investments were directed and managed from
the centre. Power shifted from the regions to the PCB, as did jobs.
He inherited a PCB with about 50 employees, including ground staff.
When he left there were several hundred and the PCB was on a path
which would take it to 900 employees by 2013.[20] The regions themselves were re-drawn and re-structured in ways which cut the power
of city associations over finance, administration and even selection of
players. One critic, the former Test spinner, Iqbal Qasim, attacked the
results as 'fictitious regions which had no history'.[21]

Both Musharraf and Tauqir Zia defended their centralising, top-
down approach as born of necessity. Musharraf said: 'Unfortunately,
very few sports bodies were run well in Pakistan. They always had politics and infighting. I thought it important to concentrate on cricket and
hockey, our main national games. I wanted to ensure that these bodies

19 S Akhtar, op.cit., p.210.
20 O Samiuddin, op. cit., p.414.
21 O Samiuddin, op. cit., p.413 and S Khan and A Khan, op. cit., pp.92-93.

were run well.' Tauqir Zia was more forthright. 'I am unrepentant because I personally feel that Pakistan cannot be run as a democracy. In any event, the PCB at that time could not have been run as a democracy. With match-fixing and all the scandals coming in, I had to take a centralising control.' However, he had always respected his five independent advisors on cricketing and selection issues and added, 'In my four years, I was never approached by any Cabinet member or senior official for any favour from the PCB.' But he then had an afterthought. 'Except for free tickets.'

Another issue which united him and Musharraf was the overt religiosity which began to emerge in the Pakistan cricket team. Tauqir Zia said: 'I had to ban a bearded man from the PCB and all its grounds – Qasim Omar, the man who had [falsely] accused Imran Khan of drug-taking. I told him he could not teach religion at our grounds.'

Musharraf's comment reflected a military man's concern for smartness as well as a politician's concern for unity. 'A very backward view of religion was imposed on the team and the game suffered. I was terribly against people forcing others to grow beards and say prayers. That is an individual affair. 'I even called Yousuf Youhana myself after he converted to Islam and grew a beard. But that beard was terribly out of shape. I told him, "I'm very happy that you have converted to Islam but I wish that you had studied Islam and got to the real issues. If you think that this beard is about Islam, you are very sadly mistaken. Why are you keeping such a shabby beard?"'

For both Musharraf and Tauqir Zia the biggest problem was one over which they had almost no influence: the continued disintegration of the national team. Its impact on public opinion was magnified by Musharraf's biggest reform, the liberalisation of the media in 2002. He remarked ruefully: 'Many think I was the victim of my own creation.' Tauqir Zia's successor, Shaharyar Khan, amplified this judgement. 'Cricket became a target for this newly acquired freedom of the media, which began to aim its slings and arrows against Musharraf's military regime that was generally losing its lustre through half-baked compromise solutions. Politically, criticising Tauqir Zia was aimed at

Musharraf's military regime.'[22] Unfortunately, the media were given plenty of targets.

In October 2002, Pakistan suffered its worst humiliation, losing in two days to Australia in Sharjah after being dismissed for 59 and 53. Tauqir Zia immediately offered his resignation: Musharraf prevailed on him to stay on.[23]

A year later, Pakistan crashed out of the World Cup, with their only victories against non-Test opposition, Namibia and the Netherlands. Again Tauqir Zia sought to resign and again Musharraf refused to accept. However, by that time their relationship was broken because of the media storm over the selection in the Pakistan Test squad of Tauqir Zia's son, Junaid. Tauqir Zia stressed that this had nothing to do with him: his selection panel had decided to include Junaid as the 15th man in the tour party to New Zealand because they thought he would bowl well in local conditions.

However, the media response had perturbed Musharraf, who called Tauqir Zia in Islamabad. 'I was asleep and had told my staff not to wake me before noon. I think Musharraf called several times again. Eventually I spoke to him. He said that Junaid's selection had caused controversy in the media and advised against his inclusion. I tried to explain the situation. I thought for the first time in his life, his tone was a little high.

'I told him that he relied on me and my advisors to run the PCB and I would have to resign if he was not willing to trust them. He refused to accept this. I told him, "No one challenges my integrity," and sent in my resignation to his ADC. He did not accept it and it sat on the table for a month. He offered me an ambassadorship in "a country of fairies" [this was Ukraine]. I said, "All the fairies speak my language in Pakistan," and refused the offer. I did not want any embassy. Musharraf asked me to suggest some names for my replacement as chairman of the PCB. I offered Zafar Altaf, Mueen

---

22 Javed Burki offered exactly the same analysis of the media attacks on his captaincy of the calamitous 1962 tour of England, as a proxy for attacking Ayub Khan's military rule. See P Oborne, op. cit., pp.172-73.
23 'Tauqir stays as PCB chief,' www.espncricinfo.com 16 October 2012.

Afzal [a former senior Treasury official], Chisti Mujahid, my secretary, and Shaharyar Khan. He chose Shaharyar and asked me to tell him. I said, "Tell him yourself."' The experience estranged him from Musharraf ever since. 'I haven't spoken to him, although he calls me sometimes.'

As Shaharyar Khan himself recognised, the change had great political significance. 'I saw my appointment as a sop to public opinion. As a civilian I would replace a general as head of the PCB.' However, Musharraf had a clear agenda for him. 'He met me with his customary geniality and, after an exchange of courtesies, underlined that my primary task was to prepare the national team to win the World Cup in 2007.'[24]

Military influence over the PCB did not disappear with Tauqir Zia. Shaharyar Khan wrote: 'Musharraf had only a superficial grasp of cricket. He was advised by a coterie of army officers – some generals who also did not have a deep understanding of cricket and junior officers in his secretariat who were active club cricketers. I found Musharraf impulsive and often shooting from the hip without assessing issues in depth.'[25]

Musharraf took the opportunity of a riposte. 'Shaharyar Sahib was a good diplomat all right, but maybe tough handling was not his forte. Take Shoaib Akhtar. He was ill-disciplined. I remember him at the time being punished for feigning an injury, so he went and formed a medical panel of his own and had himself declared unfit – all counter to Shaharyar Khan. It got into the newspapers and Shaharyar Khan formed a committee to investigate. I called him and said it was clear that this man is an ill-disciplined chap. If I were you, I'd call him in and say if you do this ill-disciplined thing again, I'll kick you out. I don't care if you are the fastest damn bowler. Why form a committee? I don't think Shaharyar could handle ill-disciplined chaps.'

This led to the notorious Oval Test match in 2006 when Inzamam-ul-Haq refused to lead Pakistan back onto the field after they were

24 S Khan and A Khan, op. cit., pp.22, 31.
25 Ibid., p.132.

accused of ball-tampering. Shaharyar Khan had given a minute-by-minute account of this in his book *Cricket Cauldron*, including his calls to Musharraf's office seeking his intervention.

'Yes. That is where you need toughness, sportsmen always need tough handling.' However, Musharraf was surprised to hear the suggestion that his personal representative, Dr Nasim Ashraf, had consulted him directly during the crisis. 'Was Nasim Ashraf then chairman of the PCB?' No, he appointed him several months later; Shaharyar Khan was still in charge. 'In that case, I would never do that. I am a military man. I don't believe in having someone over the shoulder of the man in charge. If Nasim Ashraf had consulted me, I would have said, "Get Shaharyar Khan, what does he say?"'

He was even more surprised by the suggestion that he had sent a personal message to the recalcitrant Inzamam. 'No.'

Under Shaharyar Khan, there was a notable thaw in India–Pakistan cricket relations. The two teams played back-to-back series marked by thrilling cricket and genuine amity between both sets of fans. Musharraf had vivid memories of the one-day international in Lahore in 2004, when he sat next to the daughter and grandson of MA Jinnah, the Quaid-e-Azam ('the Great Leader'), returning to the country for the first time since 1948. 'The Lahore crowds are considered very emotional and very anti-Indian, but that day they cheered both teams.'

Musharraf took advantage of the new atmosphere the following year to make his own attempt at 'cricket diplomacy', first initiated by Zia-ul-Haq. 'I went with the Indian prime minister Manmohan Singh to watch the one-day international at Delhi.' Unfortunately, he discovered that he could not depend on Pakistan's cricketers to set the right note. 'Afridi was on fire that day. He was hitting a four or a six every other ball, all in our direction. It was so embarrassing. I had to look here and there to avoid applauding the massacre of the Indian bowlers in front of the Indian crowd. We then had to leave for an official meeting, but I asked my military secretary to keep me posted on the score. He walked in every fifteen to twenty minutes and handed me a chit. Manmohan Singh probably thought it was some kind of information for our discussion. Actually, it was the cricket score. I asked him if we might go back to the match and hand out the awards together. He thought that would create a security problem, but I said that it had not been planned so there should be no problem. He agreed – but chits kept coming in and Indian wickets kept falling in their reply to our innings. I said, "Prime Minister, your batsmen are sabotaging all our efforts to go back to the match." We did not go back. It turned into a miserable match for India.'

As part of his cricket diplomacy, Musharraf made a more ambitious offer to resolve the Kashmir dispute than any previous ruler of Pakistan. There were elements which echoed the recent settlement in Northern Ireland, particularly the suspension of arguments over sovereignty, devolved rule and joint economic development in Kashmir. Had he been influenced by the Northern Ireland experience?

'No. I went around and talked to everyone involved with Azad Kashmir and tried to see a way forward to a solution. Unfortunately, no one could give me any idea of what sort of solution they had in mind. I was surprised that no one had come up with a solution since 1947. So I came up with my proposals which were purely local, prompted by the problems people were suffering: gradual de-militarisation, giving max-imum self-government, having an over-watch mechanism and finally, making the line of control irrelevant by opening up six new routes for the movement of goods and people.' The plan made no headway at the time but he has tried to keep it alive.

He condemned India's refusal to play the series against Pakistan in winter 2015 which had been agreed 18 months before. 'It is very frustrating. I think they suffer from a complex about us. They stopped playing in Sharjah because we kept beating them there. Now it's a political issue. I don't think the players and administrators are against playing us.'

Tauqir Zia was more forthright. 'India controls everything through money. If they don't want to play us, let them not play us. Pakistan cannot behave like a puppy. International cricket cannot function without Pakistan. We don't realise our importance. We're becoming slaves and puppies.'

Indo–Pakistani cricket relations may be in deep freeze, but at the time of writing the two generals were planning to break the ice, after 12 years, over a few social rubbers of bridge. This could be a risky procedure for two strong-minded soldiers. One hopes that neither will make a foolish bid nor lead the wrong suit.

29

PAKISTAN TEST AND WORLD CUP RECORD
UNDER CIVILIAN AND MILITARY RULE

(as at 1 December 2015)

We examined Pakistan's results under civilian and military rule. They are summarised in the following table. Predictably, it suggests that governments have almost no influence over them. Pakistan's performances depend on the relative strength of the team in international cricket.

	P	W	D	L	Points per Test (W=2, D=1, L=0)
Pre Ayub 1952-58	23	6	11	6	1.00
Ayub+Yahya 1958-71	39	4	23	12	0.79
ZA Bhutto 1971-77	25	5	14	6	0.96
Zia-ul-Haq 1977-88	89	26	46	17	1.10

Post Zia 1988-99	82	33	31	18	1.18
Musharraf 1999-2008*	*77*	*29*	*18*	*30*	*0.99*
Post Musharraf 2008-15	60	23	15	22	1.02
Total civilian	190	67	71	52	1.08
Total military*	*205*	*59*	*87*	*59*	*1.00*
Total*	**395**	**126**	**158**	**111**	**1.04**

*includes forfeited match v England, Oval 2006
Civilian rulers roman
Military rulers italic

NOTE: The points per Test indicator is very crude: unlike the current Test ranking system it takes no account of the quality of the opposition. It favours the era since 1993, when Pakistan started to play Tests against one of its weakest opponents, Zimbabwe (total P17 W10 D4 L3) and then, in 2001, Bangladesh (total P10 W9 D1). However, this is partly offset by the arrival in 1995 of one of Pakistan's strongest opponents, South Africa (total P23 W4 D7 L12).

World Cup achievements	
1975 (Bhutto)	First round
1979 (Zia)	*Semi-final*
1983 (Zia)	*Semi-final*
1987 (Zia)	*Semi-final*
1992 (post Zia)	Champions
1996 (post Zia)	Quarter-final
1999 (post Zia)	Final
2003 (Musharraf)	*First round*

2007 (Musharraf)	*First round*
2011 (post Musharraf)	Semi-final
2015 (post Musharraf)	Quarter-final

Source: www.espncricinfo.com.

30

STILL NEEDED: BENEFACTORS
OF PAKISTAN CRICKET

Since its infancy, Pakistan cricket has relied heavily on individual benefactors as creators of infrastructure and financial supporters for players, particularly in their early careers. Hanif Mohammad's auto-biography gave them an entire chapter entitled 'Patron Saints': one of them, the Pir of Pagaro, spiritual leader of the sect known as the Hurs, enjoyed that status quite literally in the eyes of his followers. The Pir's brother-in-law, Makhdoomzada Hassan Mahmood, was hereditary chief minister of the autonomous princely state of Bahawalpur. Both he and the Amir were cricket-crazy. They poured revenues into recruiting leading players into a team which won the first Quaid-e-Azam first-class tournament. They also built the magnificent Dring Stadium and, most unusually, gave it a turf wicket.[1]

Many early players were especially indebted to Mr Kafiluddin, chief engineer of Pakistan's Public Works Department, who put Hanif Mohammad on his payroll at the age of 16 as a roads inspector.[2] Even more improbably, Mr Kafiluddin took on Hanif's brother Mushtaq, aged 12, as a 'cement clerk'.[3]

1 P Oborne, op. cit., pp.90-91.
2 Hanif Mohammad, op. cit., p.25 and chap 4.
3 Mushtaq Mohammad, op. cit., p.31.

In those early days, Pakistan cricket was run on a shoestring budget. By comparison, the present-day PCB is awash with money from sources then unimagined, commercial sponsorship and television. But its revenues have all too frequently been dissipated by patronage, infighting and bureaucratisation. Even without these problems, the PCB's costs have regularly outpaced its income.

Pakistan cricket therefore continues to rely heavily on private benefactors, as is shown by two notable contributors, who have watered the sport's grassroots when these are not reached by official efforts.

THE SHAH FAMILY

'I was born in Birkenhead where my father was an orthopaedic registrar. When I was eight, he decided it was time to go back to Pakistan and help the country. He started a small orthopaedic hospital, but he always called himself a full-time cricketer and a part-time surgeon. He was crazy about cricket, and slept close to his bat and ball. [As did Wasim Bari and Abdul Qadir in their time, and many other cricket legends all over the world.] He ended up creating the first private floodlit cricket stadium in Pakistan, where scores of great players learnt to play cricket.'

The speaker is Dr Imran Ali Shah about his remarkable father, Dr Mohammad Ali Shah. The letter's career as a surgeon, cricketer, cricket commentator, sporting patron, sports administrator and, ultimately, sports minister of the provincial government of Sindh, is narrated in a delightful admiring biography entitled *The Legend Unfolds*. It carries over 300 photographs of the subject, and others showing his qualification certificates and even his accreditation cards to various events. He is shown with many famous cricketers: playing a match with Younus Khan, with Hanif Mohammad at a coaching camp, watching cricket with Imran Khan, making a point to Mohsin Khan, or Ian Chappell or Wasim Akram or Mohammad Azharuddin, and even signing *his* autograph for an admiring Zaheer Abbas. The supporting cast in the photographs include 'squash legend Jahangir Khan', representatives of many other sports, past presidents and prime ministers and a full collection of famous actors and singers. In one image alone, he seems to be upstaged – by a 35 kg fish which he is inspecting at a competition.

The authors can be forgiven: they had a prodigious life to illustrate. He was the only man to have won all three of Pakistan's highest civilian awards: Pride of Performance (in 1996 for his work as a surgeon), Tamgha E Imtiaz (in 2003 for services to sport), and Sitara E Imtiaz (in 2008 for social work and public service). He added an ICC gold medal in 2010.

They reveal that he carried out a world record 76,000 major surgical operations in a 31-year career (which works out at nearly 2,500 a year). His patients included Javed Miandad and his mother, Shahid Afridi, Michael Holding and Aravinda de Silva. He combined these with around 30 public appointments in medicine or sport, with 15 years as a radio and television commentator in both English and Urdu visiting every overseas Test country, and with over 25 years as a player in club and celebrity games (the captions make a point of saying number 3 batsman and demonstrating his grip for his off-spinners.)

Dr Shah's father was his inspiration. Ashgar Ali Shah was a leading public official and latterly a judge in pre-Partition India. He was renowned for probity and piety. (Patrick Eagar took a celebrated but unidentified photograph of him at prayer during the Lord's Test match in 1974 between England and Pakistan, published in his book *An Eye For Cricket*.)

Dr Shah returned to Pakistan from England in 1985, established himself as an orthopaedic surgeon in private hospitals in Karachi, and then set up his own specialist orthopaedic and trauma hospital, known as the AO Clinic, named for the surgical technique in bone surgery which it pioneered within Pakistan. It began with 20 beds and quickly expanded. Dr Shah committed 10 per cent of his revenues from the clinic to cricket, and in 1993 he was able to open his own purpose-built cricket ground in the North Nazimabad district of Karachi. It was named after his father, as was the main street in the neighbouring development: the others were named after famous cricketers. He insisted on a high-quality turf wicket and grass outfield, and within a few years it followed the Gaddafi Stadium in Lahore by installing floodlights. This enabled it to stage Pakistan's first televised T20 tournament during the month of Ramadan in 1996: it has been staged there ever since. The ground has also staged first-class Quaid-e-Azam trophy matches, national one-day and Under-19 championship matches, and the Asia Under-17 Cup in 2000. Most important, Dr Shah established free coaching camps for local children in June and July. They have continued and expanded their scope in the 25 years since.

In 2008, Dr Shah was nominated by the MQM party for a seat as a technocrat in the Sindh Assembly. He became firstly a sports adviser to the chief minister and then sports minister in his own right. He actively promoted hockey, table tennis, football and cycling in the province, as well as reviving traditional games such as *kabaadi* (the traditional game, with elements of wrestling, in which players try to occupy their opponents' terriroty), *malakhra* (a form of wrestling) and the 'donkey cart race'. He supported tapeball and had ambitious plans for the sport, which were unrealised at his death. However, he was most remembered for securing Pakistan's first international cricket visitors, a rather motley World XI, since the attack on the Sri Lankan touring team in 2009.

Dr Mohammad Ali Shah died in Houston in 2013 after a long battle against cancer. His legacy is carried on through his widow, Asma, a leading current promoter of women's cricket, and by his sons, Dr Imran Ali Shah and his younger brother, Dr Junaid Ali Shah. Both have followed him as surgeons and as patrons of Pakistan cricket.

Dr Imran (Mani) is a well-built energetic man in his early 40s. The energy survives a punishing routine of 16-hour days in the clinic and commuting at weekends to London to see his young family. They live there for security reasons: he has faced death threats. From politics or terrorism? No, simply from organised crime and extortion. Ruefully, he remarked, 'The only peace I get is on the plane.'

Was he a cricketer? Not much of one, in spite of early coaching in the garden from Javed Miandad. He was better at rugby (he still looks as though he would be useful in the scrum) and the major cricket talent went to his brother Junaid (Juni), who played for Pakistan A before taking up his own medical career. Dr Junaid is more involved in the detail of cricket issues. Owais Shah of Middlesex and England is a cousin, and played his first serious cricket at the stadium.

Dr Imran gave me a private tour. The stadium was preparing to stage a bodybuilding contest (part of a plan to expand its usage and promote other sports) but it is still primarily a cricket ground. On a beautiful day it was looking at its best with a backdrop of sunlit hills. He pointed out the Jonty Rhodes Pavilion (opened by the South African star on their tour of 1994, when they used the ground for net practice), the modern media centre, the electronic scoreboard, the Ladies Pavilion, and the spartan but secure accommodation for visiting teams. The capacity is 8,000.

The stadium earns some money from matches and events like the bodybuilding contest, but like his father, Dr Imran diverts a large chunk of his revenues from the AO Clinic to support it through the sports foundation named after his grandfather.

The coaching camps now take in 4,000 children each year. Everything is free, including a meal supervised by a nutritionist. For poor children's families, both the food and the nutritionist's advice are important. Returning children are monitored: for many this is the only check from any organisation on their health and welfare. The youngest child is only three and a half years old, 'but he's a little Javed Miandad'.

Dr Imran's mother Asma told me how hard it was to promote cricket for girls and women during the 1980s. Those days are gone, but the coaching camps are still segregated, boys in the morning, girls in the evening. She promotes a girls' Under-16 camp each year, and sponsors a women's team.

Given the demands of supporting cricket, it is as well that the clinic has expanded. Having begun with 20 beds, it now has 120, almost always in full occupancy. Dr Imran told me that Karachi produces high demand for its services. 'There are many traffic accidents with no seatbelts and no airbags, so there are many cases of head and spinal trauma. Moreover, a lot of patients have poor nutrition which produces a different pattern of fractures.' However, the clinic also has a growing number of foreign 'health tourists' for hip and knee operations.

He would like the next generation to continue the family record of service. 'My daughter is now eight [as of October 2015] and playing cricket in London. She cannot speak Urdu and I think if she does not come back soon it will be too late.' The security situation has improved and he hopes that she and her sister (age seven) and brother (three) might be able to return to Karachi in 2016.

Apart from security concerns, he knows that his family would face the stress of the infighting which accompanies cricket in Pakistan, particularly Karachi. 'There is so much backstabbing here, and people fight constantly for status and control.' He cited the example of Nadeem Omar. 'He was a genuine man. He scared people because he was incorruptible. So did my father. He stood for the Presidency of the Karachi Cricket Association but he was kept out by people who were afraid of him. My father made it eventually and changed the face of cricket in Karachi.'

Whatever decision he makes about his children, Dr Imran Ali Shah will maintain his father's legacy.

His immediate ambition is to open the nets in the stadium for 24 hours a day. 'We have thousands of shift-workers in Karachi. They deserve somewhere to play when they finish in the middle of the night.'

NADEEM OMAR: SINGER, SAILOR, RICH MAN, SPORTSMAN

Talc is a more fascinating product than anyone could imagine. It does much more than powder babies and feet. It is also needed for fire extinguishers, plastics, shoe polish, leather, printers' ink, soap, chewing gum and confectionery, and a wide variety of manufacturing processes.

Nadeem Omar's company, Omar Associates, supplies the whitest and finest talc in the world, from deep mines in Pakistan's Khyber-Pakhtunkhwa province. It also extracts high-quality sand and gravel for water filtration. Logically enough, it also rents out earth-moving equipment for major construction projects in Pakistan. Recently it ventured into pesticides. More tangentially, it also imports coffee-makers, ovens and deep-fat fryers for the catering business.

It has also supported thousands of Pakistan cricketers of all ages, some directly as players and employees, many more through a range of grassroots activities. In November 2014, it came to the rescue of Pakistan's hockey team. Apart from running this diverse business, Nadeem Omar also found time in his life to play a lot of cricket himself, to have years of adventure as a merchant seaman, and to become a singer of international reputation.

He was born in Karachi in 1957, the eldest of three children, but his life changed radically in early childhood when his family moved to Kaduna in northern Nigeria. His father worked there for four years as a consultant engineer on the construction of the local waterworks. 'I think my father and I and my younger brother were the first people to play cricket in that part of Nigeria. We had some stumps and a bat made out of some ash wood – and that's where my cricket bug started.'

He had another decisive experience in Nigeria. 'My father had four LP records. They were all of KL Saigal. I listened to them all the time and sang all the songs, so did my father.' The first superstar of Indian cinema, Saigal died of alcoholism in 1947 aged only 42, but managed to perform nearly 200 songs in 142 films, most of them composed by Rai Chand Boral, the father of Indian film music. On returning to Pakistan, Nadeem Omar studied singing under a tutor. Later, he would assemble his own band and perform Saigal's songs in public. He has given Saigal concerts and made recordings of his versions of the songs, and helped to bring Saigal back into fashion throughout the Indian subcontinent.

On return to Pakistan, Nadeem Omar went to Cantt public school in Karachi. It had nine cricket fields, more than any other school in Karachi, and was a well-known nursery for cricketers. Wasim Bari, Pakistan's greatest wicketkeeper, was there a few years ahead of him. 'My younger brother was in the first XI, I was only in the second, but we both played and watched a lot of cricket.'

Aged 17, he resisted the idea of joining the family business and instead joined the Merchant Marine Academy. On graduation he joined the Pakistan National Shipping Corporation and visited most of the ports of the world. In 1978, sailing from Gibraltar across the Atlantic, he survived a terrifying storm which sank eight other ships. His own ship's speed was reduced from its normal 22 knots to 3 knots. It took 18 days instead of the usual seven or eight to reach the United States and they had to be diverted to New York from Philadelphia.

'At sea, I dropped out of the cricket race, but we kept in touch with English county cricket scores and Test matches through our radio officer. He would have all the reports for us from the BBC. We heard about Majid Khan's exploits for Glamorgan and all the other Pakistani cricketers in county cricket.'

When he finally left the merchant navy at 34, he was a chief officer and had a master's certificate, although he never had his own ship. He was now ready to join the family firm, which was then focused on construction and infrastructure projects. His interest in cricket revived and he began to play regular club cricket. He is modest about his achievements ('nothing very noticeable and just an ordinary off-spinner') but he can be persuaded to mention two centuries and a quickfire partnership against the renowned Karachi Gymkhana club which helped his team to score 274 in a 25-over match.

More importantly, he opened up a club initially called Pakistan CC which became the Omar Associates team. Its first major recruit was the leg-spinner Danish Kaneria, and it has now become one of the leading Patron's teams in Pakistan. It has been especially successful in Ramadan T20 matches during the last five years. 'Played 138, won 132. We think that's a world record.' It has also played two finals at grade 2 level and narrowly missed becoming the first privately owned team in Pakistan to qualify for first-class matches at grade 1. Recent talent includes the Test players Asad Shafiq, Sarfraz Ahmed, Nasir Jamshed, Anwar Ali and the giant fast bowler Mohammad Irfan. 'He was always tall and we think he has now reached seven feet one inch. A very nice guy. Our manager, Azam Khan, has made a huge contribution. He had Mohammad Irfan put up at the Dr Mohammad Ali Shah academy, and looked after him.'

Significantly, the club is now helping the rehabilitation of Mohammad Amir, after he had completed the ban following his criminal conviction for match-fixing. 'There was controversy, but he has been a fine addition. I think he is a changed character. He is bowling well and I think he just needs some more matches to get his rhythm back. He has served his sentence and I always believe people should be forgiven.'

Omar Associates currently supports 70 former first-class cricketers, either by helping them establish their own businesses or, for those of limited education, finding them jobs to match their abilities within the business. 'I have never had a bad return from any of the cricketers employed by my team. None of them have ever got above themselves. There is a big gulf in income between the top players and those just below, so we encourage all our players to think of their future after cricket and present themselves well to the public. Cricketers respond to fair treatment.'

In all, Omar Associates maintains seven or eight teams, including Under-16s and Under-19s, veterans and a women's team which in 2015 won the Benazir Cup, the only women's trophy in Pakistan. Nadeem Omar is also involved as player and patron with the Pakistan Veterans (they tour as the Panthers). Apart from running a nationwide veterans trophy, they have been reviving school cricket by arranging a televised inter-schools championship for the last seven or eight years. 'But Pakistan still does not do enough for school cricket. It used to have a really good system for school and club cricket, but we are losing infrastructure and school cricket goes on shrinking.'

He has also set up the Omar Sports Fund, which helps other sports in addition to cricket. 'We are sponsoring a winter inter-schools Olympic Championship with the aim of finding some athletes for Tokyo 2020. It's a farfetched dream, but you've got to try.' (Astonishingly for a sports-loving nation of 180 million people, Pakistan has not won any Olympic medals since the hockey team's bronze at Barcelona 1992.)

In November 2014, he discovered from watching television that the Pakistan hockey team was planning to play in black armbands in the forthcoming Champions Trophy, in protest that their playing contracts had not been honoured by the cash-strapped Pakistan Hockey Federation. They threatened an outright boycott when the federation proposed to send them to India by bus and cancel their practice matches to save their hotel bills. 'When I heard that I went live on TV and said I will put up the funds. My idea was that others should pitch in – but I ended up with the whole bill.'[4]

He went to the tournament in Bhubaneswar (near Cuttack), and watched Pakistan lose their first three games. 'People said I should tell the team to remove our logo from their shirts. But I talked to the coach and the boys. They were all very positive and asked for a little time.' The team did manage to qualify for the quarter-final, which they won. Then they beat India 3-2 in the semi-final. They were jeered by the crowd, and the players retaliated by removing their shirts and making some rude gestures. Their two best players were banned just a few hours before the final, but they lost only narrowly and the silver medal was Pakistan's first hockey honour for a long time.

The result made him decide to give permanent support to Pakistan hockey. Omar Associates would run a team of its own in domestic tournament,[5] and help to restore the rundown tartan pitch in the Pakistan Hockey Club.

Nadeem Omar was frustrated in his bid to become president of the Karachi Cricket Association on a 'reform' ticket against an 'old guard' which had kept power, with a few changes of faces, for 35 years. 'I could see that boys and clubs had no funds and infrastructure was at its lowest level. I knew that we needed a new platform to pull in new funding. We had television debates and I told people that the present system simply was not working.' He was supported by an array of Test players, but as is characteristic of Pakistan cricket politics, this was actually turned against him, and he was accused of recruiting them to endorse him. 'I said I had not invited them for fun but because they could give us good advice, because they had better technical knowledge of the game. We then had no former Test cricketers running the show in a city the size of Karachi.'

He had many promises of support but refused to promise any

4 See also 'Cricket fan throws lifeline to cash-strapped Pakistan hockey team,' *Indian Express*, 2 December 2014.
5 'Omar gives Pakistan hockey shot in the arm,' *The International News* (Pakistan), 21 December 2014.

funding in exchange. So in the end, they melted away and voted back the 'old guard'.

In spite of the setback, his support for cricket and other sports will continue and his ambitions for cricket in Karachi and Pakistan are undimmed. In fact, he has just purchased one of the five franchises in the new Pakistan T20 SuperLeague to be played in the UAE, Quetta Gladiators. Kevin Pietersen, Kumar Sangakkara and Pakistan's Sarfraz Ahmed will play for them; Moin Khan will be their coach, Viv Richards their mentor.[6] Nadeem Omar is also convinced that he is not alone. 'There are plenty of possible sponsors for Pakistan cricket who would support the infrastructure which it needs – if they were convinced that their money would be properly used.'

6 They finished as runners-up in the first series.

31

GANDER OF LAHORE:
A LOCAL SHRINE TO CRICKET

Two sports shops in Lahore, both named Gander, are a bridge to the history of Pakistan cricket and a barometer of its current health.

Gander & Co and the Gander Sports Corporation were once part of a larger business in Lahore's busy Mall Road, which was founded in 1943. It had some imposing neighbours: Smith & Campbell (chemists), Jenn & Ellerton (records and musical instruments), Phipson (general trading and imported liquor). A family dispute led the original Gander business to be divided into three. However, two Gander offshoots have survived in Mall Road, although the three big neighbours have all gone. So have two other landmark sports shops in Lahore, Essa Sports and Physical Sports.

Both Gander shops are still run by the original family, Gander & Co by Mr Hussain Malik, grandson of the founder, and the Gander Sports Corporation by his cousin-in-law Mrs Azmat Humayun.

They are proper sports shops, particularly for cricket. On a much smaller scale, they are a throwback to Lillywhites of London in its great days, before it collapsed into a pitiful purveyor of labelled leisurewear. Both shops are pokey and crammed with sporting implements. They do sell clothing and footwear – but intended for use in actual sport rather than as garb for loungers and loafers too idle to dress. Even without a power cut, both shops are very dimly lit, like shrines.

Cricket still predominates but it is beginning to lose ground to tape-ball and other street-friendly sports. Mrs Humayun also does a big line in carom boards and other indoor games. Mr Malik has a bigger range for outdoor sports, particularly soccer and basketball. Revealingly, he sells quite a few lifejackets in all sizes, because outside of the best schools and the exclusive clubs there are few opportunities for local children to get swimming lessons.

Mr Malik has much to say about the old days. 'We've had a shop here since the beginning,' he told us. 'Gul Mohammed, who played for India before Partition and Pakistan afterwards, often used to drop by in the evenings. Nazar Mohammad, Fazal Mahmood, Imtiaz Ahmed were regular customers, and so was Khan Mohammad when he was in Pakistan.[1] They all bought their kit off the peg and they never made any special demands. It was not commercialised like now.'

The next generation, particularly those with English county experience, brought with them some awareness of marketing and promotion. 'Imran Khan and Majid Khan used to come and then we had Javed Miandad, Zaheer Abbas and Intikhab Alam. They were famous and got some discounts for giving endorsements. I remember that after the Edgbaston Test in 1971 we promoted a bat called the Zaheer 274.' And what about the present generation? 'We don't see any of them. It's another world now – they get all their stuff under sponsorship from Sialkot.' [The provincial city in Pakistan which has become the world's biggest manufacturing centre for sporting goods.]

In showing off their stock, both he and Mrs Humayun offered a practical lesson in the consumer economics of Pakistan cricket. Their best-quality items, including bats from English willow, are a half and sometimes even a third of their retail price in England. We totted up the cost of a complete new kit for a cricket-crazed 12-year-old – something around 10,000 rupees (around £65 at the prevailing exchange rate). The same experience in England regularly turns parents ashen-faced and leaves them with little change from £200.

However, one must then compare salaries. For convenience, we

1 Khan Mohammad was the first Pakistani to play regular English league cricket.

looked at teachers. According to the website www.salaryexplorer.com the median monthly salary for a teacher in Lahore was then 41,000 rupees (around £260). The same source gave the comparable figure for a London teacher as £2,835. Without factoring in complications such as taxation and housing costs, it was clear that Lahori teachers would have to work much longer than those in London to buy cricket kit for their children.

And where would they use it? Both proprietors confirmed the picture we had received from many others. 'There are fewer open spaces than before,' said Mrs Humayun. 'The government schools have no sports grounds,' said Mr Malik, 'although there are still some good grounds in private schools. If you have a big enough house, it is much easier to buy your kids a good basketball board and a hoop.'

Although both shops are becoming more reliant on other sports, Lahore's cricket lovers can still depend on them for the foreseeable future. 'We're holding on,' said Mrs Humayun, and Mr Malik commented, 'Our cricket business is good these days because of Pakistan's recent record in Tests.' It would be a loss to sport and history if they ever changed their minds.

32

SURVIVORS OF THE BLACKEST DAY

On 3 March 2009, Pakistan had the blackest day in cricket history. The bus carrying the Sri Lankan team to the second Test match was attacked by terrorists on the way to the Gaddafi Stadium in Lahore, as was the minivan carrying match officials. In less than ten minutes, the attackers were able to use AK-47 assault rifles, hand grenades, rockets, claymores and explosive charges against their virtually helpless targets. Seven Sri Lankans were wounded, two of them seriously. So were their assistant coach, Paul Farbrace, and four of the match officials. The minivan driver was killed, as were seven other Pakistanis, six from the ambushed police escort, the other a traffic warden.

Compounding the horror of the actual attack was the response of Pakistan's leaders, a dismal exhibition of denial and buckpassing. The PCB, led by Ijaz Butt, actually demanded that the ICC should penalise one of the wounded victims, Chris Broad, for criticising the security arrangements. The ICC ignored this and Pakistan's long international exile began.[1]

Two Pakistanis on that awful day showed conspicuously more judgement and courage than those in authority. One was Mehr Mohammad Khalil, who drove the Sri Lankans' bus and succeeded, while still under

1 P Oborne, op. cit., p.482.

fire, in getting them into the sanctuary of the Gaddafi Stadium. The other was Abdul Sami Khan, the PCB's liaison officer in the official minivan.

They told their stories of that day and its aftermath – vivid, authentic, and sometimes at odds with the established versions.

THE HEROIC DRIVER

Mehr Mohammad Khalil is a compact man with neat features and a quiet manner. He met us in the showroom of his brother-in-law's motorcycle business, in the largely working-class Bakkar Mandi area of Lahore. For some time after the attack, he and his family made a new life in Morocco. But they came back in 2012, although they were still a target for terrorists, and remain so to this day. 'Morocco was beautiful,' he told me, 'but my heart was always in Lahore. I grew up in the streets in this district, playing all sorts of games, so I had to come back.' Did those street games include cricket? 'No, I played *kabaadi* [for which, see page 235].'

Contrary to many reports, he was not working for the PCB when the attack was made, but for a specialist independent company under contract to them. A few years previously, he had been on call for eight days for another set of VIPs: President George Bush Jnr, and entourage, on a state visit to President Musharraf. 'I saw Bush try to play cricket in the net in the US embassy.'

A love of travel determined his career, after leaving high school in his teens. 'My father was a handyman. He was the only breadwinner for our family. We didn't have much money. I always wanted to see different cities, and I asked if I could join a friend of mine who was working as a conductor in a long-distance bus company. I worked with him as a conductor, but I found most passengers were very rude. They kept grabbing me and my partner. I thought this was demeaning, and that there would be more respect for me as a driver, where I would be isolated from the passengers. So I started practising manoeuvres in the bus when the driver was not there. I got my licence in 1993 and started driving inter-city buses. I have been driving ever since.'

Back on duty for the Sri Lankan visit, he drove them to the first two days of the Test match, a run-feast in which Sri Lanka were all out for 606 and Pakistan replied with 110 for one.

'I wasn't allowed to go home. The security was very strict and they kept me overnight at the Pearl Continental, where the teams were staying. Every night, I used to hear the police superintendent giving a pep talk to his officers. "If something happens, don't run, face it bravely."

'I drove the bus on the third morning and everything was fine when I reached Liberty Market and the roundabout. In front of me was one policeman on a motorbike, a jeep with the officer who gave the pep talk, two police vans, an ambulance and other vehicles.' However, there was no armed guard on the bus itself and the escort was caught totally by surprise.

'The first firing I heard came from behind me. I thought it was fireworks from people in Lahore celebrating our team. Then a white Hyundai car appeared in front of me, in a flash. A man came out and started firing at me directly, from only a few yards away. Both escort jeeps were hit. One turned left towards the market, the other turned right. That left the bus on its own. It was under attack from all sides. The bullets were like a hailstorm. The Sri Lankan players left their seats and squeezed into a little space underneath. The bus was full of noise, with people yelling and shouting.

'My first reaction was to jump out and save my life, but I heard some player shouting, "Go, go, go!"' This was Tillakaratne Dilshan: with great courage, he had raised his head and seen the only possible means of escape. 'So I made a decision. If I fled, I might get killed and so would everyone else. If I stayed, I might get killed but might save some lives. So I floored the gas.' By now the terrorists had shot out the tyres, but the bus got moving. 'The terrorists fired a rocket but I was turning the bus and it missed. Then they threw hand grenades under the bus, but I drove on and they all exploded afterwards. Then twelve terrorists started firing from all sides. I drove on and reached the stadium.' In all this time, he was not aware of anyone firing back in defence of the bus.

Providentially, the stadium staff had not realised what had happened – and the gates were opened for the bus in the normal way. 'I raised the alarm with the police officer in the stadium and told him to call an ambulance for the injured players. Although the police could hear the bullets and rockets and grenades, they did not know about the attack until I told them.'

He is certain that the terrorists planned to kill him to immobilise the bus and do what they wanted with his passengers. Six years on, he told me, 'I still get goose-pimples when I think about the attack.' Did he receive any kind of treatment or counselling for the trauma? 'That isn't done here and I never needed it. I was a kabaddi player and a sportsman. When I went to President Zardari to receive a gallantry medal, there was a brigadier sitting nearby. He asked if I had had any military training. I told him no. He said I had kept my nerves together when even trained soldiers could have lost their nerve. I told him my parents' prayers had got me through.'

Mehr Mohammad Khalil also received decorations from two provincial governments and (rather later) a certificate of merit from the PCB. With them came grants totalling 1.8 million rupees (equivalent to about £12,000). He was also honoured by the US Congress. But nothing matched his reception in Sri Lanka a few months after the attack as the man who had saved their cricketers' lives.

'The president invited me and my wife as state guests. He told them to give us the same protocol as a head of state and we were given the same hotel room as Pakistan's Prime Minister Gilani. When they took us to their temples, we were greeted like gods.' Eagerly, he showed me the photographs. One sequence was especially magical: the two of them meeting a highly decorated elephant, with what appears to be a giant smile on its face. He received a high decoration and another grant of 500,000 rupees (around £2,700). There were non-stop special features on him in the Sri Lankan media.

The highlight of his visit came from his own remarkable request. 'I looked out of our hotel room and saw a bus depot. I asked if I could visit. The Pakistani protocol officer said it would be a security risk. I said there would be no risk. I had gained prestige and respect from driving a bus and I would like to go there. So I did visit, and the owner asked what he could do for me. I asked if I could drive one of the buses. He said, "This bus belongs to you." So I had a little test drive and it made the front pages the next day in Colombo.' This must represent the ultimate busman's holiday.

He is still in regular touch with the Sri Lankan players, particularly Mahela Jayawardene, Muttiah Muralitharan and Kumar Sangakkara, who paid public tribute to him when he delivered his memorable 'Spirit of Cricket' lecture at Lord's in 2011.

Mehr Mohammad Khalil is now comfortably off. He runs his own bus business and can afford to spend money on his family. When the cash awards began to arrive, his first thought was for his mother. She told him she had long wanted to visit holy Mecca. He could have arranged a package tour, but instead procured visas at once and escorted her there himself.

However, despite his decorations and awards, we could not help feeling that this quiet hero is not valued by authority in his country as he should be. When we met him, he had just appeared as a celebrity guest at the one-day international series against Zimbabwe, the first, brief, visit of any kind to Pakistan by a Test-playing country since the terrorist attack.

But his invitation came from a private television network, not the PCB. We asked if he had ever received any commercial offers to endorse products or services, or to come aboard any special business opportunities. No. Had he been asked to take part in any kind of public campaign (driver safety would be a good subject)? No. Had he been approached by any political party or movement?

For the first time, this equable man showed some bitterness. 'That is not how things are in Pakistan. We have the same feudal system as always. An honest educated, decent person will never have a chance in politics.'

THE RESOLUTE LAWYER

It has become much harder to see Abdul Sami Khan than it was six years ago, when he served as the PCB's unpaid liaison officer for the Test series against Sri Lanka. In 2012, he was appointed to the Lahore High Court bench, and soon acquired a reputation as a hardworking judge who could be trusted to take on contentious trials and appeals. Such judges are often threatened, particularly if the case involves terrorism or organised crime. He gave an interview as an exceptional favour.

He is a tall, imposing man, but he was almost hidden at his desk behind a mountain of files. 'Ongoing cases. All death sentences,' he added with a dramatic gesture. 'This is a very crime-ridden society. People kill for nothing.'

What did his job mean as liaison officer, and how did he get it?

'Essentially, I had to look after all the match officials, and arrange anything they wanted, such as trips or shopping. I would travel with them constantly. I remember that Chris Broad, the match referee, liked to play golf and I would take him to the Royal Palm Club. I was a lawyer with a record as a first-class cricketer. I played nearly a hundred matches as a batsman who could bowl a little bit – although I was better than many regular bowlers.'

He is proud of that record and picked out some highlights. His main team was the Railways, whom he eventually captained. In only his second full season, 1981-82, he opened the batting for them in a 45-over match and set a new Pakistan record by thrashing 163 not out against South Zone.

He became liaison officer because 'there was a shortage of educated cricketers who could speak to the Sri Lankans, and the ICC officials in English.' He had three seasons as a league professional in England during the 1980s, first with Bridlington in the Bradford Senior League, then with Hunsworth in the Huddersfield League, then with Burnafield, in Newcastle-upon-Tyne. 'I left them and they hired Wasim Akram to replace me! I was popular with all those clubs because of my habits – no drinking and no visits to the casino.' After retiring as a player, he served the PCB and the Asian Cricket Council as an elite match referee for several years. With gusto, he told two stories of facing down Bob Woolmer and ICC officials in disputes over tournament rules.

He comes from a family with a strong sense of public service. 'My great grandfather was the chief judicial and revenue officer for the Maharajah of Patiala. After the debacle [his term for Partition] our family migrated and started all over again in Lahore. I was born there in 1958. My father was a gem of a person. He got me into the Sacred Heart School and from there I was admitted to Government College, Lahore, where I gained my law degree.'

He came back to the day in Lahore. 'I had no reason to think anything was going to happen. The Karachi Test had passed quietly, and so had the first two days of the Lahore Test. On the third day, Chris Broad and umpire Ahsan Raza delayed having their breakfast in the Pearl Continental hotel. I was in the van and the convoy was waiting to move. I phoned Ahsan Raza on his cellphone and told him it was getting late.' Raza and Broad joined the minivan. To save a little time, the fourth umpire Nadim Ghouri slipped into the back seat and Ahsan Raza took over his usual place. It was nearly a fatal switch for Ahsan Raza, who was shot in the abdomen. But for the late breakfast, Ghouri would have taken the bullet instead.

Judge Abdul Sami Khan rebutted criticisms of the security arrangements. 'We had security. There was a special camp of police in the hotel, twenty-four hours a day. They always provided an escort whenever anyone wanted to go anywhere. When the convoy set off, there was security in front of us and behind us. There was no slackness. The traffic was sealed off and the convoy were the only moving vehicles. We were forced to slow at the roundabout, but all the entry points to it were sealed. Unfortunately, the attack was very well planned. The police escort took the initial fire, and six or seven were killed right away, and others were injured. They did manage to fire back, although only a few shots, using whatever weapons they were carrying. Maybe that is why the terrorists did not come to our van, otherwise the story might have been different.'

He remembered hearing a blast and then firing began from the front of the convoy. 'The Sri Lankan team bus stopped and so did our wagon. Our driver, Zafar Khan, was hit in the abdomen.' The team bus was immobile for about 15 to 20 seconds, and then he saw Mehr Mohammad Khalil drive it away. 'Firing continued on our wagon, and our driver was hit again, and died. I still feel sorry for him – he was a fantastic man. I was sitting right beside him on the front seat. Ahsan Raza was wounded and I was hit in the shoulder.'

Many accounts have suggested that Ahsan Raza shielded Chris Broad and saved his life, but Judge Abdul Sami Khan had a different account. 'Suddenly, the door of our wagon opened and an elite forces officer entered and jumped on Chris Broad in order to save him. That officer was hit as the firing continued for fifteen to twenty minutes. Eventually, the firing slowed down and I opened the driver's door of our van and pushed out the dead body of the driver. I saw another elite forces officer lying injured in the road, and I asked him to drive the van. He got onto the driver's seat and took us inside the Gaddafi Stadium, where the Sri Lankan team bus had already arrived.'

He and the other wounded were taken to hospital. He made a point of visiting Ahsan Raza. 'He was in a terrible state with a big hole in his belly.' Then he was assessed himself. 'On the first day, they said the bullet was not there, but I felt a lot of pain, so I went back to the hospital and told them they were wrong and I was right.' (Clearly, this has been a common experience between him and authority.) 'They found bullets in my shoulder and my back and removed them. I have had some permanent damage.' Like Mehr Mohammad Khalil, he disdained treatment for post-traumatic stress disorder. 'God saved me. I just got on with my job. I behaved as a normal person. I thought all the time, how could I save these people? I thought that if Chris Broad or Simon Taufel were killed, there would be a reaction against the whole cricket structure in Pakistan.'

Remarkably, despite an abundance of video evidence, no one has been convicted in Pakistan for the attack on the Sri Lankan cricketers, although the alleged mastermind, Dr Usman, was executed in December 2014 for other terrorist offences.[2]

---

2 See 'Attack on SL cricket team: mastermind executed,' *Daily Mirror* (Sri Lanka), 20 December 2014 and www.dailymirror.lk/59375.

The Judge is convinced that the attack was intended as a kidnapping. Local terrorists were aiming to abduct the Sri Lankan team, and the match officials, and exchange them for some of their members then in jail. He was confident that the attackers, and other terrorist groups, were now cornered or in hiding. Terrorism had been driven out of Pakistan's major cities, but 'ordinary crime still goes on, just as in all countries. We are dealing with that here!' He made another dramatic gesture over the death penalty files in his bulging in-tray.

Since joining the Lahore bench, he has had no time for cricket, except in 2013 when he took on the sensitive job of being the PCB's election commissioner. 'Everyone in Pakistan wanted me to do something for them. I never listened.' The elections for the Karachi Cricket Association produced many writs in the High Court. There were numerous 'ghost clubs' trying to vote, but he eliminated them all. Most withdrew before he could even scrutinise their papers.

He has already been identified as a potential future chairman of the PCB. 'Maybe when I retire. All the bad people will run away the moment I step in.'

Surprisingly, he has never met Mehr Mohammad Khalil. Were he ever to take over the PCB, he might find it constructive to compare notes with the other man who did his duty for Pakistan cricket on its blackest day.

33

THE CRICKET LIFE OF DR AQ KHAN

By Najum Latif

The long passage below is taken from the verbatim record of an interview of Dr AQ Khan by Najum Latif. Securing this interview was a remarkable achievement: it is the first given by Dr Khan for ten years. We have made use of the greater part – all the passages which relate to cricket – in the words of Dr Khan and Najum Latif. The full interview, whose non-cricket passages are of great historic and cultural interest, will be published separately.

Richard Heller and Peter Oborne

After being vigilantly screened and cleared by security, I was ushered into the large sitting-room of the 'father of the Pakistan atom bomb' Dr Abdul Qadeer Khan. It was a nicely decorated room: fine paintings adorned the walls, seven or eight beautiful Islamic swords in their scabbards were mounted tastefully on one, while a gas heater maintained an ambient temperature. Dr Abdul Qadeer Khan sat on a large comfortable chair. He received me warmly and courteously and said, 'Come Mian [a respectful form of address], sit here next to me.' He was extremely cultured, soft spoken and very well mannered with a kind and gentle voice.

NL: Thank you for granting me the opportunity to come and call on you.

AQK: Well, you said that you had to meet the deadline and although I am not feeling too well with a dry cough, I thought I should see you. After all, who has the time to sit down to answer the 100 questions you sent me?!

NL: I am very grateful to you for being so considerate. You don't have to answer all the 100 questions. You may answer the ones you like to answer. Thank you.

EARLY CRICKET AND LIFE IN BHOPAL

NL: Sir, you lived in Bhopal for the first sixteen years of your life. Could you describe your early cricket experience there?

AQK: I played cricket in my high school there and there used to be a ground near our house where I played most of my cricket during those days.

NL: Did you have family members who were cricketers or cricket enthusiasts?

AQK: No, not really.

NL: Did you play at school? If so, what were your strengths as a player?

AQK: Although I could bowl fast, I preferred to bat at number 5 or number 6.

NL: Did any of your friends and schoolmates achieve success at cricket?

AQK: We had Ahmed Khan and Ansar, a fellow of small height in our team. He used to be a superb batsman.

NL: Who were your early cricket heroes and did you have an opportunity to watch them or even meet them?

AQK: None in particular and I did not meet any famous cricketers at that time.

NL: Do you remember the Pakistan cricket team touring India under Kardar in 1952?

AQK: No. My real interest in cricket was flamed by the 1954

victory of Pakistan at The Oval where Fazal Mahmood had bowled splendidly. Wazir Mohammad was also a very good player. He had batted splendidly in The Oval Test to score an unbeaten 42 runs. Pakistan could not have won without his courageous batting against Tyson.

NL: Since there was no television then, did you hear cricket commentaries on the radio?

AQK: Oh, absolutely yes. We used to live near the Jubilee cinema in a building on Bunder Road. At the corner of our building, there used to be a *paan* shop [betel leaf chewing]. There used to be a radio there and the owner used to wear just an undershirt with a *lungi* [cloth wrap] underneath. He kept a blackboard on the side of his shop and would write the scores on it with a chalk. We would ask him, '*Chacha* [uncle], what is the score?' It was so much fun listening to the commentary and see the board being updated. We were very fond of Hanif Mohammad and whenever he would get out, there used to be a hush in the listeners and the crowd at the ground. One of the listeners to the commentary used to be an old man whom we called *Barray Mian* [elderly gentleman]. We would ask him: how did Hanif get out? Now there was no television there but this *Barray Mian* would get up and take a stance and recreate the whole scene through his imagination. He would look up as if the bowler was coming and would play an imaginary shot and then would look sadly towards the slip and say, see, this is how Hanif played and there he got caught in the slips. Then for minutes he remained looking at the slip position.

NL: Did you hear the running commentaries of the Tests? How do you remember Omar Kureishi and Jamsheed Marker as commentators and who was your favourite commentator?

AQK: Yes, I was fond of listening to the radio commentaries of the Tests. Both Omar Kureishi and Jamsheed Marker

were my favourite commentators. They were the best
ever. They made a great team and were outstanding. No
one has been able to match their performance till today.
They used to create such a scene in your imagination,
as if you were watching it yourself. Nowadays, when
you are actually seeing a match being played on the
TV and someone starts to narrate it, it looks rather silly
because you can see what is happening. There is no need
of a ball-by-ball description. They should only describe
important points and other interesting things to make
it enjoyable.

NL: Your father Khan Abdul Ghafoor Khan was an educa-
tionist and also worked as the Inspector of Schools and
Superintendent of Schools. Did he encourage cricket in
schools?

AQK: Although my father believed in the 'healthy bodies will
have healthy minds' theory, he laid most of his emphasis on academics. He had graduated in 1905 from the
University of Nagpur and completed his teaching course
in 1907 at Jabalpur. Most of his service was spread over
in the region of CP (Central Provinces) at Nagpur and
Jabalpur. He was a highly enlightened person and understood the importance of sports. He led a very responsible
life and was a devout Muslim. His salary at that time used
to be 200 rupees per month but gold was priced at 15
rupees per tola [about 12 grams]. So we lived a comfortable life. In fact, we lived a lavish life at Bhopal. My father
was very strict not to let us tease any bird or animal. He
disliked cruelty and if he saw a slingshot in my hand he
would be furious. Therefore none of us were ever cruel to
birds and animals.

NL: Your father stayed back and died in Bhopal. Did you ever
visit his grave?

AQK: Yes, I did in 1961 and then in 1967, soon after I got married, when I took my wife with me.

NL: You as the youngest among your brothers played hockey, *Gilli Danda* [a traditional game played with a stick and an oval piece of wood], flew kites and swam and went fishing in the lakes of Bhopal in your schooldays, but was cricket on your mind too?

AQK: Bhopal was a very beautiful place, perhaps one of the most beautiful in the world. It had five lakes, all of them big. One was so huge that you could not see across to its other banks. Not only did I love swimming in them but I would go there fishing with my friends. The lakes were full of fish and we could easily catch quite a few and then fry them on the banks of the lakes and eat them. I can never forget those lovely days. There was also plenty of wildlife there that included tigers and leopards. Yes, cricket was there too, but I was involved in all sports then.

NL: Did you enjoy jumping over the walls of the fruit gardens to get mangoes, grapefruits and guavas?

AQK: [Laughs] You know, we had many fruit trees in our own house, but stealing fruit from a garden has its own thrill and joy. Yes, my friends and I scaled the walls of gardens with the gardeners chasing us. It was so much fun. I am still fond of mangoes, guavas and papayas.

NL: The PCB chairman, Shaharyar Mohammad Khan, is the son of Princess Abida of Bhopal. Do you have any relations with him or his family?

AQK: Indeed, I have. Our families have known each other from Bhopal. Whenever Shaharyar Mian comes to Islamabad he often comes to see me and have a meal with me. He is a very fine gentleman. Bhopal was a great place. There was no discrimination between the rich and the poor there. Everyone was friendly and courteous. There was prosperity. There was no unemployment and there were no beggars around. Shaharyar Sahib's mother herself used to feed me with her own hand.

DEPARTURE FOR PAKISTAN

NL: You left Bhopal as a boy [aged 16] and travelled alone by
       train to Munabao via Ajmer, Looni, Chittor and Baramir.
       The train conductor besides other things even took away
       your pen from you. What were your feelings?

AQK: I felt great despair and helplessness. It was 14 August
       1952 when I crossed over to Pakistan. Munabao is the
       last Indian station. It had a lovely platform. Since they
       were preparing to celebrate their independence day on
       15 August, there were lights, buntings, flags all over the
       place. There were fans running on the station and it was
       terribly hot. There were so many shops of sweets and other
       eatables.

*At this point Dr Abdul Qadeer Khan ordered me tea, and we were joined
by his wife, Mrs Henny Khan. They married in 1964 and have two daughters, Dina and Ayesha. Mrs Khan was extremely pleasant and charming.
She has beautiful deep green eyes. I reminded them that my daughter
Ambereen and a schoolfriend had been their house guests in 1987, and that
my daughter was very interested in cats and dogs. Dr Abdul Qadeer Khan
told me that there were about twenty cats in the house. We were joined by
their daughter Dina, who is tall, like her father. She greeted me warmly.*

I put a question to Mrs Henny Khan.

NL: I had read an interview of yours where you said that when
       you first came to Pakistan you were very upset by the way
       people stared at you?

HK: Oh, heavens! Yes, it was very upsetting then and still is.
       In those days I was not used to this trait, but now I just
       ignore it. I always dressed conservatively, as you can see I
       am wearing slacks and not a skirt, but people still stare.
       By the way, that was the only interview I ever gave. It was
       the first and the last.

AQK: Well, I don't mind if she wears a skirt or whatever she likes.

HK: It does not matter to me either, as long as I can keep my husband happy.

AQK: She has played a major role in the success of my life. When we lived abroad, we did not have a TV at home. After an evening stroll, we used to study together. In those days, there used to be great movies with lovely stories, unlike today's useless violent films. So once a week, we went to watch a movie.

Tea and chicken patties were brought in and Mrs. Khan and Dina excused themselves.

A nurse remained in attendance. Dr Abdul Qadeer Khan would cough occasionally. Since this was troubling him, she put a plastic mask on his face as a nebuliser. But we continued to talk and he would remove the plastic mask to speak and answer my questions.

NL: You walked barefoot in the hot sand for eight kilometres, carrying your box of books on your head to Pakistan. What kept your spirits going?

AQK: Crossing over from Munabao into Pakistan was an ordeal. It was blisteringly hot and my feet would sink in the sand which was very hot and would go into my shoes and make it difficult to walk. So I removed my shoes and hung them around my neck and walked barefoot with the box on my head. In contrast to the lit-up Munabao station, the Pakistan side looked deserted and dismal. I knew there was no point of return for me and I persevered to carry on going. I arrived by train at the Karachi city station on McLeod Road [now II Chundrigar Road]. After coming out of the station, I took a Victoria [horse-drawn carriage] to go to Nazimabad where my sister and brother-in-law lived. The carriage took the route of Garden Road–Gandhi Garden–Lawrence Road–Lasbela and on to Nazimabad. It took *many hours* to get there. When I arrived at my destination, it was already dark. After staying there for a few days, we moved to the Lyari area and from there we took up our residence in a building off Bunder Road near the Jubilee cinema which was close to DJ College [where Dr Khan continued his education] and it was easy for me to go walking to the college.

NL: How would you compare the standard of education in Pakistan when you arrived with that of India?

AQK: It was almost on a par. The British had left just a few years earlier, therefore their educational system was very much established and in place. Then there were generally very dedicated and selfless teachers in the subcontinent at the time. I started my primary education in 1948 at Ginnori School, Bhopal. Then I went to Jahangiria Middle School in 1950. I did my matriculation in 1952 from Hameediya High School. I was a *muezzin* [reciting *azan* for prayers in the mosque] at the age of eight years. The important thing is that one should work hard, no matter where one studies. So many PhDs come out of the universities every year all over the world. One never hears of them afterwards. They just disappear without applying their knowledge. Instead of becoming innovators, they simply become performers. If one wants and has the burning desire to excel, one can do so sitting in the remotest place of the world. Look at the Duke of Wellington, and how he defeated Napoleon at Waterloo. Lord Nelson lost his life on the seas defending England. These were the men who applied their know-ledge with courage, perseverance and determination to achieve their objectives. These were exemplary men of commitment.

NL: Did you play cricket in your student days?

AQK: Well, I played for my school team and the neighbourhood team at Bhopal. But when I came to Pakistan, I did not play cricket but was very fond of watching it.

NL: Your physique and height of six foot three were ideal for a fast bowler. Why did you prefer to play as a batsman? Were you a good fielder and at what position did you field?

AQK: Bowling was a tiresome chore, so I enjoyed playing as a batsman. I had a long reach as a batsman and could play spinners comfortably. I did not field in any specific position and could field at all positions, but I enjoyed fielding in the outfield because I loved to run in the open.

NL: As a batsman, who were you more comfortable against, fast bowlers or spinners?

AQK: I enjoyed batting against the spinners. With my long reach, I could kill their spin easily. I remember we used to play with a small-stature Hindu fellow about four and half feet tall in Bhopal. He had such a tremendous batting concentration and could bat all day like Hanif Mohammad. We always dreaded playing against him. He was one person I remember vividly whom we found difficult to get out.

NL: Which was the first ground where you played your first match?

AQK: The ground next to our house at Bhopal.

NL: It is said you make very good *parathas* [chapattis in butter]. Did you ever make them for your team-mates?

AQK: [Laughs] Well, my mother, Mohtarma Zulieka Begum, was never interested in cooking, although she always helped and taught at home the poor children of the neighbourhood. Both my parents tutored neighbourhood children free of charge and even gave them money. My mother taught the Holy Qu'ran to the girls of the neighbourhood and gave them clothes too. I have inherited this sense of social service from my parents. They taught us punctuality and if I was late they would get very annoyed. They taught me never to lie and always to be punctual. This is why I always arrive five minutes ahead of an appointment. Anyway, it was my sister and I who used to cook. With constant training and practice both of us became very efficient. All this training later on became very helpful for me when I went to Europe for my education. There I used to cook for my friends all the time and they would enjoy my *parathas*.

NL: You mentioned that you used to travel in the same bus from Nazimabad with Alim-ud-din[1] in 1957 after you had moved to that area. Did you speak to him about cricket as he was from Ajmer? Did you play cricket in Nazimabad?

AQK: Alim-ud-din lived near our house in Nazimabad. I remember the buses that used to ply there. They used to be of green colour and were in good condition. Alim-ud-din and I used to exchange pleasantries as we often travelled on the same bus, but we did not have conversations. He was famous then and was very polite and courteous. Not like the cricketers of present times. He was a gentleman. Many years later, I used to meet him frequently at Heathrow airport in London where he used to work for PIA and handled VIPs. Even there, he was as gentle as ever. I had received the books you sent me, Alim-ud-din's biography and *Wounded Tiger*. I am glad you wrote about Alim-ud-din. I liked it.

NL: From 1954 to 1957, you were at DJ Science College in Karachi. These were the days of glory for Pakistan cricket. Did you see any matches of the 1955 Indian and New Zealand touring teams to Pakistan?

AQK: I only saw two major matches. I saw the one against MCC A team at the National Stadium, Karachi [in March 1956]. I remember Peter Richardson fielding near the boundary. He was constantly booed by the crowd. So he turned around and faced the crowd and made some lewd gestures with his arms. I thought that was funny. This match left a

---

1 Batsman who played 25 Test matches for Pakistan from 1954 to 1962, usually as Hanif Mohammad's opening partner. See KH Baloch, MS Parvez and N Latif, *Alim-ud-Din: A Straight Bat* (Lahore: Jumhoori Publications, 2014) for the life of this upright and colourful personality.

lasting impression on me, especially the bowling of Tony Lock.

The first Test I ever watched was the one against Australia in 1956. The Australians had been badly beaten by England and were returning home. They stopped for one Test in Karachi. The National Stadium was way, way out in the wilderness, but I managed to get there and enjoyed the match very much. The match could have been played on turf, but I believe Fazal Mahmood cheekily insisted on having matting placed on the wicket. He was deadly on the matting and took full advantage of it and shot out the Aussies for 80. I can never forget Fazal's bowling in that match. I had admired Fazal since 1954 when he won The Oval match for Pakistan and now I was seeing him live. I have never seen such an exceptionally handsome man. I also saw other greats in that match like Ray Lindwall, Neil Harvey, Keith Miller, Alan Davidson and Richie Benaud. I remember Wazir Mohammad and Kardar both playing very defiant innings. Wazir Mohammad once again came in and batted beautifully, as he did at The Oval in 1954, to score 67 runs. Lindwall was still feared and his run-up was as enchanting as ever.

NL: Fast bowler Khan Mohammad was tall like you. How would you compare Fazal, Khan and Mahmood Hussain?

AQK: I think Khan Mohammad was very good. He would often get a wicket in his very first over. In the 1956 Australia Test, he bowled magnificently along with Fazal. Sadly, his cricket career was short-lived. He had a very nice run-up to the wicket. I think there was a strong rivalry between him and Fazal. Mahmood Hussain was also a very good bowler. He had bowled extremely well in The Oval Test of 1954 to give good support to Fazal. Khan Mohammad and Fazal Mahmood both used the old ball well.

NL: What were your feelings when Hanif Mohammad scored 337 against the West Indies in 1957-58?

AQK: I had always admired Hanif Mohammad for his concentration and determination. There used to be a Memon Cricket Club in Karachi and its captain, Farid Ahmed, was a friend and Hanif would play occasionally for them. So whenever I went to see their match, if Hanif was around I would make a point to speak to him. Of course, his 337 was one of the great wonders of the world. I was awestruck and very proud of him. Hanif was a fine and truly great batsman. Imtiaz Ahmed, Saeed Ahmed and Wallis Mathias were also great players. I had seen Kardar also who was known to be a shrewd and a great captain, but without Hanif, Fazal and Imtiaz he could have never reached his greatness.

NL: After you did your BSc you were one of two out of 125 candidates to get your first employment as an Inspector of Weights and Measures. Did you find any time to play cricket or any other sport after being employed?

AQK: No, I did not. In fact, I was so busy that there was no time for any sport. Frankly, when you are just employed you do not think of sports. You are more concentrated on proving your worth. In my new job, I was most certainly not thinking of cricket.

NL: Did you ever collect Test cricket souvenirs, memorabilia or autographs? Did you have cricket scrapbooks?

AQK: No, I was never interested in any of that.

NL: Was there any cricket in Berlin where you studied from 1961 to 1963?

AQK: No. None whatsoever.

NL: Did you follow Pakistan cricket from there?

AQK: Yes, occasionally, through newspapers.

NL: You were in Europe in 1962 when the Pakistan cricket team toured England under the captaincy of Javed Burki. Did you go to England to see any of the matches or follow the tour through radio or newspapers?

AQK: No, I did not go to England, nor did I follow the tour
       through radio commentaries. I only got some information
       sometimes through newspapers.

NL: There are many historic cricket clubs in the Netherlands.
       Did you play any cricket there?

AQK: No. Not at all. However, I played a lot of table tennis
       there to keep myself fit. I also played volleyball when I
       was in Belgium. But I loved to watch football. I stud-
       ied hard at Leuven University and could speak Dutch,
       German, French and English, besides Urdu and some
       Punjabi. I was the only one of the distinguished alumni
       to achieve distinction in its 650-year history. I had also
       done my Master's with distinction from Delft University
       of Technology in Holland.

NL: Your wife being from Europe, did she develop a taste for
       cricket?

AQK: Not entirely. She was always busy in the education of our
       children and their school activities, but now she keenly
       watches the matches on TV.

*At this point, Professor Dr Misbah-ud-Din Shami came to see him.
Professor Shami was a very distinguished-looking older man who had
retired as a Professor from the University Grants Commission, Punjab. We
were introduced and warmly shook hands. We spoke to each other about
our families and homes before Partition in Jullundur. More tea came and
with it some more patties.*

AQK: I don't think Punjabis were ever like refugees. They lost
       their homes in East Punjab and moved over to West
       Punjab in Pakistan where they were not treated as refugees
       and did not feel like refugees. They just gelled in. This is
       why the question of *mohajir* [Urdu-speaking immigrants]
       like the MQM [Mohajir Quami Movement] has never
       arisen in Punjab.

SCIENTIFIC CAREER

NL: Have science and scientific methods given you extra insight into cricket? And vice versa, has cricket given you any insight into science?

AQK: I never looked at cricket in that manner. For me, it was a sport that was to be enjoyed in all its innocence, free of technicalities. I have personally not delved so deeply into it. However, I remember seeing an article 'Cricket Ball Aerodynamics ... Myth Versus Science,' in *New Scientist* magazine[2] where some Pakistani bowlers were mentioned for their astonishing success with reverse swing, including Waqar Younis, Wasim Akram, Imran Khan, Sarfraz Nawaz and Shoaib Akhtar. However, I do understand that no movement is unscientific in the entire universe. Every movement must have a scientific theory. I believe this subject has been probed into since 1955, but other articles have appeared in 1980 and 1993. What I noticed interestingly in the article was that one does not have to tamper with the ball to achieve reverse swing. It can be achieved with a new ball at a speed of more than 80 mph.

NL: One of your fields of study was morphology, the shape and structure of objects. Has it given you any special insight into the phenomena of spin and swing?

AQK: As I have already said, there is no unscientific movement in the universe and similarly every shape and structure of objects has a scientific method to them. One needs to study them in their own perspective. However, doing research on spin and swing did not interest me, as I was busy with other scientific matters.

2 RD Mehta's article with this title was in fact published in eds Subic and Haake, *The Engineering Of Sport, Research, Development and Innovation* (London: Blackwell Science, 2000).

NL: Did your work on uranium enrichment leave you any time for cricket or other sports?

AQK: Hardly any. No, not at all.

NL: You had a close relationship with Mr Zulfiqar Ali Bhutto, a notable cricket enthusiast. Did you ever discuss cricket with him?

AQK: No, never. There were more significantly important national issues that needed attention and we discussed only matters of state. He was a very busy and driven man and never wasted time on unimportant things.

NL: ZA Bhutto's appointment of AH Kardar as the president of the Pakistan Cricket Board led to the creation of many more Patrons' teams with players directly employed by businesses and state organisations and competing in their names. Did you conceive at that time the idea of forming such a team yourself?

AQK: Patronage is definitely important and necessary in sports including cricket. In the state of Bhopal, the Nawab always patronised the sports. A lot of cricket used to be played at Bhopal, but the cricket-playing boys would more often move to Aligarh to play. In this way, Aligarh would become more famous for cricket than Bhopal. Therefore, for me it was not a new idea of seeing Patrons and their teams.

NL: You tried to dissuade General Mohammad Zia-ul-Haq from executing ZA Bhutto. How did you feel when he was hanged?

AQK: Just terrible. ZA Bhutto was brilliance personified which was snuffed out in an untimely fashion. I was sure that Mr Bhutto would not be spared, especially when the slogan of 'one grave and two probables' emerged. In order to make efforts to save his life, I flew to Amsterdam from Islamabad and then took an immediate flight to Istanbul, from where I flew directly to Ankara to meet Mr Mustafa Bulent Ecevit, the prime minister of Turkey, for his help and to request him to intervene to save the life of Mr

Bhutto. He immediately met me and told me that he was fully aware of the situation and had information that Mr Bhutto's life was in grave danger. He said: 'Turkey is still suffering from the aftermath of the unfortunate execution of its prime minister, Adnan Menderes, in 1961. It was a great mistake. If Bhutto is executed, Pakistan will unleash upon itself turmoil and great instability and Bhutto will be immortalised forever. Therefore, Mr Bhutto must not be hanged and should be saved at all costs. We are in touch with General Zia-ul-Haq and will try our best to save the life of Mr Bhutto.' Besides this, even Mian Tufail Mohammad, the chief of Jamaat Islami who had been ill-treated by the Bhutto regime, tried his level best to meet General Zia to ask him to pardon Bhutto for the sake of Pakistan [This was a remarkable revelation, NL]. But all requests were answered with the fact that General Zia was on his prayer mat praying and could not be disturbed. So all efforts were in vain. The conditions in Pakistan today are very different in the aftermath of Bhutto's execution. Had it not been for Mr Zulfiqar Ali Bhutto, Pakistan could never have become a nuclear power.

After ZA Bhutto's execution, I met General Zia and he put his hand on my shoulder. He said, 'I had read your request carefully. You are not only a top-notch nuclear scientist but also a very good pleader. I am sorry, but I did what I believed was in the best interest of the country. I just let the judgement of the Supreme Court be implemented.'

NL: Your work at your laboratory also gave you a relationship with Lieutenant-General Zahid Ali Akbar. Did you maintain this relationship when later on he became the chairman of the Pakistan Cricket Board at a time which included Pakistan's World Cup victory in 1992? If so, do you have any special insights into that World Cup campaign?

AQK: No, I was more involved in my professional work and as such had no time for the World Cup 1992 preparations and planning. There were better cricketing brains who were busy doing it. However, winning the World Cup was not possible without a stroke of luck and Allah's special blessings for Pakistan. Although I personally liked football more than cricket, General Zahid Ali Akbar is a good friend and we are maintaining regular contact.

NL: Over the next fifteen years, you were engaged in scientific work, but did it leave you any time for cricket or any other sport, or to relax?

AQK: Personally, I had very little time for sports or relaxation. I was hardly left with any time for even my wife and daughters. Whenever my wife met our colleagues, their wives complained that I had taken away their husbands and my wife would reply that her husband too had left his family behind. However, I am fond of poetry by the great poets of the subcontinent and I read a lot of it to relax. I even published a book called *Navadarat* of selected poetry of my choice. I was always concerned for the welfare of my colleagues and knew full well that they were working under a great stress. Therefore, I understood the importance of relaxation in order to make them perform better. So I gave them every possible facility in sports and other fields. In fact, I took over all their problems and solved them. I looked after the education of their children and even started a Khan Research Laboratory housing estate to solve their accommodation problems. I wanted their minds to be free of all worries in order to get a good performance from them.

THE KRL CRICKET TEAM

NL: In spite of all the pressures, the Khan Research Laboratory team was founded. How far were you personally involved in it?

AQK: It was the idea of my colleague, Dr Mansoor Ahmed, but with my co-operation and support we were able to raise a cricket team. We even staged a three-day 'Test' as well, where Rodney Marsh and Clive Lloyd also played. Hockey and football too were promoted there.

NL: It is fair to say that you are a national icon for our country. Your opinions are sought and respected on many issues other than scientific ones, particularly on educational issues. Have you offered any advice on the development of Pakistan cricket? If not, would you like to offer it?

AQK: [Laughs] There were three great friends at the court of Khawarzim Shah in Iran, namely Omar Khayyam, Hassan Bin Sabah and Nizamul Mulk. Each one of them was a great master of knowledge and science. Omar Khayyam being a mathematician invented an intercalation scheme to overcome the inaccuracy in the calendar which is in existence to this day and its accuracy may be off by a minute or so. Hassan Bin Sabah was a great scholar of Islamic jurisprudence and remains a classic figure. The third friend rose to become the prime minister and said, 'Always consult others, for they may have more knowledge than you.'

But in today's scenario, no one wants any advice! Everyone thinks that no one has more knowledge than themself. Whosoever sits in the chair of authority ceases to take heed from the advice of others and becomes the last word himself. Everything around him becomes a one-man show. No one has ever sought my advice on cricket and other matters and I do not wish to offer any advice either. I am sure they are more capable on cricket matters than me. When the days of one's era and influence are over, everyone runs away. Only some sincere friends are left behind with you.

NL: Khan Research Laboratories (KRL) Stadium was built in 1989 for KRL Football Club but as a multi-purpose facility it has staged 144 first-class and 90 one-day matches. It has also staged youth Test matches. How do you feel about your achievement and contribution to cricket here?

AQK: Very satisfied indeed. I am so glad that I was able to provide a platform to the upcoming sportsmen, who after using this launching pad went national. It is like in England, where if you play for Manchester United or Arsenal, with such platforms you get a chance to show your talent, get recognition and then get selected for the England football team. Similarly, many boys from the KRL team went on to play for Pakistan. The director general, Dr Mansoor, was a driving force behind it.

NL: KRL won the Patron's trophy grade II in 1994-95, and were runners-up in 1996-97. They entered first-class competition in the Patron's trophy 1997-98 and were twice runners-up in the Quaid-e-Azam trophy, in 2002-03 and 2008-09.[3] How do you feel about this great success?

AQK: I feel very good for the KRL and its players. It is their success as well as KRL's. Good players were able to find a chance to show their worth at national level that opened doors for them. I am very thankful to Allah for my humble contribution.

NL: What are the benefits to KRL from running the team?

AQK: It gets publicity. It finds talented players and also promotes football. It contributes towards making a healthy, purposeful and a peaceful society.

NL: What is the corporate and management structure of

---

3 In all KRL had played 158 first-class matches in Pakistan's domestic cricket as of December 2015: winning 56, drawing 65, losing 37, 1 abandoned. The highest individual score for KRL was 197, made by Saeed Anwar (*not* the Test opener) at home against PIA in 2013-14. He has played in 135 of their 158 first-class matches, with an aggregate of 7,502 runs and an average of 37.13. As a slow left-arm bowler, he also took 96 wickets for KRL at 27.92 each. In bowling, Yasir Arafat has twice taken nine wickets in an innings for KRL, each time on their home pitch. The fast-medium all-rounder has played 71 first-class matches for KRL, taking 304 wickets at 19.44 apiece. He played three Tests for Pakistan and was capped by Kent and Sussex in English county cricket.

KRL? Does it have shareholders or is it a state or military enterprise?

AQK: It is completely a government organisation.

NL: To whom is the team accountable within KRL?

AQK: To the director general, Mr Mansoor, who is also director general Health and Radiation Protection.

NL: How much does it cost to run the team? Do you meet these expenses from your own resources?

AQK: There is no fixed amount. It varies. But KRL manages the expenses from its own budget.

NL: Are you personally involved in its management? If so, how many matches do you watch?

AQK: I believe in sharing responsibilities and devolution of power, but I see most of the matches. This is what makes a good administrator: sharing responsibility and authority.

NL: One of your notable players from your modest start in 1980 was Pakistan's greatest captain Misbah-ul-Haq. Others included Bazid Khan, Shoaib Akhtar, Abdul Razzaq,[4] Azhar Ali, Mohammad Wasim, Azhar Mahmood and Asif Mahmood. How do you rate this success on the national level?

AQK: Personally speaking, it is a humble and sincere contribution from my side, but nationally speaking it is a matter of great pride for KRL.

NL: How easy is it to recruit players for the KRL team in competition with other teams?

AQK: Very easy. They come to us themselves for trials. KRL has a good name and a good standing. So players get attracted to it as a place from where they have a chance to reach the national team. Even the former ISI chief,

---

4 First-class playing records for KRL: Misbah-ul-Haq P 19 R1,459 HS 167* Av 58.36; Bazid Khan P 52 R 2,448 HS 140 Av 35.47; Shoaib Akhtar P 8 R 586 W 26 BB 4-24; Abdul Razzaq P 5 R 341 HS 117 Av 42.62 and R 797 W 25 Av 31.88 BB 5-73. Misbah-ul-Haq scored more first-class runs for KRL than for any other domestic team in Pakistan.

Lieutenant-General Javed Nasir, used to play for our team as a wicketkeeper. In those days he was a brigadier.

NL: Are the KRL players paid simply as cricketers, or do they have their jobs at KRL as AH Kardar and ZA Bhutto intended for employers' teams in the 1970s?

AQK: They get paid as players but they can find jobs with KRL although most of them do not. They make quite a handsome amount of money as players and usually move on without seeking jobs with us. Shoaib Akhtar was still a young boy when he was brought to me. His older brother brought him to us and said no one was giving Shoaib any chance. Shoaib stood along shyly and innocently. So I told US-educated Mr Mansoor to accommodate him. He asked me, 'Will five thousand rupees a month [then equivalent to around £55] be enough for him? 'No,' I replied. 'He deserves much more. Give him more money so that he can be comfortable and put his heart and energy into his bowling.' We had also employed Misbah-ul-Haq, the present Pakistan captain, for 5,000 rupees. I think Abdul Razzaq has not been fairly treated. He was a great cricketer who was wasted. He had the potential to become a good captain and should have become the captain of the Pakistan team. Another good player that was wasted was Qasim Umar who hailed from East Africa. He was a diminutive batsman and had a tremendous talent. He was unfairly dropped from the team after he had alleged that Imran Khan smoked hash.

NL: Could you please tell how much your first-team players earn as cricketers?

AQK: Twenty thousand to 25,000 per month [as at December 2015 between £125 and £158].

NL: Does KRL support long-serving players with jobs or pensions after their playing careers are over?

AQK: They can work for KRL if they like, but by the time they finish playing they have enough money and they do not come to work for us.

NL: How does KRL help the emerging cricketers, particularly those from poor backgrounds or remote areas?

AQK: We encourage and give financial support to such players to promote cricket.

NL: Does KRL run a cricket academy?

AQK: No, not an academy, but we do have coaches who give training to the players. Then there are senior players who teach the younger cricketers.

NL: Does KRL support cricket for women and girls and for older and handicapped people?

AQK: No, not as yet.

NL: How have the KRL team and its supporters been affected by Pakistan's international exile?

AQK: Indeed, we are very much affected. In the past, foreign teams used to come and play at the KRL ground. Our players used to get an opportunity to see and play with the famous international players and to learn from them. With the present scenario, we are completely missing out on that.

NL: Has KRL team been able to tour overseas or host foreign teams?

AQK: Of course. Our team has hosted teams at the KRL ground and has also undertaken foreign tours.

CLOSING THOUGHTS

NL: Which is your all-time favourite Pakistan cricket team?

AQK: Definitely Kardar's team that had Khan Mohammad, Imtiaz, 'Merry Max' Maqsood, Wazir Mohammad, Fazal, Waqar Hasan, Hanif, Alim-ud-din and others who played only for the honour of their country and nation.

NL: By making Pakistan a nuclear power, you made it possible for Pakistan to stand tall in the world, especially against India. What measures should the PCB take to stand on equal terms with the Indian Cricket Board?

AQK: Although it makes most of its money from playing with India to finance its great salaries – ranging ridiculously from 5 Lakhs (500,000 rupees) and upwards that are paid to the players and its employees – the Pakistan Cricket Board should not be so desperate to play against India for the sake of money. Zulfiqar Ali Bhutto had said that even if we have to eat grass we will, but we will make a bomb which we did against the threat from India. Similarly, the PCB should keep Pakistan's integrity in mind and should only play when they are treated and respected as equals. There is no need to play with India. The heavens won't fall. Pakistan should play with countries like South Africa, West Indies and Australia. The tour of a weak team like Zimbabwe does not help to build the image of Pakistan. Instead of playing against weak teams, Pakistan should play with strong and established teams.

     If no one is interested to play on an equal basis, the PCB should devise ways to improve domestic cricket by introducing league cricket of great merit. Such league matches should be played in Pakistan and not elsewhere. The benefit of such leagues should be for the spectators and the people of Pakistan. Needs can be curtailed by adopting a simple way of life instead of a lavish lifestyle.

NL: You are known for helping out the needy. You helped widows and orphaned young girls and settled them in their lives. You helped several people to receive medical treatments at your cost. You built mosques, schools and gave scholarships to the poor students. What prompted you to do all this?

AQK: Being a good Muslim is not just fasting and saying your prayers or going to Haj. You are a good Muslim and a good human being only if you serve mankind. Help out and never refuse anyone who seeks your help. You have a moral obligation to live for others and solve their problems. You have to sacrifice. [He recites Iqbal's verses: *Khoon-e-sud hazar anjum se hoti hai sehar paida,* or 'Thousands of stars breathe their last, Then only it doth dawn.'] Philanthropy should be promoted in our society and service to humanity should be encouraged. This is the real objective of life. I go to Lahore to supervise my hospital, Dr AQ Khan Trust Hospital, on and off. It was started in October 2013. Its outdoor unit (OPD) is already functioning. It will be a state-of-the-art, 300-bed, seven-storey hospital when completed, which will provide absolutely free healthcare to the poor.

NL: Sir, these days foreign universities do not give admission to Pakistani students in nuclear education. Is it not discrimination?

AQK: Well it is, but it should not matter. If one is prepared to work hard for education, one does not have to go anywhere. In my days, there were not many modern facilities of education here, so it was necessary to go abroad. However, the most important thing is the *application* of your education and knowledge. How you apply what you have learnt matters. What can a coach do if his tips are not applied properly? Similarly, cricket coaching is on the same footing. There is no point of learning in the nets unless you apply your learning in the ground in a match.

NL: You were also the subject of a series of accusations over nuclear proliferation. Was your interest in sports, particularly cricket, affected?

AQK: No comment. The question is irrelevant and out of context.

NL: Are your daughters Dina and Ayesha interested in cricket?

AQK: Yes, to some extent, but they have developed their own interests in various other things.

NL: Do you read books on cricket? Which is your favourite book?

AQK: No, I do not read books on cricket. My interest is in the Islamic history. I like to read biographies, books on philosophy and scientific knowledge. I enjoy reading the Masnavi of Maulana Rumi.[5] I like Saadi Shirazi[6] as well.

NL: Meeting you was the high note in the life of The Oval hero Fazal Mahmood. In the last five years of his life, I was his closest friend. He showed me the model of the missile you gave him and held you in great esteem. How do you feel about him as a cricketer?

AQK: He was a great cricketer and a great hero who served Pakistan cricket with great distinction in its early stages. He came to see me at the KRL ground during a cricket tournament. He kissed my hands and said, 'You are my hero.' I told him, 'No Sir, you are the great one. You are my hero and a great benefactor of Pakistan.' He was very happy with my remark and held both my hands and kissed them again and replied, 'No. You are the great one. You are my hero and a great benefactor of Pakistan.'

NL: You have always dressed elegantly. What kind of clothes do you prefer?

AQK: I like to dress up casually and comfortably. I do not use neckties much and prefer to wear safari suits.

NL: Do you prefer white cricket kits or the coloured kits?

AQK: With the changing times things have changed, but cricket used to be known as the sport of gentlemen and so white kits were worn then. Today's cricket is no longer the traditional gentleman's game. Today it has become highly competitive with so much money involved in it, so it has changed and will keep on changing as time goes by. So whatever comes along it is fine, as long as it is enjoyable and played with fairness. I still love to watch all sports, especially cricket, hockey, football, and kabaddi. If for

5 The title has been translated 'Rhyming Couplets of Profound Spiritual Meaning.' Written in the 13th century, it is a spiritual poem in six volumes written in Persian, a masterpiece of Sufi literature.
6 Another great 13th-century Sufi Persian poet, who combined sharp observation of daily life with spiritual insight.

some reason I cannot see the entire match, I still keep tabs
on the results.

NL: Do you like five-day Test matches or one-dayers or the
      T20s?

AQK: I like one-dayers. I think even in Test matches each
      innings should be restricted to 100 overs only. This will
      ensure a positive result.

NL: What is your message to Pakistan's cricketers?

AQK: They should play honestly for the dignity and honour of
      Pakistan and should not run after money and personal
      gains. Rise above self.

*It was by now lunchtime for him and we had been talking for two and half
hours. I thanked him and presented him with a Lahore Gymkhana club
necktie that I had designed in 2004. It was the first ever Lahore Gymkhana
club tie since its inception in 1880. Notwithstanding his preference for
safari suits, he accepted it and expressed appreciation. I also presented him
with a Lahore Gymkhana Cricket Club history booklet. He leafed through
it and looked at the pictures briefly. He then rose from his seat. With his
height the room looked filled. He shook hands and walked me to the door.*

34

CHITRAL: CRICKET IN A
MAGIC KINGDOM

By Alex Massie

As we sat in the departure lounge at Islamabad's Benazir Bhutto airport, waiting for our flight north to Chitral, Peter Oborne confessed, 'The only thing that could go wrong is the Taliban sending a raiding party over the mountains.' This is the kind of captain's warning that concentrates the mind.

The mountains are part of the Hindu Kush, in a province of Pakistan which for years was called the North West Frontier. For a certain sort of Briton, those words retain an aura of intoxicating romance, lost when it was renamed Khyber Pakhtunkhwa in 2010.

Chitral was an independent kingdom for hundreds of years, ruled by the Mehtar from the Kator dynasty. In 1892, a great Mehtar, Aman-ul-Mulk, died, sparking a violent succession struggle between his sons for the privilege of succeeding him. This prompted one of the most dramatic episodes in the so-called 'Great Game', the name popularised by Kipling for the long struggle between Britain and Russia for influence in India.

The British sent 400 soldiers to Chitral as a block against Russian encroachment. However, they soon found themselves besieged by Chitrali forces, with no hope of escape. The British sent two relief columns, one coming over the Lowari Pass from the south, the other hauling its cannon through shoulder-deep snow over the Shandur from the north east. This latter force eventually, and against the odds, reached Chitral to relieve the siege after 45 days. The London press rejoiced, comparing the relief to the epic defence of Lucknow in 1857. However, the British did not annex Chitral. It remained an independent princely state after independence and was absorbed into Pakistan only in 1969.

Chitral was once a beautiful place to stop on the old hippie trail. This closed years ago, but before 9/11 it still drew up to 4,000 trekkers and holidaymakers each year. But in 2014, the remote valley had fewer than 500 visitors. It is too far, too difficult, too dangerous. For at least four, and sometimes more, months of the year the roads in, from both south and east, are blocked by snow. To the west lies Afghanistan and no travellers wish to risk that road into Chitral these days.

If a tunnel through the Lowari mountains is ever completed, Chitral will become more accessible, but for now, unless you catch one of the two weekly flights from Islamabad, the journey by road from the capital can take as long as 15 hours to complete. The result is that Chitral feels like a land apart, a secret kingdom of which only a few are even properly aware.

Nonetheless, like all of Pakistan, it repays a determined traveller many times over. No place could be more welcoming; no hospitality finer. No scenery grander either.

As our plane climbed over the Lowari Pass and began its steep descent into the Chitral Valley, all Pakistan's multiple difficulties seemed to fade away. We were the Wounded Tiger XI and we were here to play cricket on the old frontier of Empire.

Seven matches had been arranged for Wounded Tigers – we took our name from the skipper's recently published history of cricket in Pakistan. We were making a small piece of cricketing history. No foreign cricket team at any level, we were told, had ever visited this part of Pakistan to play. Few, I fear, had even been tempted to do so during the six long, painful years since Sri Lanka's team bus was attacked by terrorists.

Although we were assured that Chitral was different – safer, more relaxed, less problematic for western tourists than much of Pakistan – we had constant reminders that this can be a hard country. One was our armed guards, even if their presence was chiefly meant to reassure us, and our hosts, that everything that could be done to guarantee our safety had in fact been done.

On the day we arrived in Pakistan came another unwelcome reminder. A bus in Karachi was attacked by an offshoot of the Pakistani Taliban and 46 Ismaili Muslims were slain. Since many Chitralis are also members of this minority sect, the atrocity was especially keenly felt there. We might have been many miles from Karachi but we were still in Pakistan.

Our first match, against the famous Langlands School and College in Chitral, was preceded by a moment of silence for the victims of this latest obscenity. A sobering moment in a spectacular setting. The ground, surrounded by snow-capped peaks and with falcons circling overhead, had been carved out of the hillside and afforded extraordinary views down the valley. It felt like playing at the top of the world. This clearly would be a cricket tour unlike any other.

If only our performance had matched the setting. Fifty schoolboys had been deployed to scurry down ravines to retrieve balls that would otherwise undoubtedly have been lost. They were kept busy as our hosts raced to 101 for no loss on their way to setting us 243 from 30 overs. This, dear reader, proved beyond us and already we suspected the unfamiliarity of the playing conditions was the least of our worries. It was only our warm-up match.

The next day we would face a Select XI drawn from the 40-odd clubs that constitute the District Cricket Association of Chitral. After the first over, the Chitral Select were on course to make 510. In the circumstances, restricting them to 290 in 30 overs felt quietly encouraging. The only thing worse than chasing leather in Pakistan, however, is facing leather. When the opposition's opening bowler begins his run five yards from the boundary, you worry that he might already have established a measure of psychological ascendancy. Then you remember the pitch is a yard short. Pretty shortly after that there's a rattling of timber and you're trudging from the field thankful that at least he had the decency – or compassion – to bowl a full length.

'I am very impressed and even surprised by the standard of cricket in Chitral,' said Qamar Ahmed, the legendary Pakistan cricket writer and broadcaster, who was accompanying us for the first few days of the tour. His verdict on our performances was diplomatic: 'You play and that's what is important.'

Mind you, we consistently surprised our hosts. For instance, when they asked, 'How many first-class players do you have?' they did not expect the answer to be 'none'. There were moments, I confess, when I thought our skipper might have based selection for the party on something more than 'Who would be a good tourist?'

On at least one occasion, word had spread that we were the England Under-19 team. 'Sorry,' we said, 'I'm afraid that's not quite the case.' Who were we, then? We were Tigers! What were we? Wounded!

As we limped from one defeat to another, I began to wonder if our travelling circus would look suspicious to our hosts, to say nothing of the agents from the pervasive and powerful Inter-Services Intelligence (ISI) agency tracking our progress through northern Pakistan. Would they regard our cricketing efforts as a thin cover for a deeply subtle probe by British intelligence? The nadir came in Drosh where we were dismissed for 33. 'Pathetic. Pitiful. Deplorable,' said the captain.

Chitral is, in cricketing terms, a backwater. The local association is not yet recognised by the Pakistan Cricket Board, and cricket is, relatively speaking, a new arrival in the Hindu Kush. Even 50 years ago little cricket was played here; polo, and latterly soccer, were the district's greatest sporting enthusiasms. The annual contest between the polo players of Chitral and those of neighbouring Gilgit, played at 12,000 feet up on Shandur Top, remains one of the world's greatest under-known sporting spectacles.

Until the end of the princely state in 1969, Chitralis were Chitrali more than they were Pakistani. Television, among many other things, changed that, and television also brought cricket. The development of cricket in Chitral marched hand in hand with the development of a Pakistani, as opposed to purely Chitrali, sense of identity. Viewed from the Hindu Kush, Javed Miandad and Imran Khan were nation-builders just as much as AH Kardar and Fazal Mahmood were for the rest of Pakistan a generation or two previously.

Cricket has become part of the connective tissue that binds the country together; without it the fragile bonds of community, identity and nationhood are weakened. This is so even in some of the Federally Administered Tribal Areas, further south adjacent to the Afghan frontier, where government control has always been uncertain and contested, latterly with the Taliban. The latter's attitude to cricket is complicated. Officially they frown on the game, but it remains popular with their supporters. In his history, Oborne quotes one tribal cricketer from Waziristan, who says that the Taliban 'loved Pakistan cricket ... Though they are fighting against the Pakistan Army, they love to see the Pakistan cricket team winning matches.'

Certainly no one could watch the joyful scenes from Lahore – when, on our last day in Pakistan, Zimbabwe became the first Test-status country to play an international fixture in the country in six years – and fail to conclude that Pakistan, and world cricket, needed more of this.

The Foreign & Commonwealth Office advises against all 'non-essential' travel to the Kalash valleys of Bumburet, Rumbur and Birir. We were here to play cricket, however, and so our travel, along a perilous, far-too-narrow mountain track, was essential. Each hairpin bend brought us closer to the Afghan border, as we moved ever further into the heart of old Kafiristan.

The Kalash, a polytheist sect whose festivals attract hundreds of gawping Pakistani tourists, play very little cricket and so the (few) remaining optimists in the party dared to think this might be a game we could actually win. Once again, however, we had been misinformed. We were not playing the Kalash people themselves. The opposition were a Select XI drawn from the Muslim population of the three valleys; a population that has left the 4,000 remaining Kalash a minority in their own homeland. After two overs, the Kalash Select were 32 for no loss and it became clear these people had played plenty of cricket.

Yet here again, the setting and the quality of our welcome more than compensated for our on-field frailty. 'It's like playing in Middle Earth,'

one tourist observed as he surveyed the ground. Cattle and goats wandered a boulder-hewn outfield (upon which boulders spectators would
sit, within the field of play). A grove of walnut trees, also within the
playing area, provided shelter from the heat of the mountain sun for
those fielders fortunate enough to be stationed in their shade. To avoid
balls being lost in a tumbling brook, all the bowling was from one end.

Here was our introduction to tapeball cricket – the form of the
game that accounts for the majority of the cricket played in Pakistan.
It became apparent that tapeball cricket demands extreme pace or
extreme guile, qualities in which we were disagreeably and hopelessly
deficient. Medium-paced dibbly-dobblers – our strongest suit – are
slaughtered.

Nonetheless there was something wonderfully liberating about all
this. It was cricket as it was played back when you were a lad capering
about in the garden; cricket reduced to the simplest of all equations: see
ball, hit ball. Indeed, the whole occasion had the feel of a large family
reunion at which, after the picnic, an impromptu game of cricket was
arranged. It was as pure as it was exuberant, as refreshing as it was
entertaining. Obviously we lost. Heavily.

Winning a game would risk spoiling this narrative, so it is heartening
to report that at no point did we so abuse the hospitality shown to us.
If our opponents pitied us, they contrived to hide their disappointment.
Each day, small boys chattering on the boundary would salute 'another
huge six' and suggest, with grinning pleasure but no malice, 'You lose.'

We did not always help ourselves. In our penultimate match, in
Booni, a two-hour drive north of Chitral, we somehow reduced our
hosts to 106 for eight. In a novel break with more than a century of
cricketing orthodoxy, Oborne took the view that an overs match can
be improved by some declaration bowling. Broken by this chastening
experience, we subsided to 70 all out, only 200 runs short of our target.

The day before, we had surprised ourselves by striking early and
often, and with the opposition, in Ayun this time, 15 for four, dangerous thoughts of victory had crossed more than one mind. As it was, we
found ourselves chasing 302, and in one of our better batting performances, managed just less than half that. There seemed to be an iron

law in Pakistan that, regardless of conditions or opposition, we would be chasing ten an over.

It occurred to me that we might now be doomed to trek from village to village, playing every day, until such improbable time came that we won a match and were finally permitted to return home. On and on we toiled, like the Israelites in search of the Promised Land, forever seeking a route to the Valley of Respectability.

None of that mattered, however. The game was the thing. The game and the welcome we received in this land of mountains and glaciers, eagles and falcons. We consoled ourselves with the reflection that no one, at any level of the game, has found it easy to win in Pakistan. A deep sadness, tinged with a modest measure of pride, was felt as our little plane soared up into the Chitrali sky, bound for Islamabad. We, all of us, left a piece of our hearts in Chitral. Pakistan might be a hard country, but for those who take the trouble to go, it will never leave you.

A version of this chapter appeared on www.espncricinfo.com in August 2015.

35

A MASTER PLAN FROM MAJID KHAN

Majid Khan, once a dashing attacking batsman with his trademark floppy hat, has become a grandee. The most prominent representative of the mighty Burki sporting dynasty, a product of the elite Aitchison College and Cambridge University, one of the most popular and talismanic Pakistani imports into English county cricket, he is a guardian of values learnt in another age.

During a dreadful era for Pakistan cricket, he served from 1996 to 1999 as chief executive of the PCB. He drew some fierce criticisms but no one ever challenged his probity. His former deputy Waqar Ahmed provided a vivid illustration: 'He gave himself the worst office in the PCB and sat on a broken chair.'

A visit to him at his family home in Lahore has some of the character of a Royal audience. On this occasion, he sat in a chair (not broken) on the porch, with one of his dogs in attendance. Obediently, the setting sun bathed the garden where he and his family played their first cricket matches.

As always, his manner was courteous and stately, and his speech punctuated with nostalgic slang ('some of these journalist johnnies . . .'). But behind this façade, he offered a thoughtful and sometimes mordant analysis of Pakistan cricket.

A few months earlier, he and his son Bazid had presented a comprehensive plan for reform of Pakistan's domestic structure. Bazid's lone

Test appearance against the West Indies in 2004-05 produced a volley of jealous backbiting. Nevertheless, it took his family into the record books, as only the second to have produced three generations of Test cricketers, after the Headleys of West Indies and England. Bazid has now become an authoritative television commentator.

Majid Khan described their plan in some detail, and the reasoning behind it. But first he gave a long history lesson, analysing everything that has gone wrong in Pakistan's domestic cricket. Although occasionally tendentious, it was comprehensive and incisive.

The first weakness was endless tinkering with structure. England, Australia, New Zealand and South Africa all established a basic set-up early in their history and had stuck to it since, even when new competitions and formats were introduced. (Many English cricket-lovers, baffled by constant changes to their traditional season, would find this optimistic.) The basic unit of cricket in these countries had remained constant: English counties, Australian states, South African provinces and so on.

'In Pakistan, we have had three stages in our administrative structure, districts, divisions, provinces, but there has never been any stability. In 1960, we ended provinces and we came down to a divisional structure. Then in the 1970s, this was sprinkled with some corporate teams. Then the corporates came into first-class cricket in a big way, but Kardar as BCCP president also brought back a provincial structure for some time. Then it was back to divisions, with corporates alongside, which lasted until 2000.'

The current structure, in place since 2000, now has super-sized regions at the top. The competitions have been regularly remodelled since then. 'So unlike other countries, Pakistan cricket supporters simply have not known each year which teams they are meant to support at first-class level and whom they will be playing.'

He turned to club cricket – a frequent concern of Pakistan's cricket-lovers. 'Our districts are based on clubs, which vote for district associations. But most clubs are not based on locality. They were formed by individuals for their own circle of friends or colleagues.'

Those inherited from the English were generally intended for

Englishmen in the civil service, the military or business circles. They have never become representative of the entire local community, and neither has any other private club. 'People could set up cricket clubs on their own terms without any proper playing fields or financing, but local associations would still affiliate them if they were authorised to play in local competitions.' Few of these clubs had any former Test cricketers or anyone else who knew how to run a cricket club – because they were excluded. 'Test players were seen as a threat to the authority of the patron.'

Because of this system, district associations, the lowest unit of Pakistan cricket, were generally run by club officers 'who had no money, no vision, no real knowledge of the game and poor administrative and financial skills'.

This state of affairs got worse in the 1970s. 'Before then, there was very little public entertainment in Pakistan except sport or the cinema. So sport mixed people from the wealthier and better-educated classes with others and this provided a core of educated people to run clubs and associations.'

But in the 1970s there was a big inflow of new money into Pakistan from the Middle East. The loss of East Pakistan deprived the country of its major foreign exchange earnings, but a new source appeared to replace them. The oil producers of the Middle East became vastly richer through the OPEC-engineered price rise.

They all undertook giant building and infrastructure projects, but they were chronically short of all the necessary labour. With the active encouragement of the Bhutto government, thousands of Pakistani workers went out to these countries to fill the gaps. They earned high wages for themselves and sent back remittances to their families. 'This inflow of new money from the Middle East drove out the traditional upper and middle classes. Lower-middle-class and humble people began running cricket. They still are,' he added, with a touch of hauteur.

These developments had an impact on Pakistan's leading private schools. They had been a major nursery for Pakistan cricketers, based on small class sizes, well-maintained playing fields and a strong structure of inter-school competitions, from which the best players graduated to inter-college and inter-university tournaments.

Moin Khan (centre) oversees proceedings at his cricket academy in the well-to-do Defence Housing Authority area of Karachi. (*Richard Heller*)

By contrast, Rashid Latif's academy, in the same city, is home to a more diverse group of players. (*Richard Heller*)

Aleem Dar lifts his trademark hat to perform a raincheck at the fifth Ashes Test at The Oval in 2015. *(Getty Images)*

The Khan sisters' pioneering work has helped women's cricket in Pakistan to thrive, despite much opposition, with good crowds now turning out, as here in Karachi in September 2015, when the national team played Bangladesh. *(Getty Images)*

President Pervez Musharraf (left) was very aware of the importance of cricket in terms of Pakistan's national prestige, and strongly involved himself in the sport. (*Getty Images*)

Cricket historian Najum Latif (seated) and Hussain Malik (the founder's grandson, right) in Gander & Co sports shop in Lahore, part of a business which has served cricket in the city since 1943. (*Richard Heller*)

Mehr Mohammad Khalil, the bus driver who saved the Sri Lankan tourists from terrorist attack in Lahore in 2009, is greeted by Kumar Sangakkara during his visit to Sri Lanka a few months later. (*Mehr Muhammad Khalil*)

Two Pakistanis who demanded fast reactions: Dr AQ Khan, nuclear scientist, with fast bowler Shoaib Akhtar. (*Dr AQ Khan*)

The touring Wounded Tigers take on Langlands School in Chitral, one of the more spectacular settings imaginable for a game of cricket. (*Alex Massie*)

Even in such unpromising surroundings as the road to Mastuj, there was still a chance to play cricket. (*Alex Massie*)

Majid Khan, in his familiar floppy hat, in action during a Masters tournament in Sharjah in 1996. Now, he has interesting ideas on how to revive domestic cricket in Pakistan. (*Getty Images*)

Shaharyar Khan (left) meets with Indian Senior cricketers after their one-day match in Karachi in April 2006. (*Getty Images*)

Younus Khan (right) and Misbah-ul-Haq in perfect partnership – the pair have been central to the recent revival in Pakistan's Test cricket after the spot-fixing scandal of 2010. (*Getty Images*)

Tapeball cricket is giving a new lease of life to the game in Pakistan, where for many the price of playing the hardball version is too high.
(*Richard Heller*)

Any spare piece of ground will do for tapeball cricket, and the action is fast and furious. (*Richard Heller*)

Cricket – creator of hopes and dreams for a greengrocer's boy near Peshawar.
(*Ian Vaughan-Arbuckle*)

In 1972, the Bhutto government nationalised all the private schools – just when thousands of families had been enriched by the new earnings from the Middle East. These people understandably wanted a better education for their children, but the government did not build any new schools or create any new places.

So the children poured into the newly nationalised great schools and class sizes rocketed from around 32 to 80 or even 100. 'There were children sitting in verandas and out in the open. So schools built new classrooms over their playing fields. The sports culture in schools collapsed, and even today we have no school tournaments.'

General Zia's dictatorship allowed private schools back again, but set no standards for them. Anyone could open one, without providing any sort of playing field. 'So since the late 1970s, we have had three or four complete school generations who have never played sports at school. And these are the people now running the country . . .'

Another important legacy of this period was corporate teams. They have had many strong defenders, led by Javed Miandad, but to Majid Khan they were a baleful development. 'Under Bhutto, the cricket administration looked to corporate teams to provide jobs and financial security to cricketers. They did look after their players, but they had no concern for cricket as a whole. The local divisions which had groomed first-class players lost their best players to corporate teams. This goes on today – they have to produce a double number of good players, one for themselves and one for the corporates. The media attack them for putting out weak teams, without realising that their best players are taken away by the corporate teams. Their spokesmen are too stupid to reply to all the criticisms. But they have to go on pleasing the people who vote for them – so they give team places to them, or their children or relatives, whether they deserve them or not.'

Corruption and patronage in team selection had been unwittingly promoted by English leagues in the late 1990s. Many Pakistanis sought places in their teams as professionals, but the leagues introduced a rule that only players with a first-class record could be inducted as professionals. So some cricketers had bought themselves a place in a first-class match. The going rate was around 5,000 rupees. When the leagues realised this was happening, they changed the qualification to five first-class matches in a span of 18 months. So the players bought themselves five places instead.

Majid said that corporate teams had failed to build new pitches and relied on those already in use for local teams. This generalisation might be disputed (there are fine grounds created or maintained by corporations), but when this did happen grounds became over-used and curators did not have the time to assess their pitches' performance after a match and improve them for the next one.

Moreover, Majid argued, the proliferation of corporate teams and competitions had led Pakistan to compress the first-class season into six weeks in winter. This ensured that early-morning dew interfered with pitch preparation. He added, 'The sun is weak in winter, especially in the North, and pitches do not dry properly. It makes life too easy for bowlers, too many matches finish in two or three days, but then batsmen get no chance to recover and correct their mistakes.'

To make matters worse, first-class cricket in Pakistan used inferior local balls, not a Test Kookaburra. 'Add this to poor pitches and match conditions and you promote inferior play. It is no surprise that our first-class cricket has produced very few quality batsmen in the last twenty years other than Misbah and Younus. It's all built into the structure and the system.'

He recalled the first days of Pakistan cricket when first-class matches were very scarce for all the players. 'The system was still largely a hangover from India. Competitions were on a knock-out basis, and if a match could not be finished, first-innings lead counted. So we had huge battles for first-innings lead, and teams would bat for two whole days each innings. Then the losing team might have to wait until the following year for its next first-class match. Most players simply had no experience of playing a two-innings match and acquiring the skills to win it or save it in the fourth innings. So we switched to a league structure – but then the first-class timetable got so compressed as I described. We had quantity cricket, not quality cricket.'

Finally, in an interesting digression, he presented the prime motive for the link between cricket administration and the government of

Pakistan in the early days. 'We had tight exchange control through the State Bank right up to the 1970s. All sports federations involved in international competitions had to beg for foreign exchange to pay the visiting teams. That is why, until the 1980s, we never had a full five-Test tour from anybody except the Indians.'

For all those reasons, Pakistan's domestic cricket had regularly failed to provide a proper training ground for Test players. The last full first-class season, 2014-15, illustrated many of his points. It consisted of 117 matches, all played between October and December 2014. Its competitions, the Quaid-e-Azam gold and silver trophies, mixed corporate and local teams but were dominated by the corporates. They had a complex and barely comprehensible points system. There were frequent mismatches, particularly involving the unfortunate Multan Tigers, who lost all of their matches and were dismissed four times for under 100 in front of their own supporters.[1]

The gold final was contested between the National Bank of Pakistan (did its supporters roar, 'Come on, you bankers!'?) and Sui Gas Northern Pipelines Limited ('Play up, pipe fitters!'). It occupied five days at the National Stadium, Karachi but ended in a draw. As in the old days of Pakistan cricket, the sparse crowd had to endure two long innings (173 overs and 160 overs) in which each side accumulated over 500. As a climax to a first-class season, this match was no advertisement for Pakistan's domestic cricket.

The domestic averages for that season are revealing. Pakistan's leading Test batsmen, Misbah-ul-Haq, Younus Khan and Mohammad Hafeez, did not figure at all. They did not play a single first-class match in Pakistan. That is only partly the result of Pakistan's international exile: it also reflects their choice. None of the leaders in the batting

---

1 The Tigers lost to their feline rivals, Islamabad Leopards, by 303 runs after dismissing them for 54 in the first innings. They also lost to Peshawar Panthers, Lahore Lions, and Rawalpindi Rams. Although a long way from the ocean, the Karachi Dolphins dismissed them in Multan for 46 and won by an innings and 182 runs. This completed a clean sweep of defeats against other first-class 'creature teams'. Relegated to the non-first-class Inter Region Qualifying Pool B for 2015-16, they lost their first three matches to Lahore Lions, Sialkot Stallions and the Bahawalpur Stags. Truly, a team of Wounded Tigers.

averages had played a Test for Pakistan in the previous two years (except for Azhar Ali, and he played only three first-class matches in Pakistan). Similarly, the leaders in the bowling averages had only one recent Test performer – the giant Mohammad Irfan.

Quite simply, Pakistan's first-class cricket did not reach a high enough standard to generate Test players.

The key element in the Khans' reform plan is the end of corporate teams, and a three-part structure of teams based on locality through which players could progress to first-class status. It has been strongly influenced by Majid's experience of England, particularly the way in which corporate money has been used to support the county structure.

The plan first saw the light in 2007 in a two-day grand seminar initiated by Nasim Ashraf, the new PCB chairman (and personal appointee of President Musharraf) and packed with journalists, officials and former stars (many flown in from overseas at the Board's expense). 'They offered me ten minutes to present it,' said Majid. 'I asked for thirty, and the first slot in the programme.' The meeting listened to him – and gave him no support, not even from those with experience of English county cricket.

Eight years later, he and Bazid returned to the charge in a three-hour television programme. They proposed a structure with 22 first-class teams, divided equally into two grades, playing one match against each other over six months from October to March (four-day matches in grade 1, three days in grade 2). These teams would *all* be geographically based. The present unwieldy regions would be replaced by divisions with a clear identity for local cricket followers. There would be promotion and relegation to and from each grade.

The grade 1 divisions would supply the Executive Body of the PCB and elect its chairman, whether from among themselves or from outside. The grade 2 divisions would supply the PCB's General Body, attending the PCB's AGM and doing the normal business there of approving its report and accounts, and asking questions. Promotion and relegation would automatically change the composition of each Body every year.

Feeding each division would be four district teams, playing 24 non-first-class matches on weekends over the course of the full season. Those feeding the grade 1 divisions would play three-day matches, the rest would play over two days.

Every player in every team would be paid a match fee. Every team, divisional or district, would have paid qualified coaches, scorers, curators and selectors who would watch every game.

With an eye for detail, Majid and Bazid Khan proposed that every match should use the same Test-quality ball.

Perhaps optimistically, they believed that corporations would be willing to abandon their own teams and sponsor districts or divisions instead. In exchange, they would gain a role in the governance of Pakistan cricket, locally and nationally.

Majid ticked off the advantages of the new system. It would provide a minimum pool of around one thousand paid players, coached and continuously assessed, and with a clear means of progress to the top level. The prospect of promotion and more importantly, relegation, would be a major deterrent against inadequate players chosen by patronage. They would threaten the status and financial prospects of their colleagues and would be quickly ejected. The support staff required for each team would bring new opportunities for retired players of quality to stay involved in the game. The long season would mean better prepared pitches and players. College and university teams might be revived as feeders for districts.

One can readily see obstacles to the plan, but its radical logic is evident. Was it better received than in 2007? Did it provoke a national debate?

Well, no, as Majid wryly explained.

It got a mention in the *Urdu Daily Express* after a long delay. 'A columnist from *Dawn* got in touch. He was very flattering. He even said that he had cried when he heard our plan. He asked for my email so that he could put some questions about it. I gave it to him and he sent ten questions and begged for a reply to save his career! But they were stupid questions, which had nothing to do with the plan and the structure. So I didn't reply.'

Bazid Khan was invited by Dr Naumann Niaz, the prolific cricket

historian and boss of PTV Sport, to discuss the plan with Talat
Hussain, a former first-class player who has become a respected journalist and chat-show host. 'He finished by saying openly that it would
never be implemented, because "there's no ME in it."' By this he meant
that no powerful person would be able to claim ownership of the plan.

The sun had set. The audience was over, but there was just time for
Majid to pass some dismissive remarks on the proposed T20 Pakistan
Super League in the UAE. 'Completely artificial teams, pretending to
represent cities, pretending to play home and away. Who's going to
watch? Tickets will be out of reach for most Pakistanis in the UAE.
But it will give officials the chance to stay in five-star hotels and claim
per diem expenses.'

One parting question. Would Pakistan cricket ever see a stable
administration which was independent of government?

A rare laugh. 'Not in my lifetime.'

36

A PRINCE AND A DIPLOMAT:
SHAHARYAR KHAN

By Mueen Afzal

Mueen Afzal read English at Government College, Lahore, and PPE at Corpus Christi College, Oxford and later obtained a postgraduate qualification at Wolfson College, Cambridge. He held senior positions in Pakistan's Finance Ministry, ending with the rank of Minister of State, and later in corporate and academic life. He declined the post of PCB chairman in 2004. He is a long-standing friend of Shaharyar Khan.

English cricket used to be famous for its grandees. Lord Harris, the England captain who became governor of Bombay. Lord Hawke of Yorkshire. The England fast bowler and martinet Sir Gubby Allen.

Shaharyar Khan, scion of the princely state of Bhopal and the only man to serve two non-consecutive terms as chairman of the Pakistan Cricket Board,[1] is grander than any of these.

Author, intellectual, former head of Pakistan's foreign service, Shaharyar Khan has had a rich and varied career. Our concern is with

---

1 This ignores the legal musical chairs between Najam Sethi and Zaka Ashraf, described below. Justice Cornelius, Arif Abbasi, Dr Zafar Altaf, Khalid Mahmood and Ijaz Butt held several executive positions in Pakistan's cricket administration, but none had two terms as chairman of the board.

his contribution to cricket. In both his terms as chairman, his intellect and integrity have been precious assets to the Pakistan Cricket Board. His first appointment came against a background of poor performances by the national team and a fierce barrage of media attacks on its administration. His second followed the bleakest period in the history of Pakistan cricket, with a team in international exile following the terrorist attack on the visiting Sri Lankans, a series of inadequate administrations at the PCB, and the match-fixing scandals of 2010.

That Pakistan cricket survived was due to two fortunate but accidental appointments. The first was that of Misbah-ul-Haq as captain, who inspired an on-field revival that took Pakistan to second place in the Test rankings. The second was Shaharyar's – recalled to the PCB after a year of unprecedented chaos.

His story is entwined with the early history of Pakistan and before that with the princely state of Bhopal, in pre-Partition India. He was born there and his grandfather was the ruling prince, his mother the heir apparent.

Bhopal was one of the leading princely states, with a population of 785,322 in the 1941 Census. Its ruler was entitled to a 19-gun salute. Remarkably, it was ruled continuously by four women, from 1819 to 1926. Shaharyar has left a vivid account of them in his book *The Begums of Bhopal*.[2] Each was an outstanding ruler, especially Sikandar Begum and Sultan Jehan Begum, the second and the fourth in the chain.

Sikandar Begum ruled from 1826 to 1867. During the Sepoy Mutiny she remained loyal to the British and challenged the militant Rani of Jhansi to carry out her threat of marching on Bhopal.[3] Apart from her loyalty, the British authorities were impressed with Begum's administrative acumen and her reform programme, which included initiatives to protect the rights of tenants and to promote education for women. She also reformed the police and the postal service and introduced a

2 Published by IB Tauris in 2000.
3 There is a sharp and accurate portrait of the Rani in GM Fraser, *Flashman in the Great Game* (Barrie & Jenkins, 1976).

modern railway system. She was prudent with her finances and left a healthy balance in the treasury for her successor, Shahjehan Begum.

The third Begum's reign of 33 years was chequered by her marriage to her tutor, Syed Siddiq Hassan. 'She became Trilby to his Svengali,' wrote Shaharyar, and in her latter years the British resident, Colonel Ward, took over the effective administration of the state.[4]

Sultan Jehan Begum succeeded in 1901, and revived the style of Sikander Begum, reform backed by financial prudence. Much of her time in later life was spent fighting for the succession of her only surviving son Hamid Ullah Khan.

She pursued this cause in the courts, and by intense personal lobbying of the Viceroy, the Marquess of Reading. Her chief legal adviser was Qazi Ali Haidar Abbasi. (His son, Arif Ali Khan Abbasi, would have three separate leading roles in Pakistan's cricket administration. A frequent critic of Shaharyar's, he was canvassed as a rival to him in 2014 as chairman of the PCB.) Finally, Lord Reading found in favour in 1926 of Sultan Jehan Begum. Shortly after that she abdicated and Hamid Ullah Khan became what was to be the last effective ruler of an independent Bhopal.

Hamid Ullah Khan had three daughters. The eldest was Abida Sultana, the mother of Shaharyar Khan, and a remarkable woman. She played polo, cricket and hockey on equal terms with men, reportedly shot 72 tigers, became all-India women's squash champion and brought roller-hockey to India on the hallowed marble floors of Minto Hall. She was also an accomplished musician and became the second Muslim woman in South Asia to acquire a pilot's licence.[5]

In 1933, aged 20, she married Sarwar Ali Khan from the small neighbouring state of Karwai and Shaharyar Khan was born on 29 March 1934. Shortly after that, the couple decided on an amicable separation: Abida Sultana returned to live in Bhopal and took sole responsibility for Shaharyar's upbringing and education.

She continued to be the heir apparent of Bhopal until her decision

4 S Khan, *The Begums Of Bhopal*, p.122 and ch 6.
5 Ibid., p.232.

to opt to live in Pakistan in 1949, two years after Partition. She came with few assets to Karachi, buying four acres of land in Malir from a Parsee gentleman.

Her decision to leave India may have been due to several factors. The primary one was that both she and her father, the Nawab, were very close to the political ideas and vision of Mohammad Ali Jinnah, the founder of Pakistan. After Jinnah's death in 1948, Abida Sultana remained in close touch with his sister, Miss Fatima Jinnah, and in 1964 strongly supported her in the presidential election against Field-Marshal Ayub Khan.

Shaharyar Khan was 13 at the time of the Partition of India in August 1947. He was studying at the time at the Royal Indian Military College (RIMC) in Dehra Doon. This choice was made by Abida, who did not want a 'soft' upbringing for her son. Shaharyar loved the RIMC. He found the teaching 'brilliant' and enjoyed the spartan lifestyle and the uniform he wore throughout the school day However, Partition brought unsettled times and the security situation deteriorated in the Dehra Doon area. Abida Sultana started to look for an appropriate public school in England for her only son. As with the RIMC, Abida Sultana did not want a 'soft' school, and rejected Eton and Harrow. Instead, she wanted a school which would prepare Shaharyar for a professional career, preferably as an engineer.

The school ultimately selected was Oundle, in Northamptonshire, to the north of Peterborough. Founded in 1556, it had been a minor public school until the reforming headmastership of FW Sanderson, from 1892 to 1922. Sanderson gave the school a high reputation for teaching science, engineering and modern languages.

Shaharyar arrived at Oundle aged 14. It was the first time he had been abroad. Post-war England would have been an alien experience for him. Food (including bread) and almost every essential commodity were rationed, but at least Shaharyar could enjoy the fine summer of 1948 – and the visit of Don Bradman's Australians.

Britain's Labour government was still implementing radical reforms, including the National Health Service which began in Shaharyar's first year. Class distinctions had crumbled during the war. The Fleming report of 1944 had recommended reserving a substantial number of places at public schools for children from poorer families. This was not implemented, mainly because the Labour government was too busy but perhaps also because the prime minister, Clement Attlee, was a proud public school product.

Oundle was therefore able to continue in its traditional course as a fee-paying boys' public school. The boys were strongly divided by age and by house. Younger boys 'fagged' (did personal service) for older ones. Beating could be used as punishment not only by masters but also by boys appointed as prefects. Sport and exercise were compulsory, as was participation in the school Officer Training Corps.[6] There were strict rules on uniform and timekeeping and other controls on boys' personal life, particularly anything to do with sex. Shaharyar's head-master was described thus by a slightly older Oundelian, the poet Al Alvarez: 'He was a skeletal figure called Stainforth, tall, lantern-jawed, pale-eyed, a dour authoritarian who ... had links with the Raj.' He taught English, specialising in Browning and disliking later writers.[7]

However, Shaharyar thrived at Oundle. It encouraged his gift for languages. He learnt French and Spanish and travelled extensively to both countries. This prepared him well for his ultimate choice of diplomacy as a career.

On joining Oundle, he made an immediate impact on being selected to play for the first XI as a fast bowler, aged only 15. His best perfor-mance came in June 1951, on the school pitch: five for 31 against local rivals, Uppingham. He played for the school for each of his four years and was coached by Arnold Dyson, the Glamorgan professional. Since Dyson originally came from the north, he coached Shaharyar to bat in the dour style of Len Hutton rather than in the cavalier style of Denis Compton. Shaharyar played hockey as well and developed a passion for squash. Since there were no squash courts at Oundle, he would cycle several miles to get a game at nearby Fotheringay Castle.

6 Conscription was re-introduced by the Attlee government in 1947. By Shaharyar's time at Oundle, most of his British contemporaries were expected to do two years' national service, as officers, at some point after leaving the school.
7 Al Alvarez, *Where Did It All Go Right?* (Bloomsbury, 1999), pp.94-95.

For university in those days, the first choice usually was a college at either Cambridge or Oxford. Shaharyar applied for a place at Corpus Christi College, Cambridge. This was primarily because his assistant house master at Oundle, Mike Mills, was an old Corpus man, who had served in India in the war. He was fond of Shaharyar and would accompany him on the bicycle rides for squash.

Shaharyar was given a trial in the Freshmen's match of 1954, failing to take a wicket in either innings, but earning his team a six-wicket victory with an undefeated fifty batting at number 8. It was not enough to earn him any further opportunity. Cambridge cricket was strong during Shaharyar's time: apart from himself they cruelly discarded his gifted contemporary Iftikhar Bukhari, who won the Wilfred Rhodes Trophy as a batsman for Cambridgeshire in the Minor Counties championship and later became a prolific scorer in Pakistan's domestic cricket.

On finishing at Cambridge, Shaharyar decided to take the Central Superior Services (CSS) examination. While he waited for the result, he briefly worked with Burmah Shell: he enjoyed the corporate experience and, stationed in Karachi, extensively toured the province of Sind. This gave him valuable insight into the issues facing this important province of Pakistan. Shaharyar was placed fourth in the CSS exam and opted for the Foreign Service. I was told a story from our seniors in the Civil Service of Pakistan (CSP) that Shaharyar scored 300 out of a possible 300 marks in the viva voce part of the examination. The head of the Public Service Commission, U Kramet (himself a Cambridge man), was asked to explain how a candidate could achieve this outstanding score. 'Very simple,' was the reply. 'One hundred for his public school, one hundred for Cambridge and one hundred for blue blood.'

Shaharyar Khan had a very distinguished career in the Foreign Office, ending up as the foreign secretary (equivalent to a permanent secretary in Britain) from 1990 to his retirement in 1994. He was then chosen as the special representative of the secretary-general of the United Nations for Rwanda. He worked with skill for two and a half years, serving successively with Boutros Ghali and Kofi Annan. Later, he served as Pakistan's ambassador to France as a political appointee.

He considered his stint as foreign secretary as the most challenging: a period during which the USA distanced itself from Pakistan, following the Soviet withdrawal from Afghanistan and the collapse of the Berlin Wall.

But Shaharyar's most cherished appointments were those in the UK as deputy high commissioner and later as the high commissioner. England was a second home to him and he rubbed shoulders there with his contemporaries from Oundle and Cambridge, most of whom had now reached the zenith of their careers. As deputy high commissioner he lived in Wimbledon and revived his interest in cricket by turning out for the local cricket club. He formed many new friendships and won many friends for Pakistan. He served with Mian Mumtaz Daultana, one of Pakistan's brilliant politicians who promised much but never quite made it to the top. Daultana, himself a product of Corpus Christi College, Oxford, came from one of the largest landowning families in the Punjab. He became chief minister there in his early 30s, but by the 1970s he was a declining force. To ease him out of the way, ZA Bhutto appointed him as the envoy to London. Daultana was a highly civilised person but rarely spent more than three to four hours in the office. His deputy, Shaharyar, had to keep the mission running, with the help of some of the other professionals. This gave Shaharyar vital experience for his return to London as the head of mission from 1987 to 1990. In this latter period he came to interact with Prime Minister Margeret Thatcher ('fresh as a daisy for a meeting at 7am and again fresh as a daisy for a reception at 7pm') and her foreign secretaries, Geoffrey Howe and John Major.

Shaharyar's first appointment as head of the PCB, by President Pervez Musharraf, was in 2003. Since the constitution of the PCB was in abeyance, Shaharyar's was an 'ad hoc' appointment. In principle, all authority was vested in him as chairman and although there were other members of the board he was free to consult them – and ignore them – as he chose.

In practice Shaharyar, given his experience as a consensual diplomat, did like to consult with his colleagues and invariably took decisions with their backing. However, his ad hoc appointment under Musharraf gave him far more freedom in decision-making than his second term from 2014 under Nawaz Sharif. By then, a new constitution for the PCB was in place. It would require the board's approval not merely for his own appointment but also for all material cricketing and financial decisions.

Shaharyar Khan's first term as chairman of the PCB was significant for a number of reasons. Above all his deft diplomacy and contacts with the other side resulted in the first tour in 14 years by India to Pakistan in March–April 2004. Pakistan lost the ODI series 3-2 and the Test series 2-1, but the positive gains from the tour were immense. As *Wisden 2005* put it: 'The warmth of the tour radiated beyond cricket ... Bollywood film-makers suggested that Indian films should stop pushing anti-Pakistan propaganda. About 15 Pakistani musical bands crossed the border between January and May. And the business sector brimmed with optimism at the potential for trade. The tour provided the highest possible profile for friendship and the strongest metaphorical way of saying "peace over conflict."'[8]

Shaharyar's other memorable contribution was to impress upon the selectors to pick teams on merit. This was fairly novel, since favouritism in selection had for long been the bane of Pakistan cricket.

With the appointment of Bob Woolmer as the Pakistan coach, the stage was set for a prolonged run of successes in Test cricket for the team. His first overseas assignment was grim: a 3-0 whitewash by Australia. But then followed two drawn away series against India and West Indies – and then a sequence of five victories and four draws. This included two victories over England at home – the first time any Pakistan side had achieved this.

Before their four-Test tour to England, starting in July 2006, Pakistan had climbed from number 7 to number 4 in the world Test rankings in less than a year. Their middle-order batting of Inzamam-ul-Haq, Mohammad Yousuf and Younus Khan was the best in the world. When fit and motivated, Shoaib Akhtar was the world's fastest and most hostile bowler. He was backed by performances of quality from

8 *Wisden 2005*, pp.1197-98.

Mohammad Asif and Danish Kaneria. The record was a vindication for Shaharyar Khan's efforts to improve Pakistan's Test performance.

The tour to England in July promised much but in fact ended in disaster. The 3-0 win for England in the four-match series was not a true reflection of the relative strength of the two sides, with The Oval Test being awarded to England when Pakistan appeared poised for victory.

Shaharyar became embroiled in a protracted stand-off when Inzamam-ul-Haq refused to lead Pakistan out of the dressing room in protest against umpire Darrell Hair's award of five runs against Pakistan for alleged ball-tampering. Shaharyar narrated this affair almost minute by minute over 33 pages of his memoirs.[9] The tour manager, Zaheer Abbas, was virtually a passenger in the crisis, and Shaharyar's authority was undercut by the presence of another cricket board member (and his eventual successor), President Musharraf's personal appointee, Dr Nasim Ashraf.

Shaharyar's presence at The Oval did help eventually to defuse the situation, but great damage had been done to Pakistan cricket and the incident suggested dissensions within the team despite its recent successes. These came to a head a few months later, before the autumn tour to India, when there was a public spat between Shaharyar and the new captain Younus Khan. In a thoroughly unhappy atmosphere, Shaharyar stepped down as chairman with three months of his term still to go.[10]

In retirement, Shaharyar did nothing to undermine his successors as Pakistan cricket lurched from crisis to disaster. However, he continued to keep himself involved with one of the causes close to his heart: diplomacy. He assumed important responsibilities for the teaching of Pakistan's foreign policy at one of its leading academic institutions, the Lahore University of Management Sciences (LUMS).

It was lucky for Pakistan cricket that through a series of unforeseen events, Shaharyar found himself being unanimously nominated as chairman of the PCB once again in 2014. This followed a tragi-farcical struggle for the office the previous year between competing political

9 S Khan and A Khan, op. cit., pp.229-62.
10 Ibid., p.265.

appointees, Zaka Ashraf, the chairman nominated by the outgoing PPP government, and Najam Sethi, a celebrated television journalist, chosen by the new premier, Nawaz Sharif.[11]

This process began with a dubious 'election' of Zaka Ashraf, over a candidate nominated (apparently without his knowledge) by President Zardari of the PPP, who still had a few months in office. This was overturned by the Islamabad High Court (on a motion by an irate and influential supporter), which led to the appointment of Najam Sethi as interim head of the PCB by Nawaz Sharif. But barely a few weeks later, this appointment was struck down by another Islamabad High Court judge. His order stripped Najam Sethi of all power and ordered new elections for a chairman within the tight timetable of 90 days. These elections never took place, because in October 2013 Nawaz Sharif asserted himself by dissolving the PCB's governing board. To achieve this, he made himself patron of Pakistan cricket, replacing the long-established role of the head of state. As the new patron, he set up an interim management committee headed by Najam Sethi – and including Shaharyar.

That faced another court challenge, which briefly restored Zaka Ashraf in January 2014. Nawaz Sharif sacked him again in February, and restored the committee, but a new legal challenge restored Zaka Ashraf in May. This time his reign lasted only a few days. Najam Sethi returned, was removed for one day, and returned again in July. Finally the musical chairs stopped, with the announcement of new elections for chairman by an expanded and more independent board of governors of the PCB.

Najam Sethi did not contest these and the only nominee was Shaharyar. After this year of shambles, he started his second term of office in August 2014.[12] Since then, Pakistan's media have seized on any hint of differences between him and Najam Sethi, particularly over

11 Najam Sethi's relationship with Nawaz Sharif surprised many observers: he was formerly a fierce opponent and was jailed for a month after criticising alleged corruption in Nawaz Sharif's second administration. P Oborne, op. cit., p.496.
12 See 'Shaharyar Khan elected PCB chairman,' www.espncricinfo.com 18 August 2014 and accompanying 'Full coverage of the PCB leadership crisis.'

the forthcoming T20 Pakistan SuperLeague[13] and during Shaharyar's dogged attempt to make India honour its memorandum of agreement for a programme of international series against Pakistan.

In October 2015, while Shaharyar was visiting India, negotiations were aborted when Hindu fanatics occupied the offices of the Board of Control for Cricket in India (with suspiciously little resistance).[14]

However, Shaharyar's character and experience ensure that he can still make a big contribution to Pakistan cricket. He understands that some of its key challenges have existed for a long time: the need to harness immense natural talent which is interspersed with erratic individual behaviour, as well as continued interference from political quarters. The fact that so many of Pakistan's most talented cricketers come with very limited education complicates the issue further.

With his patrician bearing and diplomatic achievements, and also with his intense love for the game of cricket, Shaharyar is singularly well placed to deal with these challenges – particularly those created by the changes in the ICC which have put international cricket and its finances into the hands of the 'Big Three', dominated by India.

There are rumblings in the cricketing world that indicate that this format may not survive. What would be the way to reform? Shaharyar knows more about international politics than any other current cricket administrator. He could guide international cricket into a more appropriate and viable system than the present ICC.

In my interview with Shaharyar Khan for this profile, I put some questions to him. He gave very candid answers. Did his mother ever regret giving up her inheritance in Bhopal and opting to live in Pakistan? He said that she never regretted this although, towards the end of her life, she did ask herself whether she had been selfish in depriving her son of his financial inheritance. I asked him if he regretted his mother's decision. His answer was unqualified: the decision to opt for Pakistan by his mother was the correct decision. He said that

13 See 'No rift with Najam Sethi: Shaharyar Khan,' *Dawn*, 28 August 2015.
14 See 'Divergent Khan and Sethi and the rising political risk in Pakistan's India chase,' *The National* (UAE), 23 October 2015.

he had never coveted wealth – as long as he felt he had contributed to Pakistan.

Shaharyar Khan's contribution to Pakistan's diplomatic history, as well as to its cricket, is immense. Among those who headed the PCB, his name will be remembered along with two others who played a critical role in taking Pakistan to cricketing greatness: the founding father, Justice AR Cornelius, and Air Marshal Nur Khan. Although they were contrasting characters, Cornelius, Nur Khan and Shaharyar were all public servants, who brought the best values of public service to everything they did for Pakistan.

37

PAKISTAN'S GREATEST PARTNERSHIP:
YOUNUS KHAN AND MISBAH-UL-HAQ

'Whenever things get hard for me or the team, I love to become the man who comes in and takes everything on his chest. At those times, my Allah helps me and that becomes my thinking.' This was Pakistan's greatest Test run-scorer, Younus Khan, on his cricket philosophy. He continued, 'I become that man …' and struggled momentarily for the right English expression. 'The Last Man Standing?' he suggested.

'In America, they often say, the Go-To Guy.' That appealed to him. He laughed, and repeated it.

Earlier that day, his captain, Misbah-ul-Haq, had expressed himself in very similar terms. 'Right from the start, in any team, at school or college or even playing tapeball in the street, if the situation was easy I always found it hard to perform, but when it was difficult, when the responsibility was on me, then I always performed well.'

Together they brought back memories of Basil D'Oliveira, the cricketer who changed history. He too produced his greatest innings when they were most needed.

It symbolises Pakistan's exile from international cricket to interview their greatest current players in the banal pseudo-opulence of an international hotel in Dubai. The Pakistanis shared this with their English opponents in their 'home' series in autumn 2015. Players from both sides milled about the lounge, carrying the same bags from the same shops where they passed the same empty hours outside of practice or match play. The English players would eventually play at home, in contact with the people and communities who know them and nurtured them. The Pakistanis would not. They faced many more days in hotels like this. In calendar year 2015, Misbah-ul-Haq and Younus Khan each played only four matches in Pakistan, all T20, in the space of a single week.

There was one advantage of the interview setting. The two players were not besieged by autograph and selfie hunters. No one looked up when each in his turn slipped into the lounge in his Pakistan tracksuit and headed for a settee in a quiet corner.

Misbah-ul-Haq and Younus Khan have become one of the greatest partnerships in cricket history. As of November 2015, they had batted together in 43 Test innings and shared 20 partnerships over 50. No fewer than 14 of these were converted into century stands. In total, they had then given Pakistan 2,846 runs together, with an average partnership of over 80.

Apart from their runs, they provided their exiled team with a moral anchor. They resumed their Test careers together when Pakistan were in the depths of disgrace, after losing three players, including their captain, to criminal convictions. They inspired their colleagues to match their standards of application and integrity and rebuild the image of Pakistan cricket.

The two have a deep respect for each other and, of course, an intimate knowledge of each other's game. But they are not personally close in the same way as the Sri Lankan brothers-in-arms, Kumar Sangakkara and Mahela Jayawardene. They have had intermittent tiffs. As recently as July 2015, Younus came close to accusing his captain and the national coach, Waqar Younis, of trying to get rid of him.[1] But – as usual – the two men came together to engineer Pakistan's Test series win over England a few months later.

1 'Younus Khan expresses displeasure with Waqar Younis, Misbah-ul-Haq,' *The Express Tribune* (Pakistan), 23 July 2015.

Physically, they are quite similar: tall, dark-haired men of Pashtun origin with angular features. Younus at 37 and Misbah at 41 shared the reputation of being the fittest men in the Pakistan team. But they had a very different manner in interviews, which gave a strong clue to their contrasting personalities. Younus's features were mobile and he gestured frequently. Misbah was more still, as he is on the crease. His expression was generally earnest, although it occasionally melted into a warm smile. Words tumbled from Younus exuberantly. Once started, he was hard to stop. Misbah's English is better and he weighed his words before answering a question.

However, each regularly used the same phrase: 'let's wait and see.' Even more frequently, each man used the word 'responsibility' in talking about his life and career.

There were moments when each sounded too good to be true. But they clearly meant everything they said. Pakistan cricket was seriously lucky that two gifted and principled cricketers joined forces when they did.

Younus (his spelling, *not* Younis) Khan was born in November 1977 in Mardan, in the province then still called North West Frontier. 'It's now a city, but then it was a country town. All the land around was very green, with a river and canals. Local people were very humble and helped each other all the time, like a family.' He was the youngest of five children, and his two older brothers introduced him to cricket. Mardan had very little cricket infrastructure but they made their own pitches (another echo of Basil D'Oliveira). 'The pitches were very dodgy, but I was there for them all the time and looked after their kitbags (there were no dressing rooms).'

When he was only four, his father had a chance to go to Karachi. The city was having a boom based on trade and construction and hard-working Pashtuns were in demand. After a year of struggle, he was able to send for his family. His youngest son's education and cricket prospects improved significantly. Like so many modern Pakistan cricketers, he played countless street games. 'Tennis ball cricket was very classy. Bowlers could squeeze the ball with their fingers to get a lot of spin. Then came tapeball. In street games, you often needed twenty runs in an over to win.' It was a fine training to become a 'finisher'.

Younus's father was an all-round handyman and craftsman, who could work with wood or metal and operate almost any kind of machinery. 'At that time, Pakistan steel mills were being developed by the Russians. If they were stuck with a mechanical problem, they called out my father. He would stand in front of these huge machines in the steel mills for just ten to fifteen minutes and work out what was wrong.' It was clearly a lasting role model: a father who repaired machines, a son who repaired innings.

His brothers continued to supervise his cricket education, and by the time he was 14 he was playing regularly with older boys already at college. They mocked him as 'a skinny boy'. As with many later opponents, they soon discovered that taunting him made him play even better. He played for Islamia College of Arts and Commerce, where he studied science until matriculation and then switched to arts and commerce (which offered a little more time for cricket). He represented Karachi at Under-14, Under-16 and Under-19 level.

Most importantly, he joined the Malir Gymkhana Club, about 20 miles from the centre of Karachi, where his game was developed further by senior players including Rashid Latif, Tariq Alam (father of the current young Test batsman Fawad Alam) and Wahid Mirza. In 1977, playing for Karachi Whites against Quetta, Wahid shared a world record opening partnership of 561 with Mansoor Akhtar, which received a sniffy editorial comment in *Wisden 1978*.[2] However, Younus Khan remembered him as an inspirational captain. The senior players tightened Younus's batting technique (without suppressing his daring late flicks to the leg-side boundary) and helped him become a reliable close catcher.

In spite of success at each age-group level, he found it impossible to break into the powerful Karachi first-class teams of the late 1990s. He chatted constantly about this problem with another ambitious teenager, Shahid Afridi, but was eventually forced to make his first-class debut for

2 See Norman Preston's Notes from the Editor, 'Dubious Records.'

Peshawar in 1999, aged 21. Characteristically, he scored the first of his 51 first-class centuries for Peshawar *against* Karachi Whites, one of the teams which had rejected him. He shared an unbroken match-saving tenth-wicket partnership with his captain, Kabir Khan.

The following year, he broke into the Test team against the visiting Sri Lankans and became the sixth Pakistani to score a century on debut.[3] His 107 in the second innings at Rawalpindi was scored from number 7. He was the last man out and added 221 in five partnerships (145 with Wasim Akram for the ninth wicket): as a consequence, Pakistan nearly snatched victory in a match dominated by their opponents for three days.

By 2004, he had played 24 Test matches, but he extended his cricket education with a short visit to England to play for Nottinghamshire. 'It taught me a lot about life. You travel a lot and you learn how to clear up your home and do your laundry.' That suggests that he had never needed to acquire these skills in Pakistan. He was popular in the dressing room, particularly in his second season, when he encouraged Graeme Swann. He showed him how Saqlain Mushtaq bowled a doosra (his repeat demonstration had a terribly bent arm) and predicted that he would play for England. 'He laughed, and asked how an off-spinner could play for England in these [batsman-friendly] conditions. I said, "Brother, you will play 100 Tests for your country." I reminded him when we met in the UAE in 2012.'[4] Later, he played for Warwickshire, Yorkshire (on the recommendation of his admirer Geoff Boycott[5]) and Surrey and for South Australia.

Younus Khan has been one of the happiest-looking cricketers of modern times. He smiles regularly in matches and even in tense passages his body language usually seems relaxed. It is surprising that

3 The predecessors were Khalid Ibadulla, Javed Miandad, Salim Malik, Mohammad Wasim and Ali Naqvi. He has been followed by Taufeeq Umar, Yasir Hameed, Fawad Alam and Umar Akmal.

4 Swann in fact played in 60 Tests before pulling out of the Ashes tour in 2013. He took 255 Test wickets.

5 'An exclusive interview with Geoff Boycott,' www.cricketarchive.com 18 November 2009.

his career has seen so many clashes with fellow players or Pakistan's authorities. He had a poor relationship with Inzamam-ul-Haq, whom he served as vice-captain. When he succeeded him, he was annoyed by issues over team selection and management, and made a public protest to Shaharyar Khan, the PCB chairman, that he would not serve as a 'dummy captain'. He rejected the captaincy under Shaharyar Khan's successor, Nasim Ashraf, because of the hostile public response, also vented on his family, to Pakistan's World Cup ignominy in 2007. He walked away from the captaincy again in 2009, upset by unfounded allegations of match-fixing and, even more, by being undermined by senior players. His relationship with Mohammad Yousuf was so bad that the PCB suspended both of them for infighting in 2010 (as it happened, he was lucky to miss Pakistan's scandal-hit tour of England that year).[6]

'Yes . . .' He paused briefly, as if reviewing all these past dramas. 'It's because of my family and my Pashtun roots. It's in my blood to speak out. But seriously, in my whole career I have never fought for myself. If something goes wrong for my team, for my country, that's when things come from my mouth.'[7] Another pause for reflection and then the words tumbled out again.

'Sometimes people think that I am a very arrogant person, but I am not. I don't go to places and say I'm Younus Khan and this and that. I am a very quiet person. If I see someone I know I will go up to him and hug him and spend time with him, but if I don't know him I think he deserves his own time and space and I leave him alone. Maybe that's why people think I'm arrogant.'

When he became Pakistan's leading run-scorer, he became the face of a Pakistan mobile telephone company, but before that his image was rarely used commercially, compared to the ubiquitous Shahid Afridi, a player of far lesser gifts. If he had any jealousy, he did not show it.

6 See P Oborne, op. cit., p.473, S Khan and A Khan, op. cit., pp.77-78, 262-64, O Samiuddin, op. cit., chap 30.
7 Shortly after the interview he annoyed Shaharyar Khan, restored as chairman of the PCB, all over again by abruptly retiring from Pakistan's one-day squad. 'PCB chairman Shaharyar flays Younus retirement,' *Daily Times* (Pakistan), 12 November 2015.

'Well ... I have been paid by my country. What I achieve goes into my account, but I have to look forward, not stay in the past. So I don't make gestures and that kind of thing. I am a famous guy but not like Wasim Akram or Shahid Afridi.' He laughed again, imagining himself as Afridi. 'Sometimes a poor person comes up to me and appreciates me. That is very valuable to me. That is what I have achieved in my career.'

Younus Khan is a very devout Muslim, but he disliked the ostentatious religiosity in the Pakistan team under Inzamam. However, he defended Muslim players who have chosen to grow beards, particularly Hashim Amla and Moeen Ali. 'I had a beard like this at the start of my career.' (His gesture suggested a luxuriant one.) 'But for me, faith is about your actions in life. I have been happy all the time in my faith, it has given me a lot of inner peace in my body, and I have always played in the same way, today as at the start.'

That faith sustained him through a series of losses which devastated his close-knit family. These began in 2002, when his sister died while he was playing a Test in Lahore against Sri Lanka. Two years later, his father died while he was on tour in Australia. Then he lost two brothers and, last year, his nephew. 'We were all very religious and close to Allah, especially my mother. As Muslims we have always thought that if Allah gives us something in life, it will go back to Allah whenever he wants.' After retiring from the Pakistan one-day team, he committed himself to fund-raising for the Indus Hospital, in Karachi, in memory of his lost relatives.[8]

His present family life gives him great joy. He married Amna in 2007 and their son, Mohammad Owais Khan, was born at the end of that year. They also have a daughter of five, Amarah Khan. 'My mother is still alive and she and my two [surviving] brothers live with us in the same house in Karachi. It is a big two-storey home. We are a very close family and every single day we have a lot of fun together. I miss them all the time when I am away, and my mother sometimes cries because I am her youngest.' Then his voice trembled momentarily.

8 'Younus Khan begins new innings with Indus Hospital,' *Dawn*, 17 November 2015.

'Quite amazingly, my son looks like my father and my daughter looks like my mother, so that whenever I look at them my mother and father are with me. I am the luckiest man alive that God gave me these things in my life.'

Younus had a strong bond with his father through fishing. It remains his favourite off-field activity, whether river or deep-sea fishing, and he has shared his passion with the next generation. His biggest catch was an eight-kilo sea trout off Karachi. With more leisure he might have shared the details, but he was due to take his young son fishing at the local marina. He agreed that fishing had helped his concentration as a batsman and as a slip fielder.

Pakistan's exile has cut deeply into his family life, and the team's. 'It is not easy travelling all the time, away from your home and family and children and friends. It can make you very weak. The players sacrifice their lives, staying in the same room for two or three months at a time. I salute the younger players especially for the way they play for their country.'

However, he was even more concerned with the impact of exile on young players in Pakistan. 'I became a cricketer because of my brothers and because of star players like Javed Miandad, Imran Khan, Zaheer Abbas, Majid Khan, Wasim Akram, Waqar Younis. We would go to the stadiums and cheer for them.' A visiting player also made a big impact on him: Martin Crowe of New Zealand. 'He made back-to-back hundreds in Pakistan against Wasim and Waqar and Abdul Qadir. I saw what kind of a player he was and I was motivated by him.[9] I feel sad for the young guys now who might have been inspired by us to become top players for Pakistan. How can we motivate them? Television is not enough, they need to see us in live action.'

During the series against England in 2015, Younus Khan moved past Javed Miandad as Pakistan's leading scorer and then became the first Pakistani to score 9,000 Test runs. 'It was really something for me to pass him. When I started my career in the Pakistan team, Javed Bhai was our coach. I learnt so much from him, not just batting but

9 Martin Crowe died in March 2016, aged 53, after a long battle with cancer.

the way he conducted himself every single day. I have always been a good learner. Learning little things, like how to clean my kitbag, that's how I stabilised my life, especially in cricket.' He had also outdistanced Javed by some way as Pakistan's best outfielder, with 117 catches in 104 Test matches. No current Pakistan outfielder is anywhere near that total.

Javed Miandad was celebrated for scoring runs when they were most needed and Younus Khan inherited that mantle. He is the best fourth-innings batsman of modern times, with the highest average and the most centuries. He has contributed more than any other modern batsman to Test victories for his country overseas. In 31 such matches (they do *not* include those in the UAE) he has scored more runs and centuries than Viv Richards (35 away wins), Steve Waugh (37) or Ricky Ponting (41): his average in them is an astonishing 91.

He has been involved in 62 century partnerships, more than any other Pakistani batsman, the greatest number with Misbah. Four other Pakistanis, Azhar Ali, Fawad Alam, Asad Shafiq and Shan Masood, completed their maiden centuries in long partnerships with him, a tribute to his benign influence at the other end.[10]

But he still has worlds to conquer in Test cricket, particularly 10,000 runs. If he maintained his recent average, he would need about seven or eight more matches. 'I think at all times, what is my next goal, what do I want to achieve now? Okay, thirty-one Test hundreds, nine thousand Test runs and I still feel I've done nothing. My country pays me, my countrymen respect me, so I must do these things. I am a senior guy, so I must perform every game.'

After that statement of intent, the fish of Karachi will be a little safer.

Like Younus Khan, Misbah-ul-Haq was the youngest child, with two older sisters. But as the only boy, he was born to face responsibility. Although his family spoke Punjabi rather than Pashto, he was part of the Niazi Pashtun clan, to which Imran Khan's father belonged. Was he a blood relation? Certainly, and his family lived on the same

10 See Umair Qazi's 'Younus Khan: humble record-breaker has left little room for doubt,' *Dawn*, 8 July 2015.

street in the town of Mianwali. It was not a great cricket centre when he was born, in 1974, but two of his cousins played cricket. Basit Niazi had a first-class career for two patrons' teams, the Water and Power Development Authority and Khan Research Laboratories, and his brother, Abdul Wasay, at Under-19 level for Sargodha. 'I learnt from them in backyard cricket, and then I played a lot of street cricket. I played with a tennis ball, then a tapeball, then with a slightly bigger soft ball, the kind used for handball or volleyball. That was good for playing at home because it didn't bounce so much and there were fewer chances to lose it. I played with my cousins and obviously I watched cricket all the time on television, so that's how I got interested.'

'He probably didn't tell you that he was a naughty boy,' said his wife Uzma, at a separate meeting during the Sharjah Test match. They are cousins and she has known him since childhood. It sounded out of character. How naughty? 'Playing sport until all hours and some broken windows from cricket.' She added quickly, 'But he was always respectful to the elders.'

Misbah's parents were both teachers and made it clear that he had to keep up his studies. When he was 14 his father died, and he became the man of his family. He worked diligently at Pakistan Air Force College in Mianwali, but also represented them at cricket, hockey, badminton and table tennis. Then, in his teens, he became a snooker star. 'I used to play carom at lot with my sisters at home [the popular board game in which wooden pieces are flicked into pockets: Amir Bee, mother of the Mohammad brothers, was a past champion]. But then snooker came to Mianwali and I loved it.' Snooker was a good training for calculating angles and placements when batting, but an even better training in strategy. 'It develops your thinking, because you have to pot a ball and then look for colours or safety. You have to make a plan for your break, so it's a thinking game.' Did he have any perfect breaks? A few, and he became District Champion in 1992.

Still following his parents' goals, he went to Lahore to do an MBA at the Institute of Leadership and Management, now the University of Management and Technology. 'The first two semesters were really tough. I hardly had time for any cricket, just some tapeball for fun. But after that I started playing club cricket for Servis Industries [the shoe and tyre concern, where Ijaz Butt honed his business skills]. I went to nets and played club matches for them for two years. It was still only for fun, but I came across many international cricketers. One day I was playing against a local Allied Bank team with three international bowlers, Aaqib Javed, Ata-ur-Rehman and Aamer Nazir. I scored forty-seven and it felt good. I thought, if I could score runs against them why not try to play first-class?'

But he gained his MBA first. It made him one of the best educated cricketers in the modern age, and his studies of leadership skills and human resource management were of lasting value to him as a captain.

Did he ever give business advice to his team? They might need it: many sportsmen lose money on bad business deals.

He broke into a smile. 'Yes, we are not good businessmen. We don't have the time, we have to concentrate on cricket. My biggest advice to cricketers is to invest in property. Especially to youngsters. Make good investments in property. In other businesses you can get distracted and your performance can go down, but with property you don't have to be there and it doesn't bother you. I tell them "our best business is cricket."'

Because of his education, he made a late entry (by Pakistan standards) at 24 into first-class cricket, for Sargodha. He had a big second season and was picked for Pakistan's tour of New Zealand in 2000-01. He played one Test, as a number 3, contributing an unmemorable 28 and 10 to a massive Pakistan victory. The 28 was his top score in five scattered Tests until 2004, and he was discarded for three years.

There have been many suggestions that he was excluded from the team for religious reasons, and because Inzamam-ul-Haq did not like educated players.[11]

Misbah dug out these yorkers. He refused to blame Inzamam and

11 See for example S Khan and A Khan, op. cit., p.202; 'Such Gup,' *The Friday Times* (Pakistan), 10-16 February 2012; Nadeem F Paracha, 'Pakistan cricket: a class, ethnic and sectarian history,' *Dawn,* 19 September 2013.

took responsibility for his exclusion. 'Looking back on my career, I think I came to international cricket late in age but early in terms of experience. I made the Test team after two seasons of first-class cricket, with no experience of Under-19 cricket, not much experience of grade cricket. That's why I think I struggled and couldn't meet the demands of Test cricket. I discovered what I had to do to improve myself, but then I went through a patch being in and out of the team. It took me years to understand properly what international cricket meant.'

As to Inzamam: 'Everything was good. Captains want players in their team who they think will be matchwinners. At that time, he may have thought his matchwinners were someone else, and he couldn't drop them.'

So he applied himself to scoring heavily in domestic cricket. There was a brief interlude in Scotland in 2002 when he played four club games for Penicuik in Midlothian. 'I met some really good people but it's not easy to bat in Scotland, it's always cold and rainy and wickets are always moist.' He enjoyed another interlude in 2006 with the Dalton club in Yorkshire. In 2013, he made three one-day appearances for Pakistan in England in the Champions' Trophy. He has never played any first-class match in England. Would he like to fill that gap in his career? 'Let's wait and see.'

He came back into the Test team with a huge series in India in 2007-08, including his first two Test centuries, but then his in-out career resumed. He was discarded for the tour of England in 2010. At 36, his Test career looked finished.

Was he shocked to be recalled as captain? 'It was a surprise but I had been captaining teams at domestic level for eight to nine years, and I had been vice-captain of the national team two or three years before. I had the experience, and I thought, "let's have a try and see." It went well from the start. The credit goes to all the players. They responded really well, and performed to their maximum potential. They took Pakistan to number three or even number two in the world.'

Before becoming captain, Misbah had scored 1,008 runs in 19 Tests at an average of 33.60. Since becoming captain, he has scored another 3,344 runs in 42 Tests at an average of 56.68.[12]

This is a record improvement by any batsman with a substantial Test career before and after taking over his country's captaincy. He was intrigued, since this record had never been unearthed, but not at all surprised. He repeated his self-assessment: 'Responsibility has always given me a lot of confidence to face the music and perform.' He allowed himself one little break from duty, against an already battered Australian team, by scoring the fastest Test fifty and sharing the fastest Test hundred with Viv Richards.[13] It was a pleasant riposte to domestic critics who called him a boring batsman.

His 20 victories made him easily the most successful Pakistan captain in history. Most of them have been gained with inexperienced attacks. Only two of his bowlers have taken 100 Test wickets, Umar Gul and Saeed Ajmal, and they have both left the scene. Of course, he has never led a team with the support of a home crowd. A tiny band of expatriates have done their best for him in the echoing stadiums in the UAE.

He acknowledged his support from Younus Khan. 'We both knew how important we were as senior batsmen. We had to score runs and guide the youngsters in the team, and show them how to build partnerships. Azhar Ali, Asad Shafiq, Sarfraz Ahmed and others have all learnt this. My relationship with Younus was therefore vital. We really needed good communication between us. I always enjoy batting with him. It happens often because we are at number four and five. We know each other's game thoroughly, so it is so easy to perform together. Over the years, we have had so many fifty or one hundred partnerships that they start to become automatic. You don't have to read the events in your mind, you can just feel them happening.'

With Younus's help he regenerated the team morally as well as technically. 'All credit to the boys, they really tried to help me. They also thought that Pakistan's image had been really hit by scandal and it

---

12 As at March 2016.
13 New Zealand's Brendon McCullum seized the fastest century record in February 2016, but Misbah still holds the fastest fifty.

was their duty to restore it. They made extra efforts on and off the field to get respect back from fans and keep out of any sort of controversy.'

He too acknowledged the stress of their exile lifestyle. 'You never know when homesickness will strike. You start to miss familiar grounds, and people and friends. Sometimes you don't know why you have become grumpy. It is tough for everyone, spending your time without the people you really enjoy.'

His task would have been impossible without the support of his family. 'I have been fully devoted to the team in the last five to six years, so huge credit must be given to my wife, my mother, my sisters, my children. I have given them, so to say, only my spare time, and they had to suffer. They have never bothered me about this.' His wife Uzma told us that sometimes he broods over a bad day for himself or the team, and the family have to help him relax and forget it. 'My wife gives me full support, my mother too. Sometimes days pass without us speaking on the telephone, but she tells me to concentrate on my duties to the game and give whatever I can to Pakistan.'

He was delighted to learn that television coverage showed a cutaway shot of his wife and son responding to his century against England in the second Test in 2015. The boy, Faham, was ecstatic, leaping up and down. 'Oh yes, he is very passionate about Pakistan cricket, and he loves international soccer as well.' At the time of writing (November 2015), Faham was nine and a half. A recent video showed him batting left-handed, very correctly, and bowling right-arm wrist spin. His daughter Noriza, an inquisitive but well-behaved five-year-old, watched him in the third Test with her mother.

Misbah could not be drawn on his retirement plans. He had hoped to use Pakistan's series against India as a farewell, but the Indians scuppered it. That left an eight-month lay-off until Pakistan's tour of England in 2016, and he worried that he would not be able to get back to international standard. Shaharyar Khan had appealed to him to stay on for the England tour. 'I'm just thinking about that, and what is important to the team. So let's wait and see.'

He has thought about life after his eventual retirement. Assuming that he has followed his own good investment advice, he should be able to make his choices without financial pressures. He would *not* like to work as a PCB employee, but he will never be lost to Pakistan cricket.

'It's really hard to disconnect yourself if you have been doing one sport all your life as a passion. Obviously, I would like to keep some association with cricket, whether through coaching or commentary, and giving youngsters facilities and opportunities. I will work something out. Whatever I got from playing for Pakistan, I must give back to Pakistan.'

38

STREETS AHEAD WITH
TAPEBALL CRICKET

N o one ever took out a patent but tapeball is a Pakistani invention. It is a form of street cricket ideally suited to a country where enthusiasm for the game is huge but space for the formal version is scarce and diminishing. It stems from a long search to replace the expense of a cricket ball, which is too easy to lose and is too likely, in small and crowded spaces, to damage people and property. There were earlier versions which many British people might remember from schooldays: cricket with a rubber ball, a composition ball, a regular tennis ball, a tennis ball with half the fur shaved off (which swung prodigiously), and then a soaked tennis ball. This was the most satisfactory version, so much so that Pakistan's great captains, Imran Khan and Javed Miandad, used it for team practices.

But the real breakthrough came when some unknown genius, or more likely several, hit on the idea of covering a tennis ball with electrical tape. In his fine essay 'Tapeball tales' in *The Cricket Monthly*, Abid Hussain suggested that it originated in the sprawling overspill development of Nazimabad in Karachi in the late 1970s. Tapeball was also popular in the Federal B area of the city, and by the late 1980s there was a recognised circuit. The K-2 Bhai Tournament at that time seems to be the first to require a set of rules. One of these suggested the commercial potential of the new sport: 'Nitto brand electric tape will be used in the tournament.' Another rule was an obvious necessity for street cricket: 'any time the ball is hit directly inside a house, the batsman is out.'[1]

Taping created a ball with many of the desirable properties of a cricket ball – it could be delivered at fair pace with an overarm action without impossible bounce, but it did not require batsmen to wear protection, it did not cause too much damage when struck out of the ground and it did not matter much if it got lost. Players could manufacture another one on the spot from another ball and a roll of tape. Better still, with small variations in the coverage or age of the tape used, they could create a brilliant medium for another Pakistani invention – reverse swing.

This version of the game caught on in every Pakistani city. It is still largely amateur and spontaneous, although there are organised tournaments with prize money and teams sponsored by local businesses. There is no structure for these tournaments but there is an acknowledged 'circuit' of events in provincial cities and in the UAE which is creating a new set of professional tapeball players. We met two of them and we believe that there could soon be many more.

A tapeball match is fast and furious, as we discovered at the Board of Intermediate Education ground in the North Nazimabad district of Karachi. It was a handsome wide space but almost uniformly ochre, with barely a blade of grass in late September. There was a spectator stand, also ochre, and a bank of ochre buildings behind one boundary. It looked like a Test match ground on Mars. In the midst of the flattest expanse was a concrete strip.

There were perhaps a hundred spectators, mostly local families of Pashtun origin, enjoying an afternoon out. They and the teams were delighted to have foreign spectators. The host team offered me the best seat in the stand, and when we preferred to watch from the other side, to avoid taking photographs into the sun, they immediately organised chairs and water and summoned vendors of sweets and soft drinks.

This match was a one-off contest set up by the two teams, best of

1 www.thecricketmonthly.com/story/929545/tapeball-tales.

three matches of six overs each, with a prize pool of 5,000 rupees (then around £36) put up by all the players. Eight overs each way is a maximum. Tapeball is especially popular in the month of Ramadan, because it is possible to complete the matches of a tournament after dusk.

Two key differences from hardball cricket are the absence of lbw and the absence of spin bowling (you simply cannot propel a tapeball accurately below a military-medium speed). In such a short innings, there is very little reward for wicket-taking – the bowlers in our match aimed for a restraining yorker and hoped for the best. With no lbw, there is no risk to batters in stepping across the stumps and carting the ball over mid-wicket. (They do not wear pads or batting gloves, but in this match the batters did wear inners.) It's a batting game: 12 an over is barely defensible, 15 an over is a par score.

Several major advantages of tapeball became immediately evident. It is cheap. The bat is a little lighter than a regular cricket bat, and made from wood or at the top of the range, fibreglass. The best bat in use in our match had cost 1,500 rupees (around £10) compared to around 9,000 rupees for the cheapest regular bat with English willow on offer in Karachi's sports shops. The number of players matters little. Our match was nine-a-side: extra players or fewer would have made little difference. Nor would the state of the ground, since the ball is generally hit on the full or the half volley. All the bowling was from one end in our match, hence only one umpire. The scorer's task was undemanding. Tapeball players do not demand statistics, averages, analyses and wagon wheels – and there is no Duckworth–Lewis calculation.

Above all, it can be played despite all manner of distractions. The players we watched ignored an escaped goat, an escaped cow, several junior versions of the game on adjacent land, a young boy showing off on his brother's motor bike, and a man performing stunts on the roof of the stand.

Virtually every modern Pakistan Test cricketer has played tapeball before regular cricket. Some, like the newly rehabilitated fast bowler Mohammad Amir, reached their middle teens before they propelled a regular cricket ball. The local boys watching the match told us that they played no other sport except tapeball. It promotes many valuable qualities for 'real' cricket, particularly athleticism, outfielding skills, fast reactions and improvisation, and of course, big hitting. Older players and coaches, such as former Test wicketkeeper and captain Rashid Latif, who himself began in tapeball, worry that it encourages batters to hit across the line, and never learn defence, while tapeball bowlers tend to sling. Moreover, there are no close catchers or proper wicketkeepers, except for an occasional visitor who is more of a long stop. Rashid Latif's academy, not far from the ground, makes a big effort to add back the skills of 'real' cricket without losing the dynamism of tapeball.

On a railway journey from Karachi to Lahore in 2013, we looked out of the window and saw over 250 tapeball matches in progress, compared to fewer than ten hardball matches. Two years later, we spoke to the two cousins who are co-heirs to the celebrated sports shop, Gander's, in Lahore.[2] Mrs Azmat Humayun told me that cricket bat sales in her shop had been virtually static over the year and all the growth was in tapeball bats. Mr Hussain Malik independently told a similar story, and gave me a simple economic reason. 'Many people raise money from their friends to buy a bat and then share it. For a cricket bat, four friends might need to put up around two thousand five hundred rupees each. For a tapeball bat, five hundred rupees or less.' He also pointed out that the tapeball bat does not need to be knocked in and oiled. Moreover, because it is not subject to the laws of cricket, manufacturers had been free to experiment. He showed me a new model with an extra-long handle and a bigger hitting surface.

Tapeball in Pakistan is here to stay. We wonder whether it will continue to be a feeder of players for 'real' cricket, or whether it will develop an independent professional and commercial structure.

Tariq Haroon is a professional tapeball player from Karachi. Now 39, he began his career in all forms of cricket at the age of 12 with a tennis ball. Three years later, he took up the hardball version as an all-rounder in Karachi club cricket, but played tapeball as well. He gave up tapeball at age 22 when selected for Karachi representative cricket, because it harmed his bowling action. He had three spells in league

2 See chapter 31.

cricket in Yorkshire and Western Australia, with Halborows CC, Salter CC and Coolbinia CC, but came back to tapeball in the last few years, as tournaments with prize money began to multiply.

From his experience, he confirmed the message that tapeball and regular cricket encourage different techniques and that it is difficult to make a transition from one form to another. In regular cricket, batsmen are encouraged to make the top hand strong and play straight; tapeball rewards batsmen with a strong bottom hand who can lever full-length deliveries over the leg-side boundary. Tapeball bowlers have to forget any lessons about using the pitch or varying their length and pace: the prime skill is to generate a fast yorker at will, although the tapeball can be made to achieve reverse swing when it is old (which happens after one over if it is not lost).

The first tapeball tournament he knew about was held at the Jinnah College ground in Karachi in 1989, and carried a winning team prize of 10,000 rupees. By comparison, he had played the previous day in an eight-team tournament with *entry fees* of 10,000 rupees for each team. The winners shared 40,000 rupees (around 3,500 rupees each), and 20,000 rupees for the runners-up. The winners' individual earnings would be around half of what a player would earn in a domestic one-day match. Although most tapeball matches were played on a cement pitch, this tournament had been set in the PCB ground at Liaquatabad, in the eastern part of Karachi, on a turf wicket.

Tapeball tournament teams usually rely on local benefactors. 'They are not millionaires, just people with their own businesses. They spend their own money kitting out their teams, buying them bats and balls and sometimes feeding them. We are lucky to have such people, who are crazy about cricket. They let other people play who could not afford to buy their own bat, such as jobless people.'

At junior level, he said that there were several different age-group tournaments for children but no national organisation. He cited the name of Dr Mohammad Ali Shah, one of the biggest private bene-factors of Karachi cricket, and creator of the AAS stadium.[3] When

3 See chapter 30.

he became minister for sport in the provincial government of Sind, he organised several children's tournaments and secured sponsorship for a nationwide night tournament at the stadium. He had ambitions for a national organisation and an international Tapeball World Cup in Dubai, but these were unfulfilled at the time of his death in 2013.

Shabbaz Kalia is probably Pakistan's best-known tapeball player. His six-hitting feats have won him a following through local television and online video. However, he was able to meet us in a small café in Lahore without being mobbed and begged for selfies and autographs as a Test cricketer would have been. He is a striking mustachioed man of 44 who looks much younger. He has played tapeball for 24 years, 20 of them professionally. Apart from being a player he is a leading promoter. This is very reminiscent of early pioneers of English cricket, such as Parr and Clarke, before the development of the county structure. Shabbaz takes his Hardahu team to tournaments all over Pakistan, particularly Lahore, Karachi, Sialkot and Islamabad, and overseas in Muscat and Dubai. There they compete against teams from India and Sri Lanka as well as Pakistan.

In the absence of any governing body for tapeball, Shabbaz is much in demand as an organiser. He raises teams, recruits new players and drafts them into teams, and secures participants for tournaments. He also participates in celebrity pro-am events: when we met him he had just guested in the Lahore Lawyers' tournament at the historic Gymkhana Club ground. There is also a new series of veterans' matches, featuring three former Test captains, Mohammad Yousuf, Inzamam-ul-Haq and Salim Malik, who is still under a lifetime ban in domestic regular cricket tournaments.

The essence of his game is extremely simple: hitting sixes. He once produced 12 of them in an eight-over innings in Sargodha at night in poor lighting. During that innings, he added 222 with his brother. The sixes are generally deposited over midwicket, but he can also hit them straight and inside-out over cover point.

Shabbaz Kalia said that the most lucrative tapeball tournaments are sponsored by Warid Telecoms and are shown on their television network. They carry prize money of 500,000 rupees for the winning team.

He is ambitious for the future of the sport. 'I want to take tapeball to the same level as professional cricket.'

Two things would need to happen first.

One is relatively easy: agree laws and match conditions. The laws of tapeball could be written by negation – the laws of cricket *minus* anything irrelevant to tapeball, like lbw or fielding restrictions. Match conditions could be pretty relaxed (as were cricket's long ago, when first-class matches could be played between unequal teams), but there would have to be agreement on the number of players in a side and minimum dimensions of pitches.

The other task is harder – creating a recognised structure of matches with an agreed timetable – but it should not be impossible for a determined business, or group of businesses, looking for a commercial sporting opportunity.

Such a business would find it far cheaper to create and sponsor a local or even national tapeball league than getting a toehold in regular cricket. It would acquire rights over a sport which already has a national following and is very well suited to television. Compared to regular cricket, televised tapeball would need far fewer cameras. PTV's highly experienced director, Asad Azeem Shan, told us that he had transmitted a tapeball tournament with eight cameras: 36 are now required for regular cricket. Tapeball needs no expensive commentators or analysts. Because a tapeball match is much shorter than even a T20 contest, within a similar timeslot televised tapeball could show more matches than one: more teams with a local following would be displayed and advertisers might reach more local markets.

For many players, tapeball might well become a more attractive career choice than regular cricket. The very best would probably still aspire to reach the top levels of regular cricket, with the highest monetary rewards and social status. But lesser talents, particularly from poorer backgrounds, could well choose professional tapeball to avoid the expense and risks of seeking a career in regular cricket, which were later described vividly by young players in Lahore.[4]

4 See chapter 39.

Regular cricket requires expensive equipment, out of reach for young players on a low income and a heavy burden to those on middle incomes. Tapeball can be played with a borrowed bat.

Regular cricket takes a long time to play and even longer to practise. Tapeball does not. Tapeball players do not put strain on their education or social life, and may well discover opportunities to improve them. Cricket at the higher levels demands thorough technical ability, maintained and enhanced by specialist preparation and analysis. Even with such help, a regular cricketer faces the constant risk of sudden loss of form – or luck – and demotion from his current level. Tapeball needs practice and athleticism but little or no analysis. Once a player has learnt to hit sixes or deliver yorkers, and can catch reliably in the deep, he is likely to stay in his team or go higher.

Regular cricket at higher levels requires a high level of conditioning and proper nutrition. Because of the shortness of the game, tapeball makes far fewer physical demands. Regular cricket carries the threat of permanent injury. Tapeball has few physical risks, except those derived from rough terrains.

Young players told us over and over that breaking through into good-quality cricket requires patronage and connections. For the time being at least, tapeball is democratic. Any skilled player will find a team.

If tapeball did get the structure and rewards which Shabbaz Kalia hopes for, we could see many young cricketers making these sorts of calculations.

Those from poorer backgrounds are now being asked to make a heavy bet on making a career at the top level of Pakistan cricket – at long odds against. If a professional life in tapeball were available, the rewards might be smaller but the odds would be much kinder. If tapeball did become a career choice on its own, rather than a childhood passage into regular cricket, Pakistan may face a serious loss in the recruiting base for its next generation of cricketers. But Pakistan – and the world – would have gained a new organised sport.

39

CRICKET DREAMS IN A SANDSTORM

By Richard Heller

As a batsman, I am now in the sunset of a career which never really had a dawn. It is rarely advisable for players like me to accept an invitation to receive deliveries from a 12-year-old bowler. It is even less advisable in Pakistan. The boy will either be the next Waqar Younis, with a late toe-crushing yorker, or the next Abdul Qadir, with an assortment of wrist-spun mysteries. But it is hard to refuse. Pakistanis are very good mannered to visitors, especially cricketing ones, since the country's international exile following the terrorist attack on the touring Sri Lankans in 2009.

Anyway, if an Englishman pauses in Pakistan beside any kind of cricket match or even practice, within a minute scores of people, mostly teenagers and below, will offer to bowl at him.

On visits to Pakistan, I have had this experience in city streets and alleyways, in parks, even on the roof of an apartment block (a setting where Javed Miandad played his first cricket, and learnt to keep the ball down). I knew what to expect when I visited the Bagh-e-Jinnah cricket ground, in Lahore, to write about a special cricket camp for city children. Alongside camera, notepads, voice recorder, normal assortment of my books to give away, I had packed batting gloves, box and thigh pad, newly purchased (for about one third of English prices) at the legendary Gander's sports shop (founded 1943, retained same décor).

It is high summer. The late afternoon sun is beating down, fitfully blotted out by relays of swooping kites. The Bagh-e-Jinnah, home of the Lahore Gymkhana Cricket Club, is one of the world's most beautiful cricket grounds, set in what used to be known as Lawrence Gardens, which also houses a zoo and a magnificent library. It is ringed by tall trees, one associated with Fazal Mahmood, Pakistan's great seam bowler of the 1950s. He would sit under its shade and, rather like his contemporary Fred Trueman, deplore the goings-on of the present generation. Benches commemorate him and other great performers or local patrons. Those in the shade are popular places to nap. The small but elegant pavilion includes the small but delightful museum founded and curated by Najum Latif.

The Bagh-e-Jinnah ground staged 148 first-class matches between 1923 and 2005, ending with Pakistan A's six-wicket victory over Michael Vaughan's English tourists. Three of those matches were Tests. The ground is now used for top-class club cricket, finals for school and university tournaments, and, increasingly, for women's matches.

I have made a point of arriving on time for the opening of the camp, which means that I am early. I linger by the side of the practice net, and sure enough someone offers to bowl at me. He looks about 12, although ages are often uncertain in Pakistan, where there is no register of births. (On official figures, Aaqib Javed, who played 22 Tests for Pakistan *opened the bowling* in a domestic first-class match at the age of 12 and two months. He took three for 15 in the second innings.) This youngster, Murad, had a broomstick in his hand, perhaps intending to use it later against my bowling.

Was he skiving from the cleaning detail? Why not? I accepted the invitation. A bat and pads were fetched from the pavilion. A helmet was offered, but I hate them and it seemed wimpy against an apparent 12-year-old in flip-flops.

Well, he wasn't Waqar Younis but he did produce a brisk military medium, just back of a length. The Fahrenheit temperature had celebrated its century some time earlier, but he put everything into each delivery. Most of them skidded on the concrete surface, and one prompted a squawk for lbw (rejected, after referral by me to me).

Like thousands of past great players, Murad was clearly ready to bowl all day on his own in the heat. However, in a short time he was joined by two security guards, who politely laid down their automatic weapons, a fat man in a Pakistan tracksuit and a chap who seemed to be a touring preacher. He was seriously quick. Now although it is good manners in Pakistan to bowl at any passing Englishman, unfortunately it is also good manners to assume that he must be a fine batsman. It is insulting not to try your utmost to dismiss him. The fat man produced some deliveries which hummed in the air (a cliché of cricket writing, but it really can happen). Murad removed his flip-flops, and the preacher lengthened his run-up (his sect evidently allowed him to wear trainers and carry a new ball). Most ominously, the security guards took up their weapons again. After several overs of groping and fending, I was able to use the formal start of the cricket camp as an excuse to break free.

The club's honorary secretary, Javed Zaman, gave a little speech. It was in Urdu, but I could tell that it contained one successful joke and one that failed. Javed Zaman is a tall, patriarchal figure in his 70s, who holds court most days in the pavilion. He belongs to the Burki dynasty, which produced three generations of Test cricketers, and a cousin of three Pakistan captains, Javed Burki, Majid Khan and Imran Khan. He played nine first-class matches as an off-spinning all-rounder, including Imran's first-class debut aged 16. ('He was a slinger then, I didn't think he would go far.') He has also held a score of administrative posts in an honorary capacity for the PCB, including being the chairman of domestic and grassroots cricket. In 2003, he held the first All-Pakistan district-wide elections in 106 districts for the PCB.

Dozens of children show up for the camp, aged from about eight to 18. It is boys only, although the barriers against girls are breaking down. Some clearly are from rich families. They arrive by chauffeur-driven car, with a retinue of attendants bearing snacks, water and energy drinks. They are in immaculate whites (or official Pakistan kit), and have expensive equipment. Sadly, some of these children clearly do not want to be there. They are overweight and argumentative. They leave their video games reluctantly and scuttle back to them at every opportunity.

But most of the boys are in real earnest. For them, events such as this are a chance to be noticed by someone important, perhaps even emulate the many great players of the past, like Wasim Akram or Shoaib Akhtar who got fast-tracked as teenagers because somebody saw them. Some of these hopefuls have walked a long way to the camp dragging a kitbag in the heat and dodging Lahore's demented traffic. Others balance themselves and their kit precariously on a relative's scooter (I once saw a family of six travelling this way). I recognise one such from an earlier visit, Shayan, then officially 12, now officially 14. He is on a roll, recently named man of the match and reported in local newspapers after helping his state school defeat a prestigious private one in a school tournament. He is a tidy off-spinner, with good variations of pace and flight, and a correct, unusually patient batsman.

As in England, cricket is in retreat in state schools. Children from poorer families increasingly depend on club cricket (also in retreat) or special events like this to develop the skills of 'proper cricket'. It is much easier to play tapeball.

I am introduced to Shayan's friend Emmad, and an older boy named Faizan. He is officially 18, but is very slight and shorter than me. He has a very typical back story. He played tapeball for six years and was not introduced to the hardball game until he was 16. This happened only because he became a ball-boy at Javed Zaman's tennis club, the Mayo Garden Railway Club, where his father was serving as a waiter. Faizan was introduced to Javed Zaman, who took him to a club match at the Bagh-e-Jinnah, where he impressed as a substitute fielder in the outfield. (This is a frequent source of opportunity when elderly club cricketers take a break in the heat.) Javed Zaman brought him to a cricket camp, where he was coached for the first time and met another leading figure in Lahore cricket, Nasir Bukhari. He was then fast-tracked into organised cricket as an all-rounder, and when I met him he had just made his debut for Lahore at Under-19 district level. The next step up would be regional selection, and from there he might go on to play for Pakistan Under-19s. Each step upwards would bring higher technical support, better care for his health and fitness, and better development of essential non-cricket skills, such as communication. At national level he might also hope for employment by one of the corporate patrons of Pakistan cricket, or as an overseas professional. I can see quickly that he has made the difficult transition from tapeball: he plays straight as a batsman and instead of trying to sling down yorkers, he bowls fizzing leg breaks.

The mercury is still climbing, and the air has acquired the metallic smell that presages an electrical storm. Even the kites have given up their swooping, but the coaches are still playing an elaborate catching game with the younger boys, and have managed to motivate even the sluggards and whiners. The older and better players are having a separate and very intense fielding session: running, sprinting, catching a skyer, hurling it in, running back into the line. I would rapidly have led the fat rich kids in the race to the pavilion, but none of those concerned show any sign of flagging. When they finally have a water break, a small group comes over to me. Would I like to join their pick-up match?

I cannot refuse the honour – but only to field. I would be wrong to deprive these young batsmen and bowlers of a chance to impress, and besides I don't want to look like an idiot in that company.

In Pakistan there is a strong culture of respect for age, so for once I make a point of mine. I tell the boys that I actually watched the great Fazal Mahmood, whom most of them knew only from his commemorative bench, in his 12-wicket triumph at The Oval in 1954. They ask, did I play first-class? Lower, lower . . . but I made the most of my celebrity matches and tours to exotic places, the day I came on first change to Dennis Lillee and Imran Khan, the day I bowled James Bond, the ground where the match ball was eaten by an ostrich . . .

Whether genuinely impressed or simply through continuing good manners, the group listens respectfully when I demonstrate the grip for the 'zombie' and when the match begins they applaud a diving stop. (Not much fun diving on Pakistani grounds in high summer.)

I have had no time to do much more for good or ill when the electricity in the air finally releases itself. Its detonations produce no rain but a massive swirling sandstorm. Since I wear contact lenses, this is the perfect excuse to dash back to the pavilion. But the youngsters stay out in the field. The sand thickens. They can barely see the ball but they can still see their dreams of a cricket future . . .

This was the romantic conclusion originally intended for this book. But we were forced to change it when Richard met many of the young people again three months later, in the same place. This time they were taking part in an organised match for the club against a lawyers' XI. They were eager to talk, and most of them quickly showed that they have very low expectations of their prospects in Pakistan cricket. Those from poorer backgrounds in particular know that they face huge odds against their success – and that talent and hard work alone will not be enough to overcome them. To have any hope of passage into the upper reaches of cricket, they would need patronage and connexions.

Faizan, Javed Zaman's discovery, is back at the ground. He has been performing well in district Under-19 matches, but in this match he has not bowled and he is batting at number 10. He has no complaints, despite the journey he made to get to the match, on his pushbike for five kilometres, weaving through the Lahore traffic carrying his kit. Many of Pakistan's great players made such journeys in the 1950s – but since then the roads have become much more dangerous and the air more polluted. For an afternoon of chasing the ball in the outfield, he has put his life and his lungs at risk.

Hassan, from a well-to-do family, was driven to the match by his mother in an air-conditioned car. He is three years younger than Faisan but looks much stronger. He has obviously enjoyed better nutrition during his lifetime and now takes great care of what he eats and drinks. He is not a spoilt brat at all, but a solemn, dedicated boy nicknamed Tiger and given to sententious clichés ('practice makes the man perfect . . . hard work can achieve any goal'). He is already a sharp opening bowler and at fielding practice he runs miles to claim catches, including many which do not belong to him.

He has a punishing routine: school (private) from 8am to 2pm, cricket and fitness from 3pm until dusk, two or three hours of homework. He is doing eight Cambridge O-Levels (he makes sure I have heard the word Cambridge) which all have a demanding, fact-driven curriculum. He will need a high mark in each to pass into a good college. There seems to be no 'downtime' in his life and the pressure will get harder if he succeeds in the forthcoming trials for the district Under-16s – more practices, more matches, more work on fitness and agility, more technical preparation and greater travelling times. I ask a silly question: will his parents expect him to keep up his school work? 'Of course, they pay the fees.' His older colleague Arish chimes in. 'It's different here from England, where parents give kids freedom. Here they can be a lot more restrictive. And they can beat the kids, and the police won't come!' Everyone laughs, but it happens to be true.

It is a reminder that young players from well-to-do backgrounds face risks of their own, juggling the physical demands of cricket with the competitive demands of private education and the high expectations of parents in a country where parental authority is still strong.

Arish and Hassan take me round some other players. I am making them anonymous in case they get marked down as troublemakers by those in authority. They tell stories of the sacrifices they or their families make to keep playing cricket at all, and, even more so, of opportunities lost to inferior players who had the right connections.

A is 25 and living off a monthly income of 4,000 rupees (then around £27) from working in a small shop. So the cheapest English willow bat on offer at Gander's would cost him over two months' gross income. Not surprisingly, he is glad to borrow kit or use cast-offs. He makes no money from any match, and is relieved on this occasion not to be charged a match fee. Some years previously, he tried for a sports scholarship to a university. There was no one to back him and the scholarship went to someone with less talent. He was given a cruelly ironic reason for his non-selection: 'they told me that I could not afford to play at the next level of cricket.'

B is 19 and relocated to another city where he thought there would be more opportunity. He is now playing for his university team, and in several regional Under-19 events under the auspices of the PCB. For these, he receives a daily allowance of 1,000 rupees, plus lunch, travel costs and one-room accommodation for away matches. 'The PCB money is not enough to pay for kit, which is very costly. If my father were not supporting me as a student and as a cricketer, I would have no chance of playing. That's the reality at Under-19 and lower levels. There are money hurdles. I simply cannot afford to play in all the matches I could. Many others who don't know how to play get in the squads because they have connections, or give money to the selectors and this and that.' (This is a much-used expression in Pakistan, particularly as a hint of something too dark to mention directly.)

C has been excluded by another local club because he would keep out another player who is a voting member of the local cricket association. This is told to me by Arish, not the player himself. 'He is way better than several of their players, but he had no backer.'

D is a senior player. He had a first-class career of 27 matches which yielded over 2,000 runs. Ten years ago, he was in contention for higher honours – but again he had no backer. He was called up for a side match against the England touring party in 2005, but somehow the invitation got delivered to another player of the same name. He is still playing at grade 2, just below first-class – for a daily fee of 1,000 rupees. It seemed that below the highest levels, all players are effectively asked to subsidise Pakistan cricket.

Arish, who has been my interpreter, sums up the situation. 'This is not like England, Australia, South Africa. We used to have school and college cricket where people got a chance, but they are not happening any more. Players are out on their own. Nobody's there to look after them, to guard them. Here you can play well but you always need someone at your back, someone to write on a piece of paper, "this guy is going to play." Go round the clubs of Lahore, every second guy has got a similar story.'

This is a very small selection of cricketers, but I believe that their experience and their sense of grievance are indeed echoed elsewhere. The problems they mentioned have been confirmed by senior figures such as Javed Zaman and Majid Khan, and acknowledged by the PCB.

Moreover, these players were at one of the finest grounds in the world, under the eye of influential people and working with highly qualified coaches. If they were pessimists about their future, what was the mood of young players in remote places with poor facilities?

However, I had a final surprise. Arish, the shop steward for the group who had expressed their grievances so fluently, had the most extraordinary personal optimism. In fact, he is pursuing one of the most enduring romantic myths of Pakistan cricket – the unknown genius who goes from nowhere straight into the Pakistan team.

40

A DREAM REBORN IN BURGER KING

By Richard Heller

Arish has left it very late to fulfil his dream of playing for Pakistan. He is 29 and has never played first-class cricket, or even regular top-class club cricket. He actually gave up the game in any form for the decade of his life that is usually formative for any other player.

The reason for this decision is revealing. Quite simply, he was heart-broken at Pakistan's ignominious defeat in the World Cup final of 1999.

He was then 13. Born in Lahore, he had spent his first six or seven years in Dubai, while his father was serving in the UAE defence forces, and then returned with his family to the provincial city of Gujranwala. There began his dream of playing for Pakistan. 'Like any kid, I was head over heels for my game. But then, when our team was beaten, I saw the reaction of our nation.' All the players were vilified, and several, led by the captain Wasim Akram, were accused of corruption and match-fixing over incidents in the final and the previous group match against Bangladesh. 'I was in shock. It broke me completely. I remember some tears came from my eyes, and I walked away from my game.' But cricket would not walk away from him.

Coming from an athletic family, he soon turned to other sports. His younger brother led him into weightlifting. Against experienced professionals, he won the gold medal for Punjab in the 67.5 kg category (he benchpressed 115 kg) and the silver medal for all-Pakistan. 'But it was just for fun, not a dream.'

He graduated from Punjab University, but as an external student, and not playing any cricket. He did not play or even watch the game when he started work in Lahore. He made a promising start in a bank, 'but I was not aiming for a banking career. It was no dream and no fun. The dream of playing for Pakistan was still hidden in my heart.'

It was unlocked by a long visit to England starting in 2010. 'I studied and did elementary jobs. It was the learning experience of my life. I discovered new communities and understood how the world actually worked.'

He had his epiphany in Burger King. 'I was working in one of their restaurants, making someone a burger and I suddenly thought, "You're good enough at cricket, why don't you go back to Pakistan?" I was twenty-seven then, maybe too late, but then I thought, "why not?"'

After 14 years' self-exile from the game, he knew that he needed some preparation. He asked around his friends to find a team to play for, and one of them took him to his local club, the Dark Horses, in east London. He produced a few quick-fire innings and some aggressive swing bowling, and the following year joined the more structured environment of a league club, Wanstead CC. He could not make the regular commitment needed for their first team, but made himself available for late summons by the fourths, thirds and sometimes seconds. 'I won a few games with fast fifties down the order, and bowled a few good spells. They made me the fourth eleven player of the year.'

So far this is still his biggest honour in the game, but it was enough to make up his mind to return to Pakistan. 'I was so excited, so happy. I thought if I could play cricket every day, life would be perfect. So I decided that I would go back to Pakistan, train hard and join the national team.'

He returned to Lahore in November 2014 and undertook intensive daily preparation. For days on end, he bowled all alone against the fence of the five-a-side football pitch beside the Lahore Gymkhana ground. (I warmed to this part of his story: the young hero of my novel *The Network* does something very similar.) He enlisted his younger brother

to bowl at him for up to three hours and analyse all aspects of his batting. Then they would change roles, and his brother would analyse his
bowling. He also watched a few instructional videos. After ten weeks,
he thought he was ready.

He wrote an eloquent letter to the chairman of the PCB offering
his services to the nation. 'In the last six months, I skipped all my
businesses and practical activities, and devoted myself into my game to
touch the international mark. I am completely aware about the Pakistan
national team, the balance we have in ODI, T20 and the Test team.
Since I have come back, I have been working hard and was trying to
adjust in the conditions quickly ... My target was to come back and
show my game to the selectors and Waqar Bhai [Waqar Younis, Head
Coach].

'I have trained hard on my own and am ready to give my fitness
test as soon as I am asked. Our culture in Pakistan is a little different
and people don't find the way into their course if they don't have any
political or social affiliations. I could have tried other avenues, but I
wanted to do everything on my own.

'I would like to show Waqar Bhai my all-round game. If I could
help my country, that would be the best job I could do in my lifetime.'

The PCB chairman, Shaharyar Khan, wrote him a polite personal
reply, urging him to work through the appropriate levels. Arish wrote
an even more eloquent letter back, calling in aid the great discoveries
in Pakistan's cricket past.

'If we take a quick look into our cricket history, we do find precedent,
when the selection of the players was done on viewing in the nets and
they were taken into national shelter on the behalf of their exceptional
talent, later proved to the best in the history of the game of cricket. This
has only happened in our country and the world has acknowledged us
for the same.'

This appeal was successful and it secured a short trial at the National
Cricket Academy. (It's impossible to imagine the chairman of the ECB
even replying to an occasional club fourth-teamer offering himself to
the England team, never mind organising a trial.) It was not successful – but yet another eloquent letter secured a more extended one at the

academy. 'I only bowled – but I was asked to give practice to Kamran Akmal, Shoaib Malik, Younus Khan and Misbah-ul-Haq. I bowled a slower ball which deceived Misbah. He kept it out, but he gave me a little nod.'

This trial was brought to an abrupt end by an official – but he managed to secure a separate session with Shahid Afridi, the captain of the national T20 XI. Meanwhile, following the more conventional road, he started playing matches for the Lahore Gymkhana Club. The dream revived at Burger King is still on the road.

I cannot judge whether Arish will make it come true. His age is against him – and so are his financial resources. Although he has help from his family with accommodation and commissions from their business, he is funding his dream from his savings.

I faced a few deliveries from him in the nets. He is a handy fast-medium bowler – but most bowlers look handy against me and it is no test of whether they are good enough for Pakistan. He would make an excellent coach. He applauded any decent shot, quickly analysed the bad ones and pointed out errors clearly but tactfully.

I shall follow his story, but even if it has no happy ending it has proved that it is still possible to dream of sudden glory in Pakistan. And Arish will be able to talk for the rest of his life about the day he almost bowled Pakistan's greatest captain.

Index

Index entries in **bold** refer to characters who are the subjects of individual chapters. Page numbers followed by n indicate a footnote.